the darkest days
of my life

the darkest days of my life

stories of postpartum depression

natasha s. mauthner

HARVARD UNIVERSITY PRESS

Cambridge, Massachusetts, and London, England   2002

Library of Congress Cataloging-in-Publication Data

Mauthner, Natasha S.
   The darkest days of my life : stories of postpartum depression / Natasha S. Mauthner.
      p.   cm.
   Includes bibliographical references and index.
   ISBN 0-674-00761-1 (alk. paper)
      1. Postpartum depression.   2. Postpartum depression—Anecdotes.
   3. Postpartum depression—Patients.   4. Puerperal psychoses.   I. Title.

RG852 .M38   2002
618.7′6—dc21   2002017258

For Dave and Sam
And in memory of my mother

All sorrows can be borne
if you put them into a story
or tell a story about them.

ISAK DINESEN

contents

the darkest days
of my life

introduction

This book is about women's experiences of motherhood and postpartum depression (PPD). It grows out of ten years of research in Britain and the United States during which I listened to women speak about thoughts and feelings that, for a long time, they felt too ashamed to reveal to the outside world. Women who suffer from postpartum depression tend to withdraw from social contact. They feel imprisoned in their own misery and experience a sense of loneliness and isolation. When they are in the company of others, they conceal their feelings and try to convince people that they are happy and coping.

When I met the women described in this book, they had all partially or completely emerged from their depression and wanted to share their stories. They believed that other mothers could learn from their experiences. They told me that if they had talked about their feelings earlier they might have recovered from their depression sooner or avoided it altogether. These mothers realized that their silence had kept them locked into a lonely and isolated world of depression.

It is not surprising that women try to conceal their feelings of depression given that society idealizes and romanticizes motherhood and readily condemns women who fall short of the ideals. Although the media, literature on pregnancy, parenthood, and childcare, and prenatal classes have begun to present more realistic depictions of motherhood, the underlying assumption remains that it is above all an experience of serenity, contentment, and happiness.[1] Many of the books on pregnancy and childcare to which new or expectant mothers turn for advice still gloss over the topic of postpartum depression. As one of the British mothers I interviewed explained, the general message of these books is, "Having a baby is wonderful *but,* as a footnote, you might get postnatal depression." PPD is a taboo topic, women told me, a condition that is stigmatized and swept under the carpet. Furthermore, there is a continuing sense among many health-care professionals that postpartum depression is somehow contagious, that the mere mention of it will lead mothers to develop symptoms, and so they shy away from any substantive discussion of the condition.[2] The women in my research also noted that mothers themselves could be very protective of the ideal of motherhood, preferring not to admit their own difficulties and vulnerabilities to one another. The women I spoke with felt inundated by messages telling them they should be happy and that their depressed mood somehow made them bad mothers. As a result, they were unable to come to terms with their feelings of sadness or ambivalence, let alone share them with others.

This pervasive silence, and my belief that it lies at the heart of mothers' experiences of depression, are what compelled me to write this book. By gathering together many women's stories, I hope to contribute to breaking the silence of individual women as well as the cultural silence surrounding postpartum depression. In this way, *The Darkest Days of My Life* might help foster understanding and ultimately acceptance of women's varied experiences of motherhood.

Traditionally, medical and academic studies have neglected women's feelings about motherhood and depression. This book, by contrast, focuses on individual accounts of motherhood and postpartum depression from the perspective of those who experienced them. It argues that depression is connected to the ways in which women interpret, construct, and internalize cultural ideals of motherhood. It also considers how cultural ideals affect the nature of women's relationships with their own mothers, their male partners, and other mothers with young children. Most important, the book examines women's journeys out of depression and the sources of support that helped them recover.

Throughout this book, I use the terms *depression, postpartum depression,* and *postnatal depression.* (Postpartum depression and postnatal depression have the same meaning, the former being used in the

United States and the latter in Britain.) Healthcare professionals, researchers, and lay people use these words in different ways; hence the importance, at the outset, of indicating what I mean by these terms.[3] Psychiatric labels and categories are used by the medical profession to describe a constellation of emotional, psychological, and physical signs and symptoms viewed as indicative of a biological illness or disorder. According to this medical model, the difficulties women experience around the time of childbirth fall into three distinct categories: the "maternity blues"; "postpartum depression"; and "puerperal psychosis."

The maternity or "baby" blues are described as a mild form of low mood affecting 50 to 80 percent of mothers three to ten days after childbirth. The feelings typically last a few hours to a few days.[4] Mothers may feel emotional, tearful, sensitive, irritable, and anxious, although they may at the same time feel happy and elated about their new baby.

Puerperal psychosis is characterized as a much more severe though rarer condition that affects one to two mothers in a thousand and is said to develop within the first month after the birth.[5] These mothers may experience delusions, hallucinations, and confused thoughts.[6] Women who have been diagnosed with puerperal psychosis are often hospitalized. In very rare cases they commit suicide or kill their babies.

Postpartum depression falls somewhere between the two extremes of the baby blues and puerperal psychosis and is believed to affect at least one in ten mothers within Western societies.[7] There is some disagreement among healthcare professionals, psychiatrists, and psychologists about the timeframe for postpartum depression, though it is usually said to occur within the first six weeks after the birth.[8] (Some professionals even argue that it can begin in pregnancy.)[9] Most cases last three to six months but can last several years if left untreated.[10] Women who self-diagnose, or are diagnosed by a healthcare professional, with postpartum depression feel a persistent sense of sadness. They feel low, anxious, tearful, and irritable. They have rapid mood swings, difficulty sleeping, altered eating habits, and little sexual interest. They lack energy and enthusiasm, find no joy in life, and feel hopeless about the future. Some women experience panic attacks, headaches, and migraines. They find it difficult to concentrate, feel an overwhelming sense of fatigue, and believe they are no longer the person they used to be before the baby arrived. They feel guilty, shameful, worthless, inadequate, and experience a profound sense of failure. Many feel unable to cope with daily tasks and with their babies. Some have suicidal thoughts and may have thoughts of harming or killing their children.

Western societies are dominated by a medical approach to the interpretation of psychic pain. As the sociologist David Karp writes, in the West there is a "culturally induced readiness to view emotional pain as a disease requiring intervention."[11] Whether we accept or reject the medical view of the world, it forms the backdrop to our thinking. Many feminist social scientists, eager to formulate an alternative means of making sense of women's feelings, argue that postpartum depression is a medical construct rather than a medical condition. They criticize the label for medicalizing and pathologizing women's distress, and for reifying postpartum depression. These scholars suggest replacing the psychiatric label "postpartum depression" with other, less loaded terms such as "unhappiness after childbirth."

Interestingly, however, the women I spoke to in Britain and the United States embraced the label postpartum depression. These women actively drew on medical discourse to make sense of their experiences—partly because there are few alternative ways for them to interpret their feelings and partly because a medical explanation absolves women from feelings of guilt, blame, and responsibility. By determining that their problems originate within their bodies—typically, in the hormones that fluctuate so rapidly during and after pregnancy—a medical diagnosis validates women's experiences of motherhood despite the fact that, in their own eyes, they have fallen short of cultural ideals.

In this book I explore how women themselves define postpartum depression and distinguish it from other, milder forms of low mood. I argue that it is important to recognize and understand women's use of the label postpartum depression, and so I use the term throughout the book. By referring to postpartum depression, PPD, and depression, I do not wish to imply the existence of biological abnormalities within individual women. My view is that postpartum depression feels real and meaningful to women who are experiencing it, but that it is also a historically and culturally specific medical construct.

Beliefs about the causes of postpartum depression are wide-ranging. They include a difficult marital relationship; a traumatic birth or cesarean delivery; breast- or bottle-feeding the baby; being an older mother; giving up paid work; women's changing roles within society; and the social structures that shape women's lives. The most common assumption made about postpartum depression, however, is that it is caused by the hormonal changes that occur in a woman's body after childbirth. As I discuss in Chapter 1, medical research has focused almost exclusively on hormonal causes and treatments of postpartum depression. In my opinion, research is inconclusive as to the biological basis of postpartum depression. Moreover, I suggest that there is more to PPD than hormones. Having listened to women who experienced this form of depression, I am aware of the interpersonal, social, and cultural forces underlying it. Undoubtedly, biological treatments may help some women (either physiologically or psychologically), but many others are seeking alternative forms of treatment that are currently not available to them. Indeed, even the psychiatric profession is becoming increasingly concerned about the over-prescription of drugs to pregnant and breast-feeding women, the long-term effects of such drugs on children, and the fact that many health plans in the United States continue to pay for medication but not for psychotherapy.[12]

One of the common threads to emerge from the stories told by the women in this book is their search for perfection. Women who had always set high standards for themselves said they continued to do so when they became mothers. They expected perfection from themselves and from their children. Their compulsion to be perfect mothers must be understood within the context of the cultural devaluation of motherhood. Despite the fact that Western cultures idealize motherhood, the high value placed on paid work in societies such as Britain and the United States compelled these women to justify devoting time to the unpaid work of motherhood. Just being a mother was not enough—they had to be perfect and exceptional mothers.

Women had different ideas about what it meant to be a perfect mother. The first-time mothers, for example, had very romanticized images of motherhood. They painted soft portraits of serene mothers gazing at peaceful, beautiful babies. They pictured themselves with calm babies who fed every four hours and slept much of the time. The women who became depressed after a second or third baby knew from experience the reality of motherhood. They realized that looking after a young baby is hard work, both physically and emotionally. Their main concern was to appear to others as though they were coping well.

There were also differences among the first-time mothers' ideals.

For some, breast-feeding was the essence of being a good mother; for others, the method of feeding their babies was not essential to their identities as mothers. Having a "natural" labor free of drugs and complications was important for some women and not for others. Many felt they had to bond with their children at birth if they were to be good mothers. For some, the ideal mother is one who gives up paid work to look after her children; for others, she has to do it all—work outside the home and care for her family.

Each woman's depression centered around the specific aspects of motherhood that were most important to her. For example, women for whom breast-feeding was important felt a sense of failure when they had difficulty nursing or had to give it up. Women who believed that good mothers leave their jobs to look after their children experienced the desire or need to return to work as a personal failure. Postpartum depression, I argue, is neither about women's ideals and experiences of motherhood, nor about the actual choices and decisions mothers make. Rather, it arises out of the discrepancy they experience between the mother they feel they are and the mother they want to be. It is a response to the distress created when what they think they should feel is very different from the reality. Postpartum depression occurs when women cannot live up to the unrealistic standards they set for themselves, and thus try to change who they are to fit their ideals.

The fact that motherhood has different meanings for different women is also a reflection of variation, and sometimes contradiction, in cultural expectations of mothers. This is particularly apparent in the dilemma many women face about whether and how to combine motherhood with paid employment. Anglo-American societies are becoming increasingly work-centered and are governed by a culture of self. David Karp calls the United States in particular a "me, myself, and I" society, arguing that we are in "the age of narcissism."[13] This self-interested, competitive world places little value on care work and can leave women (and men) feeling devalued in their roles as caregivers.[14] Limited family-friendly and parental leave policies, especially in the United States, reinforce this devaluation of parenting work. Yet society still portrays motherhood as the epitome of womanhood, as something to which all women—selfless, self-sacrificing, and caring—should aspire. Childcare is seen as primarily a woman's responsibility, and any psychological, emotional, or social problems in a child are invariably blamed on inadequate mothering. Restricted family and structural supports, such as daycare services and maternity benefits in particular, reinforce cultural notions of the importance of full-time motherhood. These conflicting messages can leave women feeling confused about how best to fulfill their parental responsibilities.

Evelyn Glenn speaks poignantly about the multiple contradictions to be found within Western notions of motherhood: "Mothers are romanticized as life-giving, self-sacrificing, and forgiving, and demonized as smothering, overly involved, and destructive. They are seen as all-powerful—holding the fate of their children and ultimately the future of society in their hands—and as powerless—subordinated to the dictates of nature, instinct, and social forces beyond their ken."[15] Jessica Benjamin reiterates these contradictions: "The all-giving woman who finds fulfilment in her home and children is no longer well respected. Yet she is *still* considered the best possible, indeed the only good, mother; she is *still* a reproach to the many who work. The moral authority of motherhood has been damaged, yet motherhood remains the backbone of socialization and care. Though maternal care is still regarded as vital for small children, its values are nearly irrelevant for life outside the nursery."[16]

Another area of contradiction concerns men's role in parenting and the household more generally. Cultural notions of the "new father" lead women to expect their partners to be caring and attentive during pregnancy, present at the birth, and involved in childcare. Women in my research who bore the brunt of domestic responsibility before having a child nevertheless expected fatherhood to transform their partners into new men. Yet cultural stereotypes of fathers continue to stress their role as providers and breadwinners. Cultural ideals of full-time mothering, and the idealization of the mother-child relationship, combine with the stereotypes to exempt fathers from family work. Conditions within today's workforce—and society's support of them —make it very difficult for fathers to care for their children, even temporarily or on a part-time basis. These constraints include, for example, limited paternity leave, the current work ethic, a culture that encourages long working hours, male-female earning differentials, and restricted opportunities for part-time work, job sharing, and flex-time. These contradictory forces leave both women and men uncertain about what to expect from themselves and their partners concerning their role as parents. In practice, however, women continue to assume most of the responsibility for housework and childcare, even when they work outside the home.[17]

These mixed messages might be seen as offering men and women a variety of parenting models rather than a single right way to be a parent. Indeed, as the psychologist Harriette Marshall comments, there is a growing discourse of flexibility in childcare and parenting. Childcare manuals suggest that "women can mother in many varied and satisfactory ways and that there is not *one* right way within the context of a loving and caring relationship."[18] Each mother knows what is best for her and her child.

The women I spoke to, however, drew selectively on cultural models. They did not embrace the notion that different women find their own individual, but equally valid, ways of mothering. Instead, they elaborated rigid and prescriptive ideals. This was partly because, as Marshall points out, alongside an explicit endorsement of flexibility in our approach to parenting lies an implicit right way of doing things, a set of moral standards to be followed rigidly.[19]

Pregnancy, childbirth, and motherhood are areas of women's lives that have traditionally been dominated by the views of a host of so-called experts—so much so that women themselves find it difficult to listen to their own views and use these as a guide to parenting. Indeed, women who have experienced postpartum depression describe losing their own voices to those of others—healthcare professionals, family members, and friends—telling them how they should feel, think, and behave as mothers. Although they question these voices because they seem out of tune with the day-to-day reality of their lives as mothers, they nevertheless feel enormous pressure to conform to them.

The women I spoke to did not necessarily feel the excitement, joy, and happiness they anticipated when their babies were born. Some did not immediately bond with their babies. Others struggled with breast-feeding, or with crying or colicky babies. Some women said they did not love or want their babies, and they had recurring thoughts of harming or killing them. Many felt overwhelmed and frightened by the responsibility of taking care of another human being. They felt vulnerable and found it difficult to care for a new baby and sometimes older children as well. Although they wanted to reach out and ask for help, they were too ashamed to do so. They felt they had failed as mothers and did not want others to know of their shortcomings. They feared they would be criticized, condemned, and rejected for being bad mothers. Some were afraid they would be institutionalized in a psychiatric hospital and their children would be taken away. As mothers, they also felt they should be able to cope on their own without asking for help; turning to others would be a sign of weakness and failure. Instead they retreated into the silent and lonely world of depression, which many compared to being stuck in a dark space, a "tunnel," a "prison," a "cage," a "box," a "pit," or a "great big hole" they could not climb out of.

In some cases women's fears of rejection and moral condemnation were grounded in reality: they had tried to reveal their feelings to other people and felt silenced and dismissed as a result. In other cases, women projected their fears of rejection onto other people. They anticipated condemnation but found that their worst fears were not realized once they shared their feelings with others. Support, understanding, and acceptance on the part of confidants was a first step in the recovery process.

The fear of being rejected by other people, combined with the fact that Western cultures do not readily recognize, accept, or validate the difficulties of motherhood or the existence of postpartum depression, led women to conceal their distress and project an image of maternal competence. The women spoke of "wearing a mask," "putting on a front," and "putting on a good face" when meeting other people. They "acted out a role" and presented the world with a "happy," "cheerful," and "coping" façade while inside they felt "terrible" and "screwed up." Many were so successful at appearing in control that they were depressed for months without partners, family, friends, or health professionals being aware of it. This happy façade was one of the reasons many healthcare professionals had not detected their depression. The women did not give themselves permission to express their feelings; nor, they said, did the culture and relationships in which they were embedded.

There is nothing unusual about the feelings of sadness, anger, frustration, and ambivalence the women experienced in the early months after giving birth; indeed, such feelings are shared by many mothers. But when society dictates that these feelings are wrong or inappropriate, depression can result. Postpartum depression, I argue, occurs when women are unable to experience, express, and validate their feelings and needs within supportive, accepting, and nonjudgmental relationships and cultural contexts.

This dual emphasis on the cultural context and personal relationships constitutes the essence of the relational understanding of postpartum depression presented in this book. In making sense of women's experiences of motherhood, I draw on a relational approach to the psychology of women (see Chapter 1 and Appendix 2), and I focus my analysis on two central issues. First, I explore how women's depression is intimately linked to the cultural context in which women live and become mothers, in particular: cultural ideas of femininity and womanhood, the gendered divisions of parenthood, and conditions and policies in society and in the workplace that operate to maintain a gendered division of roles and responsibilities. Second, I examine in detail women's interpersonal relationships. I argue that it is within the context of these relationships that cultural norms and expectations, as well as employment opportunities and constraints, take on meaning and define women's understandings of motherhood.

The women whose stories unfold in this book are drawn from two studies, one conducted in Britain and the other in the United States. My objective in both studies was to learn about motherhood from women who had experienced it, and to use women's knowledge and insights to build my own understanding of postpartum depression.

In the early 1990s, I conducted a study in Britain of forty mothers, eighteen of whom had experienced postpartum depression.[20] These forty women were not a homogenous group. They ranged in age from seventeen to forty-two at the time of the birth of their first child. With the exception of one woman who was of Afro-Caribbean origin, the women were white. One was Canadian and the rest were British. They were all living with the father of at least one of their children. At the time I met them, thirty-two of the women had one child, five had two children, and three had three children. The children were between the ages of six months and seven years. Twenty of the women were not in paid work, twelve were working part-time, and six were in full-time paid work. The social and educational backgrounds of these women varied considerably. Eleven women had completed secondary education only, seventeen had completed a vocational training course (for example, secretarial, nursing, nannying), and twelve had university degrees. The women's occupational backgrounds were also mixed: nine were in unskilled jobs (for example, nurse's aide; shop assistant; domestic cleaner); fifteen were in skilled jobs (for example, secretary; childcare provider; word processor); and sixteen were in professional jobs (for example, media manager; illustrator; home healthcare provider).[21]

Of these forty women, eighteen identified themselves as having experienced postpartum depression. The range of symptoms they described conformed to medical definitions of postpartum depression, and fifteen of them were diagnosed with PPD by their general practitioners. I chose a sample of women who self-diagnosed with postpartum depression because I was interested in the psychological and social functions that self-labeling fulfills.[22]

Twelve of the eighteen women experienced postpartum depression with their first child, four with their second, and two with their third (see Appendix 1). At the time of their depression, four of these women were working full-time, three were working part-time, and eleven were not in paid work. The length of their depression varied from six weeks to three and a half years, and lasted on average twenty months. Five of these eighteen women had had previous episodes of depression before becoming mothers, which supports research findings suggesting a link between postpartum depression and a previous history of psychiatric problems.[23]

The women who experienced PPD felt they were alone in their feelings of depression. They spoke repeatedly about their desire to talk to other mothers who had experienced similar feelings. Many of those who had emerged from their depression said that talking to another mother was a critical first step toward recovery. As the British study came to an end I became interested in the role of postpartum depression support groups in helping women through their depression. I was also curious about how culture influences women's lives as mothers. Were the stories of women living in Britain echoed in another cultural setting? In 1994 I went to live in the United States for a year, where I spent six months attending a postpartum depression support group in which I met seventeen women. The last chapter of this book focuses on these women's stories and reflects on some of the similarities and differences between British and American mothers' accounts of postpartum depression.[24]

Despite the diversity among the group of mothers I interviewed—in terms of age, class, educational background, religious beliefs, employment situation, and nationality—the stories I heard in Britain and the United States were remarkably similar. Women on both sides of the Atlantic spoke of feeling pressured to conform to cultural ideals of motherhood; striving for perfection in their roles as mothers; experiencing a mismatch between their ideals and the realities of motherhood; feeling a profound sense of shame and failure; feeling alone and isolated; comparing themselves with other mothers while at the same time wanting to share their feelings with them; concealing their feelings and retreating into silence. The differences between them lay in how they made sense of and coped with their depression. Although both the British and the American women were confused and ambivalent about the biochemical origins of their feelings, the benefits of medication, and the value of a medical approach to postpartum depression more generally, overall the American women were much more committed to a medical explanation of their distress. Although they talked about difficulties in their relationships, cultural expectations of mothers, and generally pointed to other problems in their lives at the time of their depression, most were convinced that the underlying cause of their depression was hormonal. They believed that conventional medication, in particular antidepressants, was the solution. Indeed, many more American than British women were on medication and believed in its efficacy; they were also on a greater number of different types of medication and for longer periods of time. These differences, which raise questions concerning the extent to which emotional problems are medicalized within different cultures, are issues I return to in Chapter 9.

I wanted to write about women's lives in a way that would be accessible to them, their partners, and families. I hope that by reading about other women's experiences of depression, mothers will feel less alone and isolated, and partners and families will have a better understanding of what some mothers go through. I have tried as much as possible to stay close to the words of the women I interviewed. Having said that, I had to make choices about which of the women's stories to say more or less about, and which elements of their stories to highlight and which to edit out. This book, then, is as much about women's stories as it is about my own understanding of their stories.

Because the subject of this book is of interest not only to women and their families but also to healthcare professionals and researchers, I thought it must also address academic and practitioner concerns. Thus I discuss the implications of women's own insights into their depression for healthcare professionals who see pregnant women, mothers, partners, and families. I also address some of the academic discussions concerning motherhood and postpartum depression, many of which have neglected women's perspectives on their lives as mothers. In the past, I have written different pieces for mothers, healthcare professionals, and academics.[25] Writing for all three groups of people within a single volume has not been an easy task. Indeed, there is a limit to what can be done within the scope of one book. In this sense, this book is both partial and provisional. It neither is, nor claims to be, the final word on postpartum depression. Nor does it claim to be representative of the experiences of all women confronting postpartum depression.

When I conducted the research studies on which this book is based I was in my mid- to late-twenties and had no children. I often wondered whether this made a difference to the stories women told me. At times, I considered it an advantage in that I was not another mother to whom they would be tempted to compare themselves. Other times, I questioned whether the fact that I had no children myself constrained them in what they said, particularly given their comments that their stories would put me off having children for life. The women themselves said it had made little difference to what they told me about their lives. The most important thing was that someone was prepared to listen to them.

I wrote this book, however, when I was pregnant with my first child, and the final manuscript was completed after my son was born. My experiences of pregnancy and motherhood have not altered my intellectual understanding of these women's lives, but they have made a difference to my emotional reactions to their stories. Even though my experience of motherhood is different from that of the mothers in this book in that I have not experienced postpartum depression, I do have a more personal understanding of some aspects of their stories. I certainly have more insights now into the physical and emotional demands and intensity of the early weeks and months of parenthood—the sleep deprivation, the hours spent breast-feeding, the energy required to soothe a young baby, the exhaustion, the mountains of laundry, the effort it takes to get oneself and the baby ready to go out, and the paraphernalia that is required for any venture into the outside world. I understand better the cultural and interpersonal pressures women feel to do the right thing for their children, and the sense of being watched and judged by other people. I have also gained an insight into the desire mothers feel to conceal their vulnerabilities from one another, to present a picture of contentment and competence, and in this sense to protect the ideal of motherhood. Recognizing aspects of my own experience of motherhood in other women's stories reminded me that my difficulties and feelings were not unique. They gave me a sense of perspective when I experienced disappointment at having a cesarean section after a long labor; when I struggled initially with breast-feeding; when I grew frustrated with the difficulties I had settling my son after his nighttime feedings; when I felt exasperated by those first few weeks of sleepless nights; and when, like them, I struggled with the way in which our work-centered culture devalues the hard work of caring for and raising a child. The voices of the women in this book accompanied the start of my own journey through motherhood, and the knowledge that I was not alone in the challenges I faced has played an important part in making my own experience of parenthood a fulfilling and enjoyable one.

lifting the veil of silence

Pam is a large twenty-six-year-old woman with short, dark hair.[1] She lives with her husband, Bruce, who is twenty-seven, and their daughter, Charlotte, in a two-bedroom home in a housing development a few miles outside a small city in England. Pam works part-time as a childcare provider and today is one of her days off. Her daughter is at daycare.

Pam has been depressed ever since Charlotte's birth four years ago. She was not planning to have children when she married Bruce at the age of nineteen. She had spent most of her adolescence looking after her two sisters, who were thirteen and eighteen years younger than Pam. This experience put her off having children of her own. After three years of marriage, however, she began to feel broody, and she and Bruce decided to have a baby. Pam conceived easily, had a healthy and exciting pregnancy, and experienced an uncomplicated birth.

Pam's depression set in a few days after the birth. She felt disappointed by the lack of care and support she received from the midwives in the hospital. She had a host of physical complaints that she had not expected, including anemia, high blood pressure, and a bad backache. After the birth, Pam's mother-in-law came to stay for a week. She helped with the housework but was not very involved in caring for Charlotte. Whereas some women might have appreciated this lack of interference, Pam wanted her mother-in-law to take over

Charlotte's care so that she could rest and recover. When her mother-in-law left, Bruce took two weeks off from his advertising job.

After these first three weeks of support, Pam began to feel lonely. She had few friends. Her next-door neighbor had a baby about the same age as Charlotte, but she was surrounded by family. Pam tried to share her feelings with this neighbor, but the woman's experience was so different from her own that Pam ended up feeling even more alone:

> This girl I knew who lived next door but one . . . I said, "Oh, do you feel like that, do you?" and she'd say, "Oh, no, no, no," and I said, "Oh-oh, pull yourself together dummy . . . you're all right." And then I'd get home and think, "She doesn't feel like that, perhaps it isn't normal" . . . That was the one thing that really got to me through it all, that I couldn't find anyone who felt like I did, and I felt like I was going through it on my own . . . I really thought I'd gone mental. I really thought that was the end of my life. I thought I'd flipped completely and I couldn't find anyone who said, "Oh yes, I felt like that, don't worry, you'll get better" . . . I felt really isolated and lonely through it.

Pam went to a group for new mothers but felt they were unsympathetic when she talked about her depression and the fact that it discouraged her from having another child. She described one woman's response:

> She just flew at me, she said, "How dare you, how can you make a decision like that." She said, "You're so young, you're in no frame of mind to make a decision like that. It's so wrong of you to do that." And she just went on and was really nasty to me, and that made me even worse. I came home and I was crying.

After these initial attempts at disclosing her feelings, Pam withdrew, finding it increasingly difficult to confide in others. She felt guilty and ashamed and experienced a sense of failure because she did not enjoy being a mother. Like so many women with postpartum depression, she was reluctant and unable to reach out to other people even though she craved human contact: "When you're really ill," she explains, "you can't do it, you know what I mean, you can't phone somebody else up although you want to."

Pam also found it difficult to talk to Bruce, whom she describes as "a dream husband." He was very supportive and often stayed home when she could not bear being on her own. Despite the practical and emotional support he provided, Pam wanted to talk to another mother who had some understanding of her feelings:

> Bruce was really, really good. How he stayed married to me, I don't know, he's such a patient person, really laid back. He took it all . . . and he really looked after me . . . But it wasn't the same . . . You'd say, "I feel like this," and he'd say, "Yes, I know," and you'd think, "You don't know because you've never been through it" . . . So that is what I found difficult. I always wanted to talk to somebody who'd been through it and knew what I was going on about.

When Charlotte was six months old, Bruce got a new job and they moved closer to Pam's family. Despite the move, Pam continued to feel depressed, and she wondered whether going back to work might make her feel better. She returned part-time and felt much better about herself when she was at work, but she continued to feel depressed when she was at home:

> I was fine at work. I was perfect. I coped, I ran all these people's lives, I was organized, I did my job and then I'd get in my car and I'd come home, and I'd cry all the way home. I'd just be completely, you know, like jelly [jello]. I'd cry and it would be awful and I couldn't cope. I was really ill.

In the first few months after the birth—Pam cannot recall exactly when—she went to see her doctor. She was initially unwilling to seek medical help because she feared that she would be hospitalized or that her daughter would be taken away. Finally, her mother persuaded her to go. Pam was disappointed with the doctor's response to her complaints. He ran tests for thyroid conditions and anemia and, when the results were negative, told her she was depressed because she was overweight. Appalled and upset, Pam left his office. During the next six months her depression worsened. She experienced panic attacks and a change in her personality:

> I was moody all the time. I snapped at people all the time, which wasn't my personality at all . . . and I couldn't bear being here on my own. I'd go to my mum's all the time when Bruce was at work. And like at week-ends, if we were here, and he'd say, "Oh, just going to cut the grass," I used to go mad. I used to hate him even going outside to cut the grass. I didn't want to be left on my own, at all, even when he was just out the front there. I couldn't bear it and I used to get quite violent. I used to lose my temper, not towards Charlotte at all, but towards Bruce. I'd throw

things at him and hit him . . . I was just awful, and it was just so frightening but I knew that I didn't have any control really. I couldn't control what I was feeling. And I would just feel so low and lifeless all the time.

During this time Pam also had recurring thoughts of suicide:

> When I was really depressed I was really quite suicidal . . . One day I walked off down the road and Bruce came running after me, and said, "Where are you going?" and I said, "I'm going to the motorway," and I wanted to lie under this lorry. I wanted to just lie on the motorway and I just felt really calm about it . . . I said, "I just want to lie there and everything will be over." And I'm sure I would have done it . . . because there was just this feeling that I had. I just wanted to get it all over with.

Another feature of Pam's depression was her fear of being criticized and judged for being inadequate. This fear led to a preoccupation with housework:

> When I was ill, I was really wound up about the housework because everything I thought looked such a mess. And my husband goes, "It doesn't matter, it looks fine to me. It doesn't matter." And I think I was more house-proud then in a way though I couldn't be bothered to do it . . . But I didn't want people criticizing me, do you know what I mean? . . . I'm quite a laid-back person really and now I'm not so bothered. I certainly, you know, let it go, I'm enjoying my life sort of thing—what's housework? But when I was ill . . . there was something in me that I had to get it done because I didn't want people coming in and criticizing me, saying I was a messy person.

The one area of Pam's life that was not affected by her depression was her love for her daughter. Charlotte kept her going throughout her depression. "[Charlotte was] my whole life," she says, "and if it wasn't for her I wouldn't have got up in the mornings."

For months, Pam struggled with her feelings on her own until eventually her mother dragged her to the doctor again. This time, she saw a different doctor who diagnosed postpartum depression, prescribed antidepressants, and referred her to a psychiatrist. At first Pam felt embarrassed at seeing a psychiatrist because, she admits, it made her feel like "a real nutcase." As it turns out, however, she found the psychiatrist very helpful and saw him for a year:

> I could go in there and say exactly what I was feeling, and I couldn't always say that to family members or friends. It's easier to talk to someone

you don't know and get it all off your chest. So I used to feel better after seeing him.

Pam remained on antidepressants for three years. Her depression gradually lifted although she still feels moody, tearful, anxious, and experiences panic attacks. She continues to feel guilty that she was depressed and fears that her depression may have negatively affected her daughter. She also feels a great deal of sadness at the lost years of Charlotte's babyhood:

> I can't remember a lot of Charlotte being a baby really, a lot of it is just a blur to me now . . . It used to really upset me to look at photographs of her when she was a baby because it brought it all back, you know. It was horrible because I just thought that's a part of my life that I've missed out on . . . you can't relive it again.

Although Pam describes herself as much better now, she still regularly attends a postpartum depression support group in her village. She values this group because it provides a safe place where she can talk freely about her feelings. She goes partly to seek support but also to help other mothers:

> I can talk about my experience and . . . because you can't talk to anybody else, like I don't talk to my family about it because they know and also you think that it gets a bit boring, doesn't it. But you feel you've got to get it out of your system, for some reason, and also I couldn't really talk to my friends because like they're all having babies and I think if I tell them I'll frighten them to death.

Pam has been able to overcome her feelings of torment and despair, but she still struggles to understand why depression happened to her:

> It was pretty frightening. It was just the fact that there was no reason for it, you know. Like we had a good marriage, we didn't have money problems . . . the baby wasn't crying all the time, she was a good baby and everything so I couldn't work out why do I feel like this, I couldn't understand why . . . It was awful not being able to control your own body, feeling so out of control. It just put me off having children.

Pam's depression was so terrifying that she is unwilling to risk experiencing such a dark, bleak period again. She once thought she would never survive her depression—she believed it would last for the rest of her life and eventually consume and destroy her. As a result, Pam and

Bruce have decided not to have any more children. A few months ago Bruce had a vasectomy.

Pam's story is both different from and similar to the stories I heard from other women in Britain and the United States. It is different because the circumstances of each woman's life and depression varied. Some became depressed after a first child, others after a second or third baby. For some, the child was planned, for others it was not. Similarly, the women's experiences of pregnancy and childbirth were not uniform. Some babies were wakeful, some cried a lot, some had difficulty feeding. Others slept, were content, and fed well. Some women breast-fed, others bottle-fed. Some felt very close to their babies, some were indifferent, and a few rejected them. All the women were living with a male partner, but these relationships were more or less problematic. The women differed in how close they lived to their families and how much support their families provided. Some women returned full-time or part-time to their jobs or careers after the birth, while others gave up paid work altogether. The women were of diverse ages and social, educational, and economic backgrounds. Each woman's depression was also different in its symptoms, time of onset, and duration. There were variations in the types of medical care and other help women received, in how soon they got help, and for how long.

Yet there are also striking similarities among the women's experiences. As Pam makes clear in her story, there is often a contrast between a woman's expectations and her physical and emotional experience of motherhood. Pam tells of feeling alone and different from other mothers. She speaks of the silence she maintained, of her inability and unwillingness to disclose her feelings and reach out for help, and of her fear of losing her child or being institutionalized should other people find out about her feelings. She voices her fear of what other people will think of her if she does not maintain certain standards, if she does not appear to herself and others as a perfect housewife and mother. Despite a very supportive relationship with her husband, she talks of nevertheless wanting to confide her feelings to another mother who would have a more personal understanding of her experiences. She describes her difficulties in seeking medical help, how she needed assistance getting help, and how her depression was not initially detected by her doctor. She speaks of the stigma associated with being depressed and having to see a psychiatrist. She talks about the antidepressants she was prescribed but of her need, above all, to discuss her feelings. Although the details of the women's lives differed, these central themes described by Pam dominated their stories.

Pam's story also reveals the lucid and articulate quality of these mothers' accounts. It illustrates how much we can learn about women's psychological and social worlds by listening closely to their words.

DEVELOPMENTAL RESEARCH

My interest in finding out what women themselves had to say about their experiences of motherhood and postpartum depression arose when, as a doctoral student in a department of experimental psychology, I embarked on a developmental study of the impact of postpartum depression on mother-child relationships. This study was in a long tradition of experimental, laboratory-based research designed to examine the emotional, cognitive, and social capacities of infants and children, in the context of interactions with their mothers, and in response to their mothers' behavior.[2]

This body of research suggests that postpartum depression adversely affects children's mental and motor development. Children of depressed mothers are believed to show less sharing, a lower rate of overall interactive behavior, less concentration, and less sociability to a stranger. They are described as insecurely attached, and mothers report that their children show behavioral problems including sleeping and eating problems, temper tantrums, and separation difficulties.[3]

Within weeks of beginning the research I grew increasingly critical of the theoretical and methodological framework underpinning the proposed study and this tradition of research more generally. My initial concern was that although the study was ostensibly about the relationship between mother and child, there was little interest in the mother as subject in her own right. The mother was closely observed and scrutinized but only in her role as provider of the emotional and psychological environment in which her child was developing. Her mothering was examined only from the point of view of the child, while her own view on her experience and relationship was ignored. Indeed, this point has been echoed by feminist psychologists, sociologists, and psychoanalysts who have criticized developmental research in general for failing to consider the mother as having an existence of her own, or a perspective on what she does as a mother.[4] The mother, they note, appears only as a "shadowy figure," an "absent presence" who is rarely given a voice.[5]

Research on the impact of postpartum depression on child development focuses exclusively on the mother-child relationship. Isolating the mother-child relationship in this way, however, is at odds with the reality of family life in which fathers, siblings, grandparents, or other caregivers often take an active part in child-rearing. Indeed, Michael Rutter has also noted that the possible impact of these other relationships, as well as social problems (for example, marital difficulties, socioeconomic disadvantage, alcohol and drug dependency, isolation, lack of support, little contact with other parents or children), tends to be ignored within these research studies.[6]

Perhaps the most disturbing aspect of this type of developmental research is that it promotes idealized and unrealistic models of mothers and mother-child relationships. The ideal mother in these experiments is responsive, receptive, and sensitive at all times. The ideal relationship is child-centered, absent of conflict, and one in which mother and child are in tune with each other. These characteristics are portrayed as the touchstone of successful mothering. Deviations from this model of mother-child interaction are attributed to the detrimental effects of depression on the mother's behavior, on the mother-child relationship, and on the child. Yet research carried out by the developmental psychologists Edward Tronick and Andrew Gianino shows that being in constant tune with each other, and what they call optimal "mutual regulation," are not the norm even within mother-child relationships in which the mother is *not* depressed. Interactions between mother and child are not always smooth and consistent; they constantly move back and forth between conflict and resolution. Indeed, they note that the infant's experience of "repairing" interactions with his or her mother has positive developmental effects because it serves as a guide to interactions with other people.[7] Interestingly, after they had recovered from their depression, the mothers in my own research also spoke about what they regarded as the developmental benefits of exposing their children to a mother's varied emotions, and to real rather than idealized relationships. Their depression, they said, had made them better mothers because by recognizing and taking into account their own needs, as well as those of others, they were providing their children with more realistic models of parenting, parent-child relationships, and indeed relationships more generally (see Chapter 8).

Developmental studies reflect, reinforce, and contribute to cultural ideals of the all-loving, all-giving, perfect mother who is attuned to every emotion in her child while denying her own needs and feelings. As the psychotherapist Rozsika Parker writes, "observational studies of mothers and babies [have] lent the authority of science to representations of the ideal mother as sensitive, measured, attentive and naturally at one with her children."[8] In this sense, this research produces what Adam Phillips calls "canonical fantasies about mothering," which not only fail to reflect the reality of motherhood, but can also reinforce women's sense of inadequacy in their role as mothers.[9]

THE MEDICAL MODEL

My concerns with the developmental research led me to devise a qualitative study centering on women's accounts of their experiences of motherhood and postpartum depression. I transferred to the social and political sciences faculty, where I began reading social scientific work on motherhood and exploring how medical, psychiatric, and experimental psychological literatures made sense of postpartum depression.[10]

This latter body of work, which I refer to here as the medical model of postpartum depression, investigates its epidemiology and etiology.[11] Postpartum depression is understood as a disease or illness, and research efforts have been devoted to describing, predicting, preventing, and treating it.[12] I searched for evidence of women's own accounts of their depression but found none. Indeed, within this quantitative research tradition mothers' views tend to be regarded not only as irrelevant but also as an obstacle to understanding postpartum depression. In 1980 Eugene Paykel, a leading researcher in the field, along with his colleagues reported on a study exploring whether postpartum depression was linked to the occurrence of recent stressful life events such as moving and bereavement. Paykel and his colleagues were not interested in the women's views on the impact of certain events on their lives; they were concerned only with an objective measurement of impact. They assessed "the degree of negative impact the event would be expected to have on someone when its full nature and particular circumstances were taken into account, but *completely ignoring the patient's subjective report of reaction*" (emphasis added).[13] When it came to assessing the mother's personal history, details of pregnancy and delivery, and social circumstances, the researchers were forced to include elements of the mothers' views by default. They write, "For a few items subjective feelings of the patient were recorded. For the others, although some effects of patient perception cannot be ruled out . . . attempts were made to construct detailed anchor points and to elicit objective information based on actual circumstances in order to make judgments."[14] This passage is revealing because it implies not only that the researcher is deemed a better judge of the mother's life than the mother herself, but also that the researcher's (subjective) judgment is regarded as objective.

Within this research women's views are not only ignored; they are actually regarded as a source of contamination to the research enterprise. Critics of psychiatry such as Erving Goffman, R. D. Laing, and others have commented that, within psychiatry, depressed individuals are perceived as having a negative and distorted view of reality reflecting a disturbed mind.[15] Their subjective perceptions are therefore deemed of little value because they fail to offer an objective perspective. Similarly, within the field of postpartum depression, women's accounts are seen as confounded, confused, and distorted by their depression.[16] They are regarded as untrustworthy because, it is argued, they are too biased and subjective to tell us anything about what is really going on. As the psychologist Rhonda Small and her colleagues have pointed out, there is a persistent belief among many researchers that being depressed renders women incapable of meaningful insights into the experience of postpartum depression even though research indicates that depressed mothers are not universally negative in their recollections of their experiences.[17]

This devaluation of women's own perspectives arguably accounts for the failure of medical, psychiatric, and much psychological research to shed light on why and how women come to be depressed after the birth of a baby. Although this research has been ongoing for nearly forty years, it has revealed few conclusive findings. It aims to find objective risk factors that predict who will become depressed. It asks whether postpartum depression is associated with, or caused by, certain factors. For example, is postpartum depression linked to hormonal or other biochemical changes in the body? Is there a genetic predisposition to postpartum depression? Do depressed mothers have a family history of postpartum depression or other psychiatric conditions? Do they share certain personality traits or a similar attitude toward children? Is depression associated with any of the following: an unplanned pregnancy, a cesarean delivery, a hospital or home birth, complications during the birth, early discharge from the hospital, breast-feeding or bottle-feeding the baby, experiencing the baby blues, having twins, trying to cope with a "difficult" baby, a lack of previous experience with children, a poor relationship with a male partner, poor relationships with family and friends, the occurrence of stressful life events, or whether or not the mother is employed outside the home? What about the sociodemographic distribution of postpartum depression—is it linked to age, social class, ethnic background, marital status, education, or income? And is it more common after the birth of a first child or after subsequent births?[18]

With a few exceptions, these studies fail to yield conclusive results. Consistent evidence does seem to point to the fact that women who become depressed experience difficulties within their relationships with their male partners, though, as I explain in Chapter 6, this is not to say that women are necessarily unhappy in their relationships, or that difficult relationships cause postpartum depression.[19] Research also suggests that, compared with non-depressed mothers, women with postpartum depression are more likely to have a previous history of psychiatric problems and to have experienced stressful life events around the time of the birth, such as a death in the family, illness, a move, or childcare-related stressors.[20] Overall, however, it is difficult, if not impossible, to build a profile of the typical woman who becomes depressed postpartum given that PPD affects a diverse group of women. Depression knows few boundaries, I would suggest, because it is not about what objectively happens to an individual, but about how the individual subjectively interprets and experiences what happens to her. Women's perspectives, then, are the key to understanding postpartum depression.

Women who suffer from depression are locked into a certain way of perceiving themselves and the world around them. In order to make sense of their depression, we must understand these perceptions. By failing to include mothers' perspectives, studies that follow the medical model overlook the fact that different women experience similar events or situations in different ways, depending on their individual circumstances and point of view. Until such research gives women a voice, those who are struggling with postpartum depression will continue to be portrayed as passive victims of their biology, personality, or social context.

HORMONAL THEORIES

Hormonal theories of depression have captured popular imagination and infiltrated lay beliefs about PPD. Media stories in particular tend to emphasize the hormonal nature of postpartum depression. When friends and colleagues hear of my research their first question is invariably, "Is postpartum depression caused by hormonal changes?" The most widely read publication on postpartum depression among the women I spoke with in Britain and the United States was Katharina Dalton's book *Depression after Childbirth,* in which the author puts forward a hormonal theory of postpartum depression.[21] Despite the lack of solid evidence for a biochemical cause, there is a widespread but unproven assumption within the medical profession, the media, and the general public that postpartum depression has a hormonal basis.[22] Indeed, many of the British and American women I spoke to embraced a hormonal theory of postpartum depression in order to make sense of their feelings (see Chapters 2 and 9). For these reasons it is important to consider this theory, and in particular the ideas put forward in Dalton's book.

Katharina Dalton is a British general practitioner. Although her theory is regarded by some sectors of the medical and psychiatric profession as extreme, it typifies many aspects of medical and psychiatric understandings of women's psychological problems in that it emphasizes women's unstable, weak, and deficient bodies.[23] Dalton argues that postpartum depression is "an illness due to a biochemical abnormality in the brain, which controls the workings of the body, and also a biochemical abnormality in the blood which perfuses all the tissues of the body."[24] The primary cause of the depression, she notes, is the abrupt change in hormonal levels in the woman's body after the birth and delivery of the placenta, in particular, a drop in progesterone and estrogen. She suggests that a disheveled appearance and a disorganized home are sure signs that a mother is suffering from postpartum depression:

A home visit reveals the patient as quite different from the carefully made-up, well-coiffeured lady who attended the prenatal clinic. She's now dishevelled with no make-up, and no recent sign of a shampoo and set. The home is a bit of a muddle with the baby's clothes on the floor, a pile of nappies waiting to be washed, and several cups on the draining board.[25]

This caricature of a depressed mother is very misleading. Many mothers who have not experienced depression would recognize themselves in this description, especially during the first demanding and exhausting weeks of motherhood. Moreover, as Pam and many of the other mothers explained, they went to great lengths to have an immaculate home and "look the part" of the coping mother—not only because they were afraid they might be judged bad mothers if they appeared to be "in a state," but also because they wanted to conceal their depression from other people. As one visiting nurse pointed out to me, she was less concerned about the messy homes than she was about the immaculate ones.

Dalton also argues that the irritability seen in postpartum depression is the result of low blood sugar levels. In a passage that reveals remarkably little sympathy or understanding for women, she writes:

The irritability is reflected on the husband, for too often he is at the wrong end of his wife's bad temper. He finds she has changed from the elated, vivacious person she was during pregnancy into the ever-moaning bitch of today. Can you blame him if he stops in for a quick pick-me-up on his journey home before he faces another irrational flow of verbal abuse or physical danger?[26]

Given the insensitivity of this passage, it is perhaps surprising that the majority of the women in my study who had come across Dalton's book found it helpful. By attributing depression to biochemical causes, however, the hormonal explanation paradoxically relieves women of responsibility for their feelings and behavior. Nevertheless, Dalton's book is problematic because it reinforces the ideal of blissful motherhood while pathologizing negative and ambivalent feelings. Most important, Dalton fails to acknowledge the psychological, interpersonal, and social factors to which women themselves attribute their depression.

SOCIAL SCIENCE PERSPECTIVES

In recent years, a growing body of work has developed largely as a critique of the medical model and in particular its failure to consider women's perspectives. Social scientific studies explore women's accounts, experiences, and perceptions of their depression, in particular, its time of onset and duration; its perceived contributing factors; its consequences for women, their children, and their families; women's views of professional support as well as other sources of support; and the recovery process.[27] An important strand of this work is feminist analyses of postpartum depression, which are rooted within broader feminist critiques of medicine and psychiatry.[28]

Like social science perspectives, feminist accounts of postpartum depression challenge medical theories because they cast women's depression as an individual, often biological problem, and leave the broader social, political, and cultural context unexamined. They also take issue with the notion that postpartum depression is treated as a disease with clear symptoms and characteristics. They argue that postpartum depression is a category elaborated by the medical and psychiatric professions to describe a cluster of signs and symptoms; and in this sense it is a medical and social construct.

My characterization of a particular group of scholars as feminist is based on their use of gender as an analytical tool in understanding postpartum depression. Feminist approaches share an emphasis on women's gendered subjectivities, and on the inequalities women face in public and domestic spheres—inequalities that researchers believe lie at the root of depression.

There are divisions within feminist thinking about postpartum depression. For example, one strand of research is dominated by a structural approach in which PPD is seen as a normal and understandable response to the oppressive conditions of motherhood within Western societies, including the devaluation of motherhood and caregiving; the medicalization of childbirth; inadequate provision of childcare; limited parental leave; problematic re-entry into the labor market for mothers; and difficulties combining motherhood with paid work.[29] This tradition of work has tended to emphasize the losses associated with motherhood, and it sees them as responsible for postpartum depression. According to proponents of this theory, becoming a mother entails a loss of self, occupational status and identity, autonomy, physical integrity, time, sexuality, and male company. A mother also loses her established relationship with her spouse or partner because the division of domestic tasks tends to become more pronounced along gender lines after the birth of a child. Postpartum depression is therefore seen by some feminist thinkers as a form of bereavement—it is a grief response to these losses and, above all, to the mother's lost identity.[30] For example, the feminist social psychologist Paula Nicolson argues that because most of the women in her sample suffered some degree of depression or negative feelings following childbirth, "postnatal depression needs to be reconceptualized as part of the *normal experience of most women when they become mothers.*"[31] Depression, she suggests, is "a healthy and normal grief reaction" because of what she terms the "universal/common experience" of motherhood.[32] This experience includes problems with breast-feeding, lack of sleep, lack of closeness with one's partner, and oppression within a patriarchal society. This feminist approach to understanding postpartum depression reflects a broader strand of feminist thinking on motherhood that accentuates its negative side and focuses on the oppressive aspects of the role, including gender inequalities within the workplace and within society more generally (see Chapter 2).

A different strand of feminist research explores not only the structural and material conditions of women's lives, but also cultural attitudes toward femininity, motherhood, and postpartum depression. These scholars argue that structural approaches are overly deterministic and neglect women's agency and the ways in which they actively negotiate the social contexts within which they live. For example, the psychologist Janet Stoppard espouses a "material-discursive" theory of depression that she applies to postpartum depression as well as depression occurring at other times in women's lives. Her theory has three key concepts: subjectivity, gender, and embodiment. She argues that postpartum depression can be understood as "a set of experiences arising at the intersection of women's lives and their bodies. These experiences are socially constructed in relation to cultural meanings of marriage and motherhood and socially produced by the practices of being a wife and a mother. These meanings and practices are both shaped and regulated by discourses of femininity, as well as by structural conditions characterizing the societal context within which women live their lives as wives and mothers."[33]

Feminists also have different views on how women's feelings come to be labeled postpartum depression. Some argue that women are unwilling and passive victims of psychiatric labeling. Labels such as postpartum depression, they suggest, are a form of medical and social control and should therefore be abandoned in favor of such terms as "depression following childbirth" or "unhappiness after childbirth."[34] Other feminist thinkers, however, observe that many women embrace the label postpartum depression and are active participants in the medicalization of their experiences.[35] These scholars have turned their attention to the intriguing question of how women self-label, and some argue that women's appropriation of this psychiatric label can be viewed as a form of resistance to gender roles, norms, and expectations (see Chapters 2 and 9).[36]

Feminist thinkers also differ on how to alleviate women's feelings of distress. Some advocate structural change in order to address the political, economic, and social inequalities that are seen as responsible for postpartum depression.[37] Others argue that individual support and help is not only necessary but can lead to broader changes in society. For example, in her research on postpartum depression and the self-help movement associated with it, the feminist sociologist Verta Taylor argues that self-help groups promote not only personal but also societal change. Although they appear to offer an individual solution to women's problems, in seeking to rework cultural assumptions about what it means to be a woman and mother they actually challenge and change the gender order. These groups, Taylor argues, are central players in the redefinition of gender relations in American society.[38]

While feminist work has done an excellent job of mapping the cultural and structural restrictions on women's lives, there is still a need to explore the different ways in which individual women deal with the ideologies, meanings, practices, and social conditions of motherhood. The tendency within some feminist work to assume that social structures and cultural discourses affect women in a uniform way, and to present women's responses to motherhood as homogenous and universally negative, leaves unanswered the question of why some women become depressed while others do not. In practice, as I discuss in Chapter 2, women vary in their emotional reactions to motherhood. Moreover, individual women experience a range of conflicting feelings about being mothers. Feelings of frustration, distress, and depression can exist alongside feelings of joy, reward, and fulfillment. Motherhood may bring with it losses, changes, and constraints, but it also brings positive changes, not least a new child. As many writers have argued, motherhood is above all an experience of ambivalence.[39]

Furthermore, whereas dominant feminist theories of postpartum depression present it as a problem of identity and autonomy, my own understanding is that depression is a relational problem. Because many feminists view depression as a consequence of the lack of autonomy, independence, power, and paid employment assumed to accompany motherhood, they regard the autonomy and separate identity acquired through paid employment as the route to psychological health for women. My own research contradicted this theory, however. I heard women speaking about depression as a sense of psychological isolation and difference. Their experiences of motherhood did not reflect the ideals supported by the culture in which they lived, and this caused them distress, particularly when healthcare professionals, partners, relatives, or friends reinforced these ideals. The sense of shame and failure this created led them to withdraw, isolate themselves, and conceal their feelings from other people. In these women's stories depression could be understood as a relational problem; their experiences of motherhood left them feeling disconnected from parts of themselves, from other people, and from cultural norms and definitions of motherhood.

RELATIONAL PSYCHOLOGY

To make sense of women's stories of depression, I turned to relational psychology because it gave me a theoretical and methodological (see Appendix 2) way of exploring the relational dimensions—both cultural and interpersonal—of motherhood and postpartum depression. Relational psychology has been described as "one of the most influential strands of feminist social psychology today."[40] It grows out of more than two decades of research and clinical work, predominantly with girls and women, but increasingly with boys and men, in the United States.[41] Early relational writings were dominated by the experiences of white, middle-class, heterosexual, and educated women. The last decade, however, has seen a growing appreciation of the need to consider diversity among women and men, and to broaden and deepen relational thinking through the incorporation of issues of race, sexual orientation, socioeconomic standing, able-bodyness, and age.[42]

The relational model of women's psychology has been developed by two groups of psychologists: clinicians working at the Stone Center, Wellesley College, and empirical researchers at the Harvard University Graduate School of Education. In the late 1970s, Jean Baker Miller at the Stone Center and Carol Gilligan at Harvard University simultaneously began to question traditional theories of human development.[43] Within these theories, separation, individuation, and independence are seen as the hallmarks of adult development, maturity, and health. Development is seen as the growth of an autonomous and contained self with firm boundaries, as well as movement toward self-sufficiency. The notion of an isolated individual dominates not only psychology but also sociology, philosophy, and Western thought more generally, as Ian Burkitt writes:

> The view of human beings as self-contained unitary individuals who carry their uniqueness deep inside themselves, like pearls hidden in their shells, is one that is ingrained in the Western tradition of thought. It is a vision captured in the idea of the person as a monad—that is, solitary individual divided from other human beings by deep walls and barriers: a self-contained being whose social bonds are not primary to its existence, but only of secondary importance.[44]

This view of the self seemed at odds with the experiences of the women Miller and Gilligan were listening to in clinical and research settings. Whereas women's views have generally been discounted or regarded as deficient within classical theories of development, Miller and Gilligan stayed with the women's voices and began to hear and develop a relational way of thinking about women's psychology and development.

They, and subsequent relational theorists, argue that women experience themselves fundamentally as caught up in a web of intimate social relations.[45] Identity is defined in a context of intimacy, care, and relationship.[46] Jean Baker Miller notes that "women's sense of self becomes very much organized around being able to make, and then to maintain, affiliations and relationships."[47] She and others have added that "self, other and the relationship are no longer clearly separated entities in this perspective but are seen as *mutually forming processes*."[48] Other aspects of the self such as creativity, autonomy, and assertion are seen to develop within this primary context in which relationships are the central, organizing feature of women's development.[49] Women are primarily searching for connections with others, rather than struggling toward independence and autonomy.

Theories of "normal" development implicitly or explicitly contain within them theories of psychopathology. Within classical theories, psychological problems are generally seen to arise when a person fails to separate from others and become an independent and autonomous human being. Women with psychological problems have tended to be seen as too "dependent" and insufficiently autonomous.[50] From a relational perspective, psychological problems result from a sense of disconnection from oneself, other people, and the surrounding world.[51] For example, a recurring theme within relational writings concerns the sense of disconnection girls and women experience from themselves and the world around them when they come under pressure to conform to cultural standards and norms of femininity and womanhood.[52]

Disconnection occurs when, for different reasons, an individual feels that she cannot discuss her experience with other people, or that her experience does not conform to cultural norms and expectations.[53] Such disconnections happen throughout a person's life and only lead to problems when the person cannot bring her experience into the relationship, or when other people make a reconnection in the relationship impossible. Within these situations, the individual is left feeling profoundly isolated. Jean Baker Miller and her colleagues suggest that this psychological isolation, "the feeling of being locked out of the possibility of human connection," is one of the most terrifying human experiences.[54] Women will go to great lengths to try to maintain or re-establish their relationships, including altering parts of themselves to turn themselves into what they believe others want them to be. At the same time, this leaves them feeling cut off from their own experience, which in turn leads to psychological problems. As Miller and colleagues write, "Psychological problems represent the mechanisms people construct that keep them out of connection while they simultaneously are seeking connection."[55]

This analysis of the origins of psychological problems has parallels within other theoretical traditions. For example, in his symbolic-interactionist study of depression, the sociologist David Karp writes that "depression is an illness of isolation, a dis-ease of disconnection."[56] His study of fifty men's and women's experiences of depression shows that depressed individuals crave connection but feel unable to realize it. Much of the pain of depression, he writes, arises out of the recognition that human connection is what the individual wants most and yet finds impossible to achieve when gripped by a paralyzing episode of depression.

*   *   *

Relational psychology helped me understand not only women's stories but also existing research on postpartum depression. Dominant feminist interpretations tend to cast motherhood in a negative light. By emphasizing the importance of autonomy, independence, and paid work to women's psychological health, they advocate a return to a pre-motherhood identity. This position implicitly adopts a male model when looking at women's lives by emphasizing the importance of paid work while devaluing women's traditional caregiving and homemaking roles. Relational theory, in contrast, seeks to valorize the caring activities traditionally associated with women and mothers, and challenges the value accorded to them by society. In placing the spotlight on relational issues in women's lives, both cultural and interpersonal, this book seeks to extend current feminist thinking on motherhood and postpartum depression.

the landscape of motherhood

During the eighteen months I spent traveling around Britain, visiting women in their homes and talking to them about their lives, I heard many different reactions to the experience of motherhood. Many women said that it was the most fulfilling and meaningful event of their lives. Others explained that though their spirits were low and they found motherhood difficult, they did not experience postpartum depression. Of the forty mothers I spoke to in this study—and on whom I focus in this chapter—eighteen said they experienced a debilitating and distressing episode of depression after the birth of a child (and in some cases also during pregnancy).

These women, who used the term *postpartum depression* to describe their feelings, were surprised by their reactions. They did not recognize the person they had become, nor had they experienced anything like this before. Although they knew that motherhood was challenging and often devalued, with many new mothers receiving little support or understanding, they also struggled to understand their extreme reactions and feelings of deep despair. These women, most of whom were prescribed antidepressant medication, felt they were losing their minds and feared they might wake up one morning to find themselves institutionalized in a psychiatric hospital.

This book is concerned mainly with the experiences of these eighteen women. Before considering their stories, however, it is important to explore why some women who have also struggled with motherhood have not defined their experiences as depression. They offer insights into how the feelings of sadness, low mood, and ambivalence that many mothers experience can become feelings of depression.

Sasha describes motherhood as a mostly enjoyable and unproblematic experience. At twenty-two, she lives with her husband, Keith, twenty-eight, in a small home in a housing development. Sasha is at home full-time looking after their eleven-month-old son, Gregory, while Keith works at a nearby factory. For Sasha, motherhood has been all she expected and hoped it would be:

> When Gregory came along . . . our whole life changed round to . . . suit him. I loved it, though, I've always wanted children, so it was great. My friend suffered postnatal depression and I can never understand why because I was just so happy . . . I think it's the best thing that's happened in our life.

Amanda is an older mother who works full-time as a tax consultant. On a Wednesday night, after a long day at work, she has found time to see me. Her eighteen-month-old son, Liam, is tucked in bed and her husband is making us a cup of tea. As we sit talking in her comfortable house in a rural village, she explains why, like Sasha, she is unequivocal about the joys and rewards of her life as a mother:

> I thoroughly enjoy motherhood. Whether I would be if I was doing it all day, probably not. Yes, it's great, I don't find *any* of the tasks irksome . . . I did think, before, that I'd get very impatient at all this fiddling around putting clothes on . . . and I'd resent the time, and that I'd think there were more important things to do, but I don't. I mean . . . our life as a couple has changed, but only in ways we welcome because . . . Liam is there, and that's really nice, and all the changes are nice changes.

Of the forty women I interviewed, seventeen had similar tales to tell. Despite differences in their ages and class, the quality of their relationships, whether or not they were in paid work, and the type of work they did, these women embraced and welcomed their new babies and their identities as mothers.

In contrast to these women, a group of the mothers clearly struggled with the experience of motherhood. At the time of the interviews, and especially during the months I spent reading the interview transcripts, I began to notice differences among these women. Some defined their feelings as postpartum depression whereas others did not. Their descriptions of their feelings and how they coped with them varied significantly. Five of the forty women said that, while they felt "low," "depressed," and "stressed" during the first few months after the birth, they did not experience "postnatal depression." They blamed their feelings on a range of problems including a traumatic birth, difficulty breast-feeding, a crying baby, a baby who hardly slept, tiredness, marital problems, and loss of time to themselves.

Hannah, for example, experienced mixed feelings about motherhood in the first weeks after her daughter, Zoë, was born. She attributed these feelings to a "bad birthing experience." Although she expected the birth to be relatively uncomplicated, and the healthcare professionals caring for her in the hospital to be supportive, she had a long and difficult labor during which the hospital staff failed to consult and inform her about her progress. She felt very angry with the doctors and midwives and blamed them for her negative experience. She attributed her low mood to her disappointment about the birth and the hospital, but not to any negative feelings about Zoë or about being a mother:

> I was very disappointed by the birth and the hospital, but I've never been disappointed by Zoë. More than anything I was sore, exhausted, angry with the hospital and felt my enjoyment of Zoë had been seriously marred.

About four to six weeks after the birth Hannah started to feel better. Throughout this period, she was always able to talk to her husband about her feelings, no matter how awful she felt. She also enjoyed a close and confiding relationship with her mother. Now twenty-four and a full-time mother of fourteen-month-old Zoë, Hannah explains that these relationships have been important in helping her through the difficult times she experienced as a new mother.

Like Hannah, Vivienne is close to her husband and mother, both of whom were "extremely supportive" when she had difficulties in the first few months of motherhood. Vivienne found the first two months of Laura's life very stressful as a result of problems breast-feeding and a lack of sleep:

> The first few weeks after the birth were hell . . . I always assumed breast-feeding would be easy and natural—not true. It was *always* painful . . . This discomfort made me *dread* Laura feeding and I was often in tears. So this combination of pain and lack of sleep just increased my anxiety and tearfulness.

The breast-feeding caused abscesses and broken skin. Vivienne was angry with her doctor and visiting nurse for their lack of support and their failure to recognize that she was having real physical difficulties. "They tell you you have a psychological block," she says, "when one knows perfectly well it's physical. I certainly was highly committed to breast-feeding."

Vivienne also found Laura a demanding and "clingy" baby. Whenever she was awake she insisted on being held. Vivienne, who is now thirty-six and works full-time as a probation officer, explains that her husband and particularly her mother were invaluable in helping her manage during the first few months after Laura's birth. "More than once," she says, "I rang my mother in tears to say I couldn't cope any more. She would come straight over, and she never criticized." Her mother-in-law, by contrast, has been very critical of Vivienne and her husband's child-rearing practices and unsympathetic about Vivienne's difficulties. In the thirteen months since Laura's birth, Vivienne has been able to contend with the "deep rift" between herself and her mother-in-law because of the support she has received not only from her own mother and her husband, but also from other parents. She has found reassurance and comfort through sharing her difficulties with other mothers, met through prenatal classes and postnatal support groups.

Vivienne's story begins to shed light on why some women who experience difficulties in motherhood do not become depressed whereas others do. We learn from Vivienne that the key to coping with the challenges of motherhood is not just supportive, sympathetic, and accepting family and friends—indeed, she struggled with a critical mother-in-law for a year—but also the support of other women who have experienced the same feelings. Beatrice offers further insights into how women cope without becoming depressed.

When I meet Beatrice on a cold winter morning, she is on maternity leave from her job as an editor in a publishing house. She is thirty-five and her son, Jack, is six months. Beatrice is now finding motherhood much easier than she did in the early months. She found the first weeks frightening, exhausting, and monotonous. The most difficult aspect of her life as a mother is the contrast between the control she feels she used to have over her life, when she was working full-time outside the home, and what she now experiences as a loss of control over herself, her time, and her space:

I think the critical thing was the lack of control, and I hadn't expected that, that with a small child you have no control over your life whatsoever . . . And I mean I've always known that control is a very important thing to me but I hadn't realized, well, either quite how important or quite how much it would be taken away . . . It was not being able to have any time to myself . . . a predictable period of time . . . I found *really really* hard . . . I mean I just made sure lots of people came to see me most days . . . just to stop the sort of wall closing in . . . So I must say the first month was appalling, the second month wasn't much better . . . and then after three months it got really much better, it was lovely.

Beatrice took a crucial step toward improving her situation when she decided to create more time for herself. She has arranged for Jack to have part-time childcare and has decided to return to work part-time. Her close relationship with her mother and her friendships with other mothers have also helped her through the past months. These women have contributed more to her feelings of well-being than her relationship with her husband, whom she feels offers her little practical or emotional support.

Initially I found it difficult to pinpoint differences between these women and those who said they had experienced postpartum depression. Women within both groups talked about struggling with the realities of motherhood, difficult births and poor professional support, problems breast-feeding, wakeful babies, disappointment with themselves as mothers, and sometimes difficult relationships with their husbands, mothers, or mothers-in-law. Also, for every woman who struggled with a particular aspect of her life as a mother, another woman found this same aspect unproblematic. As Hannah, Vivienne, and Beatrice made clear, women who find motherhood difficult do not necessarily experience postpartum depression. In other words, depression or lack of it cannot be attributed to any particular events, circumstances, or difficulties within these women's lives. It was not until I spoke with Ruth and Anna that I began to make sense of this confusing picture.

Since becoming a mother, Ruth has received the most support from other mothers. She feels able to talk to other women about the challenges of motherhood, and she values the psychological support and understanding they have to offer:

Moaning to other mothers . . . was vital. It was very important at the time . . . You spend a lot of your time moaning, but it isn't really like that, I don't think. It's actually just a way of helping you not feel quite so isolated in your inadequacies and incompetencies. It's very important.

Since her son, Russell, was born twenty months ago, Ruth has been coping with the demands of motherhood, a difficult baby, and a rocky relationship with her husband, Tom. Ruth, who is thirty-two and works part-time as a domestic cleaner, says that she was "depressed" for the first nine months of Russell's life "but for quite *real* reasons." Becoming a mother has been "the hardest and most challenging period of my life," she says. Russell didn't sleep well, wanted to feed all the time, and was very demanding. She also found that the "relentless, monotonous routine was very hard to adjust to." As Russell became more independent and settled into a routine, she began to feel better.

One of Ruth's main problems has been Tom's lack of practical and emotional support. "More than anything," she says, "I was disappointed with my husband." Just before she became pregnant with Russell, Tom had an extra-marital affair. Within two weeks of the birth, he stopped looking after Russell, leaving the baby's care entirely to Ruth. Tom's contribution to housework was equally minimal. Ruth feels disappointed by her husband's lack of involvement with Russell. She is hurt not only by his refusal to help, but more important by his lack of desire to be involved in Russell's life. Despite her feelings of disappointment and resentment, they rarely talk about the problems in their relationship.

When Ruth tells me her story, she explains that although she felt "depressed," what she experienced was "marital problems," not "postnatal depression." Intrigued by her comment, I ask her why she thinks she did not experience postpartum depression. She tells me about her close relationship with her own mother, with whom she regularly talks by telephone and occasionally sees. She also talks about a male friend, Julian, with whom she became briefly involved when she was having problems with Tom and difficulty adjusting to motherhood. Julian offered her a lot of emotional support at a time when she was not getting any from Tom. She also feels that she did not become more deeply depressed because she is a person who acknowledges the importance of confronting the difficult issues in her life. She accepts the way she feels and is not bothered much by the fact that her feelings about being a mother are different from those of other mothers. When she sees other women who seem to be coping better or having an easier time, she accepts that her experience is different, neither better nor worse. "After all," she says, "we're all different people anyway, with different natures. People cope with things in different ways." She also knows that there are two sides of motherhood: a public "façade" of the mother who "seems" or "looks" to be coping, and the often quite different private reality. Ruth knows about this private reality from her own experience and also from sharing her feelings with other mothers. She knows that "a lot of people feel exactly the same as me."

Anna is thirty years old and looks after her one-year-old daughter, Rose, full-time. She found motherhood very difficult for the first six months. Rose did not sleep well and cried a lot, leaving Anna feeling exhausted. Anna and her husband, Graham, lived in a small village where she knew few people. She felt lonely and isolated. But the main source of her depressed mood was breast-feeding. Rose often threw up after a feed, which Anna found very distressing. After three months, she switched to bottle-feeding but experienced considerable guilt. At the time of our interview, Anna had recently written an article for her local National Childbirth Trust (NCT) newsletter describing her experiences.[1] In the interview, she read it to me:

> The three months I breast-fed Rose were very traumatic and unsettled. I suppose they probably are to most first-time mothers. All she seemed to do was vomit after every feed and cry all day, and I spent most of the day in tears too and sitting for hours on end trying to feed her. At my wits end, I decided to experiment with bottle-feeding and during the next few days I alternated two bottle feeds with two breast feeds. By the end of the week I knew that both she and I were happier with the bottle, and I decided that I would bottle-feed her totally. She changed overnight from my crying bundle to a very contented baby and we never looked back. Except for all the guilty feelings I then began to have. Had I really done the best for my baby or was I letting her down? What would other people think? How on earth was I going to tell my doctor that she was now *on the bottle,* let alone face my NCT reunion class, and I very nearly didn't go. I found myself justifying my actions to everyone, and I felt such a sense of relief when I saw someone else bottle-feeding their baby. All in all I worked myself up into a private frenzy. I did get over it. After all it was *my* baby and *my* body . . . There is a lot of propaganda and pressure to breast-feed, and rightly so, but I don't think we should forget those who *really* do find it difficult or for whatever reasons decide to bottle-feed their baby. Rose is a year old this week, and I'm proud to say

she's never had a day's illness. Despite the guilty feelings I experienced I'm still convinced that bottle-feeding was right for Rose and me.

Throughout the difficult early months, Anna's husband, Graham, had been very supportive emotionally and, to a lesser degree, practically. Nonetheless, she felt that Graham did not understand fully what she was experiencing. But she was able to confide in her mother, with whom she had a very close relationship.

When I asked Anna whether she thought she had experienced post-partum depression, she said that although she had felt "depressed," she had not felt "depressed, depressed." Yes, she had found mother-hood "difficult," but she had not experienced postpartum depression. Her previous experience of severe depression in late adolescence, for which she took antidepressants for a year, had taught her the impor-tance of acknowledging her feelings. When she had her daughter, she realized that in order to avoid becoming severely depressed she had to accept her difficult and ambivalent feelings about motherhood. Anna articulates clearly the difference between feeling "depressed" or "low," and feeling "depressed depressed," as she puts it. When I asked her how she understood postpartum depression, she responded:

> I think perhaps having the same feelings that I was having, but really not being able to sort of come to terms with them, and to really let them get on top of you . . . One of the things I've learnt from . . . being depressed before, was that you have to have room for your feelings, and there are times when you don't feel happy or you feel angry or you feel sad, and that you shouldn't pretend that you don't feel those feelings. So when I felt low after the birth, I didn't pretend that I didn't feel low. And I think . . . my interpretation of being sort of depressed, in that respect, is feeling low and feeling really bad about feeling low.

By drawing on her experience in adolescence Anna offers an astute analysis of depression. She explains that feelings of low mood, sad-ness, and anger only become feelings of depression when a person does not allow herself to experience these feelings, when she tries to deny them to herself and hide them from other people. Anna's insights, along with the stories told by Hannah, Vivienne, Beatrice, and Ruth, suggest that many women experience difficulties, feelings of low mood, and ambivalence when they have a baby and that these feelings are perhaps the norm.[2] Nonetheless, some women find it harder than others to discuss, accept, and come to terms with their negative and ambivalent emotions. And when this happens, feelings of low mood and sadness can escalate into depression. In the chapters that follow I explore the extent to which this understanding of postpartum depression, derived from the stories of women who have not experienced it, is echoed in the stories of women who have. I examine what it is about the lives, circumstances, and relationships of women experiencing depression that made it difficult for them to acknowledge, accept, and voice their feelings and difficulties.

For the moment, however, I want to examine how the eighteen women who experienced postpartum depression described, defined, and characterized their experiences of motherhood and their feelings.

When I interviewed the women I chose not to perform any diagnostic assessments of their mental health, and it was they who identified themselves as having experienced postpartum depression. Their assessments were informed by what they had been told by healthcare professionals (fifteen of them were diagnosed with postpartum depression by their general practitioners), and what they had gathered from the media, pregnancy and childcare advice books, literature from voluntary agencies, and friends and family. Just as the five women discussed above were adamant that what they had been through was *not* postpartum depression, these eighteen women were clear that what they had experienced *was* postpartum depression. Although the severity and duration of the depression varied considerably across the eighteen women, they all emphasized the differences between feeling "depressed" and "ill," and simply feeling "low," "down," "fed up," "tired," "run down," and "exhausted."

Frances, thirty-seven, has three children, twelve, ten, and six years old. She works part-time as a nurse and runs a kennel, and her husband is a doctor. With three children Frances knows that motherhood can be a stressful and demanding job, especially given that her husband works long hours and rarely looks after the children or household activities. When she became depressed after the birth of her planned and much-wanted daughter Mathilda, she recognized neither herself nor her feelings. Even though she had experienced depression and anorexia at eighteen, this depression was different. For Frances, motherhood the third time around was quite unlike her six previous years as a mother. Within six months of Mathilda's birth, a depression descended on her that was to last three and a half years. She describes the effect her depression had on her, including how she became very superstitious:

> I've always been a very superstitious person, unfortunately, but it got to the point I was incredibly superstitious. I mean this is going to sound absolutely weird to you, but I mean the number of thirteen, as far as I'm concerned, was absolutely horrendous. I mean if we had a dog in the kennel of that age, I wouldn't go near it. I mean it was really awful. If I touched anyone of that age, I'd come home, wash my clothes, have a bath. It's laughable now, I can laugh at it now, but at the time it was a really awful thing.

It is only in the last six months that Frances has started to "feel more normal." For a long time she felt she was going "mad" and becoming a "nutcase," to use her words. Toward the end of my second visit, Frances says that she knows from her own experiences and those of other women that mothers do get down and depressed. But she emphasizes the difference between these predictable feelings and the depression she suffered with for three and a half years:

> I'm sure you get people that get depressed, you know, just depressed from sheer exhaustion really, but it's knowing the difference between just being exhausted depressed, and going a bit further down the road.

The distinctions Frances draws between different emotional responses to motherhood are echoed by other mothers. Sonya tells me that "there's . . . a difference between feeling tired and run down, and feeling like you're doing this depression." Pam says, "When I was depressed, I used to think, 'I wish I could feel fed up,' because being fed up is nothing like being depressed." And Celia explains: "I think people can be very flippant about it . . . as if it's like a Monday morning feeling . . . People use the word *depressed* very casually, 'Oh I feel depressed today, nothing's going right'—well, that's just feeling low, that's not what depression is." In distinguishing between different emotional states, these women draw attention to the severity of their feelings in contrast to the feelings of low mood and the regular ups and downs that many mothers, and people generally, experience much of the time. One of the reasons these women welcome the psychiatric term *postpartum depression* is because it captures the severity of their feelings. The label postpartum depression is also a source of relief and reassurance to these women precisely because it suggests that they are *not* going mad. Rather, they are experiencing a medically recognized problem that is shared by other mothers. Dawn has been depressed since her son's birth three and a half years ago. When her depression was finally recognized by her visiting nurse, it came as a relief. By that point she had been depressed for two years but had not told anyone—not her husband, her mother, nor her one close friend. She successfully hid her inner despair behind her cheerful appearance:

> You put on an amazing face sometimes for people's benefit. I used to put on a good face, I'd get made-up, and I'd wash my hair, and I'd look cheerful and bounce around in the sun and be this happy person that I used to be, and nobody would guess, nobody could tell. But as soon as I shut the door when I got home, I used to feel really miserable.

Although she was disappointed that the only medical help she received consisted of a prescription for antidepressants and not a professional to talk to, Dawn welcomed the diagnosis postpartum depression:

> The health visitor that was on the case at the time didn't really pick it up and I didn't 'cos usually when you have depression you don't admit it anyway. You just think you're being unusually unreasonable. It usually takes a professional to say, "Look, I think you're suffering from depression," and it's quite a relief when they say it.

When asked why the diagnosis was a relief, Dawn replied, "Well, I thought I was going mad."

For two years Dawn struggled alone and in silence because she felt inadequate. When the doctor recognized her feelings as a medical condition, this validated and legitimized her distress. Dawn and the other mothers explained that having a label for their feelings rendered them "rational," understandable, and legitimate. Sandra described her reaction when, three months after the birth, her doctor told her she had postpartum depression:

> I was relieved almost that somebody had pinpointed that I'd actually got a problem, rather than that I was just being totally unreasonable. She was putting a name to it, you know. I think I felt well yes, perhaps that explains why I've been weird.

Having a label and diagnosis confirmed that their feelings were different from the ordinary mood swings experienced by most mothers.

Celia's depression came on gradually; it was not until six months after the birth of her child that she realized something was wrong. She wanted to "cocoon herself away from the world." "I felt like I was living in a nightmare," she said, "you just wanted to be able to wake up and enjoy the good things." She also had recurring suicidal thoughts and visions. "I would get in the bath," she said, "and think 'well, if I just sank underneath the water, that would make it all go away.'" She continued: "I would be driving down the road, and I'd think, 'Oh well, if I just went over this bridge, it would all be over.'" Celia went to see her doctor, who said her depression "was quite normal. Have a few tears. What you need is a holiday, take yourself out a bit and it'll soon pass." Celia felt "appalled at what [the doctor] had to say 'cos after six months it's not baby blues anymore." Still feeling depressed, she returned to her doctor four months later:

> I went back to the doctor . . . and she said, "Oh, you definitely need some help," you know, "we've got to put you on some antidepressants, you're obviously suffering from depression." So she prescribed them to me and I thought, "Well, at least I know what's wrong with me now." That made me feel a bit better.

In using the term *postpartum depression* these women were drawing on culturally dominant medical models, explanations, and discourses of PPD. But they were not passively reflecting these medical constructions. Just as some women actively rejected the label, others actively embraced it because it released them from feelings of guilt, blame, and moral responsibility, thereby protecting their identities and self-image as "good mothers." The label validated their experiences, distinguished their feelings from other, less severe feelings of low mood, and meant their emotions were taken seriously. It justified their seeking help, empowered them to do so, and promised the possibility of relief. As Verta Taylor writes, "As long as women are unable to identify their problems in a way that connects their experiences to both the lay resources and professional treatments available to help them, they remain powerless to overcome their problems."[3] Although a label and a medical diagnosis were not enough to help them overcome their depression, they did provide some relief, and as I discuss further in Chapter 8, for many it was a first step on their road to recovery.

It is interesting that whereas women embrace the psychiatric label *postpartum depression,* much of the research community and medical profession reject it and question whether PPD should be treated as a discrete medical condition. Researchers from different disciplines and traditions—from feminist social scientists, to psychiatrists, to psychologists—question what is specifically *postpartum* about PPD and the extent to which it differs from depression that occurs at other times in women's lives and from depression in men.[4] This is why postpartum depression is not featured as a distinct diagnostic category either within the American Psychiatric Association's *Diagnostic and Statistical Manual* or within the World Health Organization's *ICD-10 (International Classification of Diseases).*[5]

For the same reasons that the women embraced the label *postpartum depression,* many also welcomed hormonal explanations of their condition, though often with some ambivalence. When I asked them what they believed was the cause of their depression, many mentioned hormones, but in the same breath they pointed to interpersonal, situational, circumstantial, societal, and cultural issues that they felt contributed to their low mood. On the one hand, hormonal explanations were appealing because they relieved the women's feelings of guilt, shame, and responsibility. As Sonya explains:

> You see it's easier on me to think it's hormonal because that is completely outside my control and hormones go wrong and then hormones go right. That is much easier to grasp than: "Well, you're always a person who's had this deep-seated obsession of always appearing successful and good and having a baby has now magnified those fears that you're going to be found out and the illness has just fed on that and multiplied itself." That's more complicated.

On the other hand, the women also rejected the theory that hormones are solely responsible for their depression. Tina, for example, became depressed while she was pregnant with her third child, Emily. Her depression was linked to her mother's death two years before Emily's birth and to difficulties in her relationship with her husband. When I asked her why women get postpartum depression she drew on hormonal explanations, referred to the interpersonal and relational issues in her life at that time, and then not only rejected the hormonal argument but did not even consider it an explanation at all:

> What I think personally happened with me, right, is that my hormones obviously are very like in a turbulent state after having a baby and that

makes you far more vulnerable to anything that's gonna get to you . . . It made me far more vulnerable to depression which thinking about it I must have been slightly depressed during my pregnancy. And then all the issues of mum's death and all the other issues of our marriage you know just made me far more vulnerable to things and so I got depressed. I mean the doctor said, you know, "It's your hormones," and everything, and I thought well, if it were my hormones then surely they would have sorted themselves out by now you know . . . He didn't really offer any explanation.

The relationship among women's feelings of depression, their knowledge and understanding of their depression, and their experiences and views of medical explanations is an intriguing one to which I return in Chapter 9. While most of the women criticized the medical approach for failing to provide adequate support, other than the prescription of antidepressants, they also welcomed the medical label, diagnosis, and hormonal explanation, while at the same time explicitly or implicitly rejecting hormonal causes. This was partly because of the psychological benefits of having a medical diagnosis that I outlined above. Also, a medical, hormonal explanation of postpartum depression is culturally dominant. Although the women knew from their own experiences that their depression was linked to interpersonal, social, and cultural issues in their lives, it was difficult for them to accept this explanation because there was not much discussion of it. One of the aims of this book is to create such an alternative discourse of postpartum depression that women can draw upon in making sense of their experiences.

Women described a variety of feelings, and displayed a sophisticated analysis of different emotional and mental states, when they talked about their experiences of motherhood. Some felt that motherhood was stressful but overall described their lives as mothers as deeply satisfying, rewarding, meaningful, and enjoyable. Even women who became depressed did not describe motherhood as a wholly negative experience. For some, such as Pam, whose story we heard in Chapter 1, love for their child got them through their depression. For these women, motherhood had both positive and negative aspects. They were also able to distinguish feelings of low mood or ambivalence from feelings of depression. Some women experienced difficulties that, although distressing, they characterized as expectable responses to childbirth and motherhood, rather than as postpartum depression.

Another group of mothers, however, experienced debilitating feelings that they defined as postpartum depression. They regarded such feelings as abnormal in the sense that their behavior and personality changed so dramatically that they did not recognize themselves.

As noted, feminist literature on postpartum depression has for the most part treated women as a homogenous group in terms of their reactions to motherhood. Feminist writings on motherhood generally have tended either to idealize motherhood and see it as a source of special power or to devalue it and regard it as a source of oppression. As the sociologist Martha McMahon writes, "feminism has attempted both to *validate the hitherto devalued identities and experiences of being a woman and mother and to reject and transcend the restrictions and oppressiveness of those identities.*"[6] This tension, which lies at the heart of feminist accounts of motherhood, has been the focus of much discussion and debate.[7] Evelyn Glenn, for example, writes that

> feminist thinking about mothering is not all of a piece: there remain fundamental divides. Some feminists have seen women's role in biological reproduction as the original source of women's subordination . . . In these formulations, liberation for women would have come only when women were freed from having to be mothers, or released from primary responsibility for mothering. In contrast, other feminist writers have sought to reclaim motherhood for women, seeing it as a source of special power, creativity, and insight . . . This divide grows out of a basic fault line that Ann Snitow identified as running through the history of feminism. What do feminists want? Do we want to do away with the category of woman—minimize the significance of sex differences and claim our rights on the basis of our essential sameness with men? Or do we want to claim the identity of woman, valorize women's culture and organize on the basis of our commonalities as women? The fault line is especially "sore" in feminist discussions of mothering. We are reluctant to give up the idea that motherhood is special. Pregnancy, birth, and breast-feeding are such powerful bodily experiences, and the emotional attachment to the infant so intense, that it is difficult for women who have gone through these experiences and emotions to think that they do not constitute unique female experiences that create an unbridgeable gap between men and women.[8]

Glenn and other scholars rightly point out that this dilemma in how we view motherhood cannot be resolved. More important, they note that thinking about motherhood as *either* special *or* oppressive is unhelpful. It fails to reflect the reality and lived experience of mother-hood, the contradictions and complexities of women's lives as moth-ers, the ambivalent feelings mothers experience, and the fact that any particular woman's relationship to mothering is both the same and different from that of other women.[9] This last point has been made particularly strongly by feminist scholars of color. They criticize the work of white feminists in both camps for putting forward universal theories of motherhood which imply that all mothers face identical issues.[10]

Similar criticisms apply to many feminist writings on postpartum depression because, by normalizing PPD, they fail to acknowledge differences in women's experiences of motherhood. As noted, a domi-nant feminist perspective on postpartum depression portrays mother-hood as an oppressive, inherently negative, and depressing experience for all women. Ann Oakley, for example, writes that "it is hard to avoid the fact that there is something really depressing about mother-hood."[11] In her book on postpartum depression, Paula Nicolson ar-gues that "most mothers in industrial and non-industrial, urban and rural, societies are oppressed. They may have particular responsibili-ties, but not the accompanying rights to choose how they mother or whether to mother at all. The popular perceptions of maternal influ-ence and power are mythological and the origins of this myth lie within patriarchy."[12] Nicolson concludes that motherhood entails a loss of self and excludes women's own development. Yet in her study of Canadian women's experiences of motherhood, Martha McMahon shows that many women view motherhood not as a source of oppres-sion, but as a means of fulfillment as human beings. Her research sug-gests that "it is a mistake to think of mothers' connectedness with their children as costing a loss of self or as a threat to the women's personal identity."[13] Although motherhood brings with it increased work and, for some, perceived economic disadvantage, it also pro-vides women with opportunities for personal growth and moral transformation into less selfish and more responsible and caring indi-viduals. As the work of McMahon and others suggests, feminist por-trayals of motherhood have often failed to reflect women's complex and ambivalent feelings.[14]

Early feminist work on postpartum depression mirrors early femi-nist analyses of motherhood in general as mostly negative. I suspect that personal experiences of motherhood also had a role to play in shaping individual research studies.[15] A comment in Ann Oakley's popular book on motherhood and postpartum depression, *Becoming a Mother,* implies this was the case in her own work:

> Some readers may feel that the portrait of motherhood given here is too bleak, too depressing, an inaccurate rendering of the satisfactions many women derive from having and looking after a baby. I have tried to show the positive side, but of course it is to some extent true that the best news is bad news: happiness doesn't hit the headlines because it is boring. In some ways, too, the picture is deliberately black. What many of the women who were interviewed said was that they were misled into thinking childbirth is a piece of cake and motherhood a bed of roses. They felt they would have been better off with a clearer view of what lay in store for them. I have constructed the book around this conclusion, perhaps amplifying it somewhat, because only in that way are messages made impressive. But the insight itself is authentic—theirs, not mine, even if it does help to interpret the way I felt back in 1968.[16]

The suggestion made within many feminist writings that postpartum depression is the norm following the birth of a baby unwittingly reinforces the very position feminists seek to criticize; namely, the fact that psychoanalysis, psychiatry, and medicine equate femininity with pathology and regard pregnancy, childbirth, and motherhood as inherently pathological events for all women.[17] Nor is it clear that attempts to normalize postpartum depression are helpful to women, or to health professionals and other caregivers. Writing in a midwifery journal, Katherine Paradice notes that "all the symptoms [of postpartum depression] defined, which are regarded as pathological, could easily be considered as a normal response to the demands of motherhood."[18] This position is unhelpful in a clinical context because it trivializes women's feelings, and it can also lead clinicians to ignore depression because its symptoms are seen as "normal" concomitants of childbirth.[19] As Celia explained earlier, she felt her feelings were invalidated when her doctor told her that what she was going through was normal. She felt he was treating what she was experiencing as the baby blues when she herself knew that it was more serious. Ultimately, her doctor's response was unhelpful because it meant Celia did not get any support.[20]

What seems to me a more useful approach is to try and understand women's different emotional responses to motherhood, and in particular differences between feelings of low mood and feelings of depression. Indeed, the literature on depression more generally recognizes these differences, as do depressed individuals themselves.[21] As James Coyne notes:

> Similarities between everyday depressed mood and the complaints of depressed patients have encouraged the view that clinical depression is simply an exaggeration of a normal depressed mood. However, patients sometimes indicate that their experience of depression is quite distinct from normal feelings of sadness, even in its extreme form.[22]

Insights from research and clinical practice within a relational tradition further elucidate the experiential, psychological, and interpersonal differences between feelings of low mood and feelings of depression in women. Drawing on their clinical experience, and writing about what they term "sadness" as opposed to "depression," the relational therapists Irene Stiver and Jean Baker Miller suggest that

> phenomenologically, significant and qualitative differences exist between sadness and depression. It is a difference between a "feeling state" and a state in which feelings are hidden; what is left is a "nonfeeling state" but with "clear dysphoric components."[23]

They continue:

> Perhaps the major difference between sadness and depression is that the depressive experience is very isolating and nonrelational. It is exquisitely self-centered in that the person has withdrawn from others and has focused on her personal defects, often around concerns about appearance and performance.[24]

Stiver and Miller, along with other relational clinicians and researchers, have argued that when feelings such as anger and sadness are not experienced, expressed, and validated, depressive reactions develop.[25] They point out that the relationships in which the woman is involved are key to the expression of emotions. If her relationships are inadequate, such that she feels she can neither experience nor express her feelings, depression can ensue. Stiver and Miller explain:

> Our basic notion is that many women who suffer depression have not been able to experience their sadness and, most important, have not been able to experience it within a context of empathic and validating relationships. There is one major reason why this occurs: The people in the surrounding context of relationships (and often society) in general do not recognize that a disappointment or loss has occurred. Alterna-

tively, they may recognize that some kind of loss has occurred, but they do not recognize its significance or magnitude *for* the woman. Not only do they not help the woman acknowledge the loss, they often actively prevent her from doing so and, therefore, contribute to severe confusion and self-doubt. Sometimes the woman initially may have some sense of her feelings, but people around her are conveying the strong message that she shouldn't have them. There's no reason to have them; so if anything is wrong, it must be that something is wrong with her.[26]

This analysis is helpful in understanding how women become depressed following childbirth. The birth of a child creates problems and ambivalent feelings for many women.[27] However, for a combination of individual, interpersonal, and cultural reasons, some women may find it more difficult than others to acknowledge and disclose their feelings. They may believe they have no supportive individuals in whom to confide. They may withdraw into silence, at which point their feelings of low mood give way to a more serious and debilitating depression. Others may come to terms with their feelings and discuss them early on, thereby avoiding postpartum depression altogether. Indeed, it appears that there is a critical time of withdrawal and silence that marks the transition from feelings of low mood and sadness to feelings of depression. If healthcare professionals and mothers are made aware of this critical period, and if mothers are encouraged to speak about their feelings early on in a supportive, non-judgmental relationship, PPD might be prevented. This innovative approach to preventing postpartum depression also points to the importance of creating a cultural and social atmosphere in which the stresses and strains of motherhood, and the range of feelings mothers experience, are accepted and acceptable.

the perfect mother

It was midday when I arrived in the quiet village where Dawn lived. I made my way to a small home in a housing development and rang the bell. Dawn answered the door wearing make-up, jeans, and a red cotton top. I was struck by how young she looked, much younger than her twenty-five years. She was slim and petite. Dawn took me straight through to the kitchen where her mother was getting twenty-one-month-old Lisa ready to go out. Dawn's son Tim was at a playgroup. Her husband, Len, twenty-eight, worked as a car mechanic. After a few minutes Dawn's mother and Lisa left to go for a walk. Dawn brought two cups of tea to the kitchen table, and we began the interview.

Dawn got married when she was eighteen, had a miscarriage when she was nineteen, then gave birth to Tim when she was twenty-one and Lisa when she was twenty-three. Although her depression was only detected eighteen months ago, she has been depressed since her son's birth three and a half years ago. She describes many factors contributing to her depression. Tim was a difficult baby who cried a lot and threw up his milk. When he was a year old, Dawn got pregnant with Lisa, a decision she now says was "foolish." When Tim was fifteen months old he developed behavioral problems and started biting other children. He had bitten Lisa the day before our interview, and Dawn showed me two bite marks on her daughter's back. Because of his biting he was taken out of local playgroups and the other mothers were unwilling to socialize with her or have their children near Tim. She lost all but one of her friends and became very isolated and lonely. She remembers feeling very depressed during the last two months of her pregnancy with Lisa, when Tim was about twenty months old. Two weeks before Lisa was due, the family moved, which she found stressful so late in pregnancy. She also found it a financial hardship because they moved to a bigger, more expensive house. Then, two weeks after Lisa's birth, Dawn had a hemorrhage and had to be rushed back to the hospital. She also suffered from mastitis and had to give up breast-feeding when Lisa was five weeks old.

Dawn feels devalued in her role as a mother. Since having children she feels "unimportant" and like "a second-class citizen." She believes she has lost her youth to her children: "I sometimes feel like I've aged about ten years when I'm peeling the spuds looking out of the window at the children. I feel like ten years of my life has just gone." She says again and again that motherhood is a "thankless task," and she resents the lack of recognition, both from other people and from society more generally, for what she does as a mother. She says, "You look for praise and reassurance, but never get it, because 'it's what women were meant to do.'" She resents the fact that as a mother she is always expected to be there for everyone else when no one is there for her: "You have to become selfless once you've got kids, you have to think about what everybody else wants first before you can think about what you want."

Dawn feels that her expectations of motherhood have been shattered by what she calls the "dreadful" reality of her daily life. When asked what she thought about motherhood before she had children, she replies:

> I always pictured myself in floral dresses in the summer, pushing prams with these idyllic little blond-haired children. It never worked out that way . . . I'd got such a naïve outlook on children . . . I just had pictures of cute little babies, that was my plans for when you become a mother, like you see them on telly, slim, pretty.

From textbooks on pregnancy and childcare, magazines, and television programs, Dawn had pieced together a "rosy view of babies being these cute little pink things . . . with lots of downy fur and sort of blond things with great big blue eyes." Her vision was one in which babies "had lots of bottles and then would go to sleep and leave you alone." She imagined "lovely pictures of this glorious nursery with the happy mother looking terribly serene." When, later in the interview, she spoke about the prenatal classes she attended, I asked whether they had addressed the difficulties of motherhood or postpartum depression. This question tapped into a great source of anger. Dawn told me that she blamed the prenatal classes more than anything else for failing to discuss what motherhood is really like. She would have liked less emphasis on the birth, pain relief, and feeding and more time on postpartum depression, tiredness, crying babies, babies who throw up, and generally what it is like to care for a new baby.

Dawn is not alone in her romantic view of motherhood. All the women I spoke to who had experienced postpartum depression, and particularly the first-time mothers, gave similar accounts using words such as "serene," "glorious," "rosy," "lovey-dovey," "calm," and "idyllic." They had embraced an image of motherhood as a state of perfection, and they expected nothing less. They craved perfection from themselves and from their children. They talked about "trying to be this perfect mother," struggling to "keep a perfect house," and wanting their children to "look perfect and smile prettily."

These portrayals of motherhood are more reminiscent of the images and ideals of the 1950s than of the more sophisticated and nuanced nature of contemporary representations of motherhood. While the 1950s saw the introduction of rigid doctrines and ideologies in which mothers were expected to stay home, care for their children, and follow strict feeding schedules, today's norms, expectations, and what Ann Willard calls "cultural scripts" of motherhood are more diverse.[1]

Cultural norms and values surrounding motherhood, as well as women's expectations and experiences of motherhood, vary historically and culturally.[2] Evelyn Glenn and her colleagues provide excellent examples of the ways in which ideas of mothering vary according to race, ethnicity, class, sexual orientation, and historical period.[3]

For most of the twentieth century, however, an idealized model of motherhood derived from the situation of the white, American, middle-class mother was projected as universal.[4] The sociologist Sharon Hays characterizes this as "the ideology of intensive mothering," a gendered, child- rather than parent-centered model of childrearing in which women are encouraged to devote their time, energy, and resources to raising their children.[5] Embedded within a seemingly wide-ranging diversity of cultural scripts of motherhood is an implicit set of moral standards. Culturally speaking, there are good and bad ways of mothering children.[6]

The women I interviewed embraced this prescriptive nature of motherhood with all its rigidity. They did not consider the complex, contradictory, or flexible nature of current ideas about motherhood, or accept the notion that there is no single right way to be a good mother. Nor did they draw on the experiences of mothers around them—whether their own mothers or mothers-in-law, sisters, other female relatives, friends, neighbors, or acquaintances—to build realistic expectations. Indeed, when they did talk about these women, they tended to idealize them as "good" mothers while deriding themselves as "bad" mothers. They projected the "fantasy of the perfect mother" onto these women.[7]

Although the women held idealized notions of motherhood, these ideals varied from one woman to another depending on which aspects of motherhood were most important to them. For example, having a "natural," drug-free delivery was part of Dawn's idea of what constituted a good mother, but it was not equally salient for other women. Many, but not all, saw breast-feeding as the pinnacle of good motherhood. Some believed that good mothers bond with their children from birth, and thus felt "evil" when they did not experience love at first sight. For some, being able to stay home to look after their children was central to their identity as mothers and was simply what good mothers do. Others felt that these days a good mother is expected to do it all—work outside the home, keep a tidy house, and look after her children. The women's high expectations carried over to their children, and each mother had her own notion of what was the right way for a child to behave.

Whatever their expectations, the women felt deeply disappointed with their experiences of motherhood. They did not turn out to be the perfect mothers they wanted to be, and many were disappointed that their babies were not the peaceful, content little creatures they had anticipated. This discrepancy between their expectations and their experiences was devastating because they interpreted it as a personal failure. Rather than question the cultural images that gave rise to their expectations, or challenge the relationships that upheld them, they blamed themselves for being bad mothers.

PENNY

Penny, twenty-nine, became depressed soon after her son Adam's birth. Her fear of doing something wrong or not doing enough in caring for Adam was so extreme, and her sense of responsibility for his life so overwhelming, that she became almost paralyzed in her role as a mother:

> I thought, "Oh yeah, I can bathe a baby, I can change a baby, I can feed a baby but they need more than that" where really they don't. They just need someone to feed them and change them. They don't need someone to watch them twenty-four hours a day, which I was doing, you know, just sitting there watching him the whole time. I can remember when my husband worked till midnight. On one of his late nights he went from half-past one, when he goes to work, and I . . . think he got back at half-past twelve. And he stepped out that door and I'd sat there holding [Adam] till half-past twelve. I hadn't had a drink or anything to eat. I daren't put him down 'cos I think, "if I put him down he's gonna die."

Penny's feelings of inadequacy and fear that her son would die in her care led her to return to her factory job, even though she had never intended or wanted to go back to work. "I hated my job," she says, "but I would rather return to a job that I hated than sit there trying to watch him to make sure that he didn't die on me."

Penny's fear is perhaps surprising given that she had years of experience looking after other people's babies and children. She spent her teenage years minding her sister, who is thirteen years her junior. Six of her seven siblings had children before she did and she had a lot of experience looking after her nieces and nephews. Nonetheless, Penny's overwhelming feelings of responsibility are understandable given the cultural associations of mother, morality, and responsibility for children.[8] As discussed in Chapter 1, children's physical, emotional, and psychological development and well-being are seen as ultimately dependent on the mother's behavior. The gendered discourse and experience of parenting, and what Martha McMahon terms "the ideology of privatized caring" that goes with it, place a huge emotional, psychological, and physical burden of care and responsibility on women.[9] Penny's story illustrates the consequences of this burden and women's struggle to come to terms with it. Ultimately, Penny finds the burden unbearable. Rather than risk, as she sees it, "failing" to care adequately for her son, she decides to return to work and share the responsibility for Adam with other people. But this, too, leaves Penny with a sense of personal failure for, as McMahon points out, "the feeling of responsibility for their children is more than the expectation of a social role; it becomes constitutive of self, making the denial of such responsibility almost unthinkable. Thus for a woman to be remiss in feeling responsible for her child would implicate her whole moral character. Being responsible for her child is about being moral as a person."[10]

Penny had high expectations of herself as a mother partly because of the experience she had looking after children. "I thought I knew it all," she says. Paradoxically, her expectations were unrelated to her previous experiences and were derived from images of mothers and babies gleaned from magazines, books, and television programs. Referring to one of the soap operas she watches, she asked: "How often do you see the children and how often do you hear them crying? You don't." Later she adds, "What you read in books, it's not like life, you know, they don't tell you the bad things in books, do they?" Like Dawn, Penny had a highly romanticized picture of motherhood that bore little resemblance to the real mothers and children she knew:

> I thought it was going to be so easy, could have nice relaxing baths, little wander up town, you know. It's not like that at all, you know, it's *very hard* work and *very* emotional, very tiring . . . You look at all the magazines of happy, smiling mums and of their lovely, shiny, pretty baby and he wasn't, he wasn't *pretty* . . . he had these awful spots all over his face . . . I'd imagined this lovely little bundle, this beautiful skin and he only woke up to be fed and be cooed at, you know. When they're tiny babies they don't do anything like that, you know, it was *totally* different . . . I just felt useless, incapable . . . frightened . . . I just wish someone had said, you know, "You're gonna feel like this."

Penny realizes now that her expectations of herself, of motherhood, and of babies overwhelmed her, as did her fear for her child's life: "the thought of someone giving him the flu, and him dying or him choking or him having a [crib] death or being stolen" were all too much for her. She lost confidence in herself.

Penny never spoke to anybody about her feelings—instead she "bottled them up." "I had no one to talk to," she says, "I was totally alone." She describes herself as not "one to confide in anybody." Her husband is a very caring and understanding person but she kept him in the dark, partly because she did not want to disappoint him, and partly because she needed him to have confidence in her. Most of her friends did not have children, and this kept her from speaking about her feelings. Because she had worked full-time until she had Adam, she knew few of her neighbors. Although her parents and siblings live close by and she saw them frequently, she feared that they would be disappointed in her if she told them how she felt:

> My mum was quite helpful but, you know, you don't like to let your mum know that you can't cope, you know, your mum sees you as some-one who can, who's okay . . . Because I was older than my three brothers . . . who've all got children, no problem. And I was older than them and I was the one who had all the problems and I just didn't want them to know. How come they can manage and I can't. You're embarrassed about it.

Penny remained depressed for sixteen months. Once she realized that other mothers shared her feelings, she no longer felt individually responsible, regained her confidence, gave up her job to look after Adam, and enjoyed motherhood for the first time.

VERA

Vera was twenty-six when she and Matt had their first child. Within four days of the birth Vera started to have odd thoughts and feelings. She felt she was going "crazy" and "round the bend." Throughout the eight months of her depression she experienced, above all, a deep sense of failure as a mother. She relentlessly condemned and blamed herself for being "a bad mother," for being "useless" and "inadequate," and for falling short of her expectations of herself:

> I had such bad thoughts in my head, that's the only way I can really describe it, bad thoughts about myself in my head that I just thought, I couldn't bear the thought. I really couldn't bear the thoughts I was having, like you know, "I'm going to be like this forever, I'm never going to be right again. I'm going to damage him by being like this, it's not fair on my husband."

Vera felt inadequate, guilty, and shameful about virtually every aspect of her life as a mother—not bonding with her son, her difficulty breast-feeding, giving her child a pacifier, not doing enough house-work—even though others often reassured her that she was doing fine as a mother. She says, "I just felt everything I was doing was wrong and it was all my fault." She struggled with breast-feeding but forced herself to continue despite suggestions from her doctor that she switch to a bottle given the distress nursing was causing her:

> The doctor said, "Stop breast-feeding," and I *wanted* to stop breast-feeding but I wouldn't let myself 'cos I thought, "Well, *that's the thing you're meant to do*," and you know, "you're not to bottle-feed." And I *never* bought any bottles . . . And I *wanted* to be told by somebody it was okay to do it, but I wouldn't let myself do it myself.

Rather than be guided by her own experience, or listen to the advice of other people, Vera was desperately and rigidly trying to follow some abstract notion and ideal of what good mothers are supposed to do:

> I wouldn't let things go. I wouldn't let myself give in. I was doing the housework, polishing every day, and all that sort of thing. Still trying to keep up with things, not giving in at all, you know, everything had to be done.

She describes a similar struggle with herself over whether to give her son, Felix, a pacifier:

> I always felt I was doing things wrong. Like the midwife told me, "Give him a dummy [pacifier], you know, he likes to suck." But I thought, "Oh, but I shouldn't be doing this." I was so strict with what I thought was right and if I did give in, I'd feel . . . "Oh you've failed."

One of Vera's greatest sources of shame and distress was the way she felt about Felix when he was born. She expected to fall in love with him immediately but found it took her a long time to develop these feelings:

> I didn't love him. I didn't feel any sort of mother love or anything. He was the biggest mistake in my life as far as I was concerned. I was frightened to tell anybody that, even the psychiatric nurse or even my husband really. You know, he was the first grandchild for my in-laws and they were absolutely over the moon and I would think, "Oh God, what on earth they must think, 'She's going round the bend.'" I was really ashamed about that . . . I felt really tortured about that, you know, that I didn't love him. I know it's not that unusual, you know, with people who, I mean, even like haven't got depression, but I felt evil for not feeling the way I thought I would, you know. I cuddled him 'cos I felt I ought to, not because I particularly wanted to.

This theme dominated Vera's interview. For a mother not to feel love for her child and to admit to it is one of the greatest taboos in a culture that idealizes motherhood, mother-love, and the mother-child bond. Within this context it is not surprising that Vera felt her lack of love for her son was an unspeakable crime she had to deny to herself and others by trying to force herself to love Felix:

> I didn't want contact with him. I didn't want to hold him . . . *I made myself* but if I'd have been a bit stronger I would have said, "Just take him away for a while," *not* forever, I didn't mean it forever . . . just until I'm feeling better . . . and feel I can cope with him . . . I still loved my husband much more than I loved him . . . and I thought that was wrong. I just expected to fall in love with him totally straight away, which I didn't . . . but I hate myself for that. I felt ever so wicked. I felt really what is it when you can't love your own baby . . . So I was going through all the motions. I was cuddling him, playing with him, and all that but my heart wasn't in it. And I was always aware of it and it just felt like an act. I felt like a fraud.

When I asked Vera where her fixed ideas about how to behave as a mother came from, she responded:

> It's not from anybody putting pressure on me, so it must come from myself and what I've read, you know. I thought I *knew* it all. I was so cocky . . . I'd read every book under the sun from Leach to Spock. I've read so much and most of it is rubbish I realize now . . . I was probably battling against myself all the time like, "He must have a bath every day, he must do this, he must do that" . . . It's like with the housework, after I had him I'd be, you know, even if I didn't do it, I'd be worrying about it, you know, so maybe not doing it is not the answer simply. But I *have* to seem, especially I think 'cos I was at home, I have to seem to have done something.

The pressure to be the perfect housewife and mother, Vera explains, is not overtly imposed on her by other people. It comes from within her but reflects cultural images, ideals, and expectations. Vera picked up many of her ideas about motherhood from pregnancy and childcare books. She also points to a broader cultural context that influences how she feels about herself as a mother and that feeds her compulsion to be perfect. Vera values motherhood highly and so has decided to give up her job as a nurse in order to look after Felix. But she lives in a culture that paradoxically both idealizes and devalues motherhood, and she is caught within this paradox. She internalizes the devaluation of motherhood, giving rise to feelings that she is "just a mother." In order to justify her life as a mother she feels she has to be more than "just a mother" and so is driven to be a *perfect* mother.

Within ten days of the birth, Vera found the courage to tell her midwife how she was feeling, but to no avail. Her experience of trying to voice her emotions early on and feeling silenced was echoed by other mothers. Indeed, it was often this kind of rebuff that led them to withdraw from other people. The fact that a healthcare professional, or in other cases a relative or friend, failed to affirm their reality made it all the more difficult for them to validate their feelings.

SONYA

Sonya felt surrounded by people who failed to appreciate her difficulties. Her story illustrates how women's unrealistic ideals of motherhood, and feelings of failure when their experiences fall short of their ideals, can be further reinforced within difficult relationships. Sonya had worked for fifteen years before she and her husband, Johnie, decided to have a child. At the age of thirty-seven, Sonya became pregnant. Although the birth was complicated, eventually leading to an emergency cesarean, she did not experience it as traumatic. Despite some physical pain and discomfort, she thoroughly enjoyed the time she spent in the hospital as well as the first six months of her daughter Suzie's life. Her words convey the emotional intensity and euphoria she experienced during this period:

> I spent seven days in hospital and I *loved* it. I was on a high, you know, I was *absolutely* over the moon. I was like tripping . . . To me it was like a holiday camp, you know. I mean it was hard work 'cos I was feeding and I still had drips [IVs] on, but all that seemed irrelevant, you know the drips, the catheters, feeding, you know blood everywhere and engorgement, and I reveled in it. I mean I had very clear third-day baby blues but I even enjoyed them in a funny sort of way, you know. I took myself off into the day room and looked at the sunshine and thought, "Gosh, you know, I knew this was coming and this is quite cathartic and only lasting a while," and then it went away. And I came out of hospital and everything was fine. I'd wake up in the morning you know just really excited to bring Suzie down and start the day, you know. I was rushing about, I wouldn't walk anywhere. I was running down to the washing line and rushing back to see her . . . It was like that for six months.

When Suzie was six months old, Sonya's emotions suddenly changed. The catalyst for this change was Suzie's growing independence. Suzie was an easy baby. As she got older, like most children, she became more willful, active, and mobile. Sonya found Suzie's independence difficult to cope with because Suzie was no longer the perfect, quiet, smiley baby she wanted her to be. "I liked her to sit where I knew she was that she couldn't move without me," she explains, "and then at six months she was obviously . . . being her own person." She continued:

> I suddenly thought to myself, "Why is she not that sweet little baby any more in my mind," you know. She was so easy, you know, she hardly cried unless she was hungry . . . It was like this bolt out of the blue came to me and I suddenly wasn't enjoying it anymore and I was finding it a difficult job to deal with Suzie. I mean even if she sat in her high chair and spilled a bit of food then I'd start *really* shouting at her, you know, and I was losing my cool and I could feel that something wasn't right.

Although Suzie's behavior was typical for her age, Sonya blamed her daughter for behaving badly because she did not conform to her expectations of the perfect baby:

> I could feel panic rising up in my stomach if she wouldn't put her coat on to go out, if she cried a bit and you know if we had a little tussle before we were going out. It would be a big thing to me . . . So it was all these exaggerated feelings of not being in control. And panic . . . I could feel it rising like bile in my stomach . . . as soon as she did anything that was not what I expected. I expected her to be like a robot, you know, I'd dress her, she'd put her arms up and I mean that's not reality. If she wants to run around a bit before she puts her nappy [diaper] back on then that's normal. But to me, I was thinking, "She shouldn't be doing this, she should have her nappy on now," and it was almost like when a housewife is obsessively tidy. It was like an obsession about "she will always look clean, she will always eat her dinner without a spot going on the, you know." It was almost that sort of I'm imposing standards on her that are much much too high and I was trying to fulfill them and making myself feel ill.

Sonya's story is particularly remarkable in that she is so lucid, aware, and articulate regarding her depression. She knows that the image of the serene and calm mother and baby that she aspires to is a "fantasy" that is making her "ill":

Part of the fantasy that made me ill in a way is thinking she's got to be sweet and nice and never raise her voice . . . It's just a picture of what you think a baby is going to be.

When I met her, Sonya was still depressed and on antidepressant medication. Despite her insights into her depression, she still struggled to let go of her high standards and expectations. As she tried desperately to live up to her ideals, but continued in her mind to fall short of them, she condemned herself more and more for failing not only as a mother but as a human being:

It's like if someone comes for a cup of coffee . . . when you're ill you think, "Well, I have to clean the house from top to bottom so they can sit and have a cup of coffee." Do you understand? And this obsession drives you . . . It's these silly obsessions. And when I'd stayed in and I was sort of in this house for too long I'd look around and I'd be almost looking in the corners of the room and thinking, "God, it's dirty down there, I feel really depressed because there's a piece of fluff down there." Can you imagine feeling like that? And it's *stupid* but it's what you feel. I used to think, "The kitchen floor is dirty, therefore I'm a terrible person, which goes to prove that, you know, I'm even worse than I thought I was." You know, you're *crucifying* yourself all the time . . . When you're in the illness everything is the end of the world. It's black and white, good and bad. "You were bad, you didn't do the cooking right, you didn't socialize enough, you didn't make enough witty sparkling conversation," you know, as soon as someone's gone you're saying to yourself, "You're bad, you're bad, you didn't do this, you didn't do that," but why, why do you do this?

Sonya also blamed herself for her depression:

I feel the guilt for it which is not fair really on myself but I punish myself and say, "If you'd been more relaxed this wouldn't have happened. If you'd taken each day as it came and didn't worry if Suzie made a mess, it wouldn't have happened, you know. Because you're an obsessive personality this happened," you know, and I carry on like that in my mind and think, "Well, you know, I did it to myself."

Like Sonya, all the mothers criticized themselves relentlessly on moral grounds while they were depressed. They also feared that their depression might scar their children. The fact that any faults or failings in children tend to be blamed on their mothers weighed heavily on these women and operated as a powerful source of pressure to conform to cultural norms and standards. To some extent, this pressure and the feelings of guilt that accompany it are a universal feature of motherhood within Western societies. Feelings of guilt are exacerbated, however, when women are depressed, making it difficult for them to see themselves as anything but bad mothers.

Other scholars have similarly noted the moral and condemnatory dimension of depression. Most notably, in an article on depression or what he termed "melancholia" first published in 1917, Sigmund Freud notes that "in the clinical picture of melancholia, dissatisfaction with the self on moral grounds is far the most outstanding feature."[11] More recently, in her study of depression in North American women, Dana Jack detected the presence of an internalized moral voice within women's accounts. She termed this voice the "Over-Eye" because of its surveillant, vigilant, and moral quality. The Over-Eye, she notes, carries a patriarchal flavor both in its collective viewpoint about what is good and right for a woman and in its willingness to condemn her feelings when they depart from what is expected, as well as from cultural standards, norms, and imperatives. This voice

> speaks with a moralistic, "objective," judgmental tone that relentlessly condemns the . . . self. It says "one should, you can't, you ought, I should." It speaks to the self, and like the classical psychoanalytic concept of the superego, it has the feeling of something *over* the "I," which carries the power to judge it. Or like the object-relations notion of the false self, it conforms to outer imperatives and perceived expectations in order to gain approval and protect the true self.[12]

Jack also elucidates an inner division and two-voice dialogue in women's narratives of depression between this moral voice and "the voice of the 'I'" that speaks from experience and knows from observation. Depression, she notes, is associated with an inability to believe and legitimate the voice of the "I" and act on its values.

Jack's analysis echoes the inner dialogue and struggle about which the women with postpartum depression spoke. Sonya, for example, describes her depression as a state of constant "*mental* strife and fighting with yourself." During the depression, she says, "there's too much dialogue going on with yourself, and you believe what you're saying because you only know you." She feels torn between two voices and two parts of herself that offer competing perspectives on her life. One voice tells her what she should be doing—as she says, "I must put on a good face. I must always be marvelously dressed.

Suzie must always behave well"—while another voice questions these imperatives. For example, she felt a constant pressure to provide intellectual stimulation and emotional reassurance for Suzie even though another part of her realized it was unrealistic to impose such expectations on herself:

> I try not again to have this obsession, like she's playing there now and I think well, that's fine . . . But in the past I've thought you know, "God I should be sitting down reading a book with her, cuddling her, holding her." But they need space, you know. I'm trying to be *easier* on myself and say, "Well so what? She's playing in the corner on her own. My main job is to make sure that she doesn't fall off her chair and crack her skull open . . . I'm here to keep her safe" . . . I keep putting this pressure on myself to be *The Intellectual Mother,* to hot-house her . . . and I think, well, I don't particularly have all those skills anyway . . . I always have this thing, "Am I giving her enough," but I mean they don't need bombarding twenty-four hours a day, do they?

Another source of inner conflict for Sonya is whether to return to paid work. While she recognizes that she may be happier going back to work, she also feels pressure to look after Suzie herself. In the following passage we hear Sonya alternate between competing positions on this issue:

> Sometimes I think if I hadn't been ill, would I have gone to work quicker possibly and maybe felt happier? Because it's more my natural personality to have part work, part Suzie, but I kept thinking, "No, if I'm going to do this mother thing properly, I'm going to be at home, I'm going to watch *Neighbours* [soap opera], I'm going to make jam and I'm going to go to the local playgroups." What I did was again sort of sweep the businesswoman under the carpet and say, "Ah, but I'm this now," but by denying the skills there, right, I was harming myself . . . I think I damage myself by trying to shut that off . . . I was intent on this is my big sacrifice, this is me changing my lifestyle for the good of Suzie and pushing my own needs completely down to the bottom of the bag . . . which is a stupid thing to do but that's what I did because I thought . . . "I will be the best mother of all time," you know, like people do and then they start putting pressure on themselves because of unrealistic expectations.

Where was this image of the perfect mother coming from? What was compelling Sonya to mold herself to it to the extent that she was harming herself? What internal and external pressures was she experiencing? Part of what Sonya is expressing is the damaging effects of the intensive child-centered mothering that defines the good mother in many Western societies and reflects a white, middle-class conception of appropriate maternal behavior.[13] This model of parenting exempts fathers from taking an active role in looking after children and compels women to prioritize their children's needs at the expense of their own.

Sonya's story suggests that she has been strongly influenced by these cultural ideals. Her feelings as a mother, however, are also connected to feelings she has experienced earlier and in other areas of her life. She comes from a working-class background and was among the first in her family to go to college. While she was at college she tried to commit suicide, did not complete her studies, and left with a deep sense of failure. Sonya also expresses shame about her background. She has spent much of her life in the shadow of her working-class roots, trying to escape them by excelling at being middle class. Striving for recognition is tied to her class and gender. She has spent her life "trying to please everybody," trying to be a good woman:

> I'm constantly striving for recognition for things that I do without getting the peace, that's the problem. I'm *driven, driven* by wanting people to say, "Isn't she successful, doesn't she do this well," but I don't internalize the praise . . . I'm insatiable for praise and recognition and . . . I'm on a tread-mill of constantly trying to please everybody for them to think "I'm a jolly good person," you know, all the bad things a woman does 'cos of conditioning.

Sonya's preoccupation with trying to be "the perfect mother" and "the best mother of all time" is another manifestation of her need for approval and validation as a human being. Her strivings as a mother, however, appear more extreme partly because, like Dawn and Vera, she feels devalued in this role. At some level, she feels that just being a mother does not justify her existence. In order to feel a sense of moral worth, she thinks she has to be an exceptional mother and have an exceptional child. Sonya is struggling to give value and meaning to what is devalued by society and by her husband.

Sonya's thoughts and feelings about combining motherhood with paid work provide a stark illustration of how the devaluation of motherhood can negatively affect women's experiences. When Suzie was six months old, Sonya's friends with babies the same age started to return to their jobs and careers, and Sonya started to question her identity and role as a mother. It was around this time that she began to feel unwell and depressed. With the return to work by other mothers came the realization that children do not necessarily need their mothers full-time. This led her to question many of her assumptions about motherhood and expectations of herself, including her ideas about having to look after Suzie full-time. She realized that trying to live up to her ideal of the full-time mother was "damaging" her, but she could not stop herself. Caring for her children full-time represented, for Sonya, the epitome of motherhood; it was what she had grown up with and what she came to expect of herself:

I suppose if you look back to my mother I was thinking that, you know, once I have a baby then I'm no longer the businesswoman, I'm you know the person who should always be there with the hugs and does the ironing. And I was almost pushing the rest of me out of the way saying, "Okay, I had those skills but those are not useful in what I'm doing now," you know. I wanted to revel being at home and doing the housework and this, that, and the other but I wasn't really being true to myself.

When asked if she was trying to be the parent she felt her mother had been, Sonya replied: "In some ways yeah . . . I was hankering back to days when mothers used to walk round with big blankets around them and walk up and down with the babies and that was their job."

In trying to live up to this ideal of motherhood, Sonya was denying the person *she* was. She realizes that, in her case, she probably needs to go back to work and regain her identity as a businesswoman. However, she finds it difficult to value and authorize her own feelings and thinking about her situation because she is caught between a confusing array of internal and external voices. Her childhood images of motherhood, her beliefs about what good mothers should do, and the cultural idealization of motherhood compel her to look after Suzie herself. By contrast, the professional woman in her, the return to work by other mothers, the cultural devaluation of motherhood, her husband's apparent lack of appreciation for what she does as a mother, and her own need to be valued, approved of, and recognized by others lead her to question the sufficiency of her life as a mother. What is striking about Sonya's story is how difficult it is for her to know what she wants and who she is amid all these voices, images, and pressures. She is so concerned about what other people will think of her that she no longer has a clear sense of what is good for her.

Sonya's struggle to value herself as a person and as a mother is made worse by the fact that her husband, Johnie, values paid work highly and puts little value on what she does. She feels he appreciates neither her job as a full-time mother nor her volunteer work because they are not financially remunerated. She says that Johnie has "got strong feelings that when I work for the NCT I'm wasting my time because I'm not making money for me." Inevitably, Johnie's attitude begins to affect how she feels about herself:

> Occasionally I think, "Well, he doesn't ask me what I do during the day, therefore it's no surprise that I don't value it," do you see what I mean? As soon as he comes in I am ready to give *him* comfort because he has a bad time . . . I wish he would say to me, "Well, what have you done today?" you know, not in a nasty way but you know, "Did you go out today?" . . . I mean he's aware that I do go out . . . but he doesn't know if I'm going to lunch with Janet or whether I go to a playgroup or you know. So I suppose to me that time has no value, it's starting to have no value to me because it has no meaning to him. Do you see what I mean?

Although Sonya is still depressed when I meet her, she is beginning to feel better. The worst of the depression is over and so she is able to sit and talk to me. Six months ago she had reached such depths of despair that she would not have agreed to see me. As she emerges from her depression, she finds it easier to listen to her own voice and rely on her own thoughts, feelings, and experiences as a guide to how to live her life. She begins to question the ideals she has absorbed about motherhood. It is unrealistic, she now believes, to expect that she can or should provide constant emotional support and intellectual stimulation to her daughter. Sonya's has been a slow and gradual resistance to the models and ideals that she feels are prized within the society in which she lives. At the time of our meeting she still struggles with her realization that paid work is valued more highly than the unpaid work she does:

> When I think, "Well, you undervalue yourself because you think, well I'm just at home with Suzie," I also think, "Well what about all the people who've got these high-powered jobs?" Like my friend who rang up the other day and she's earning a fortune but she's having problems with her husband, she seems to throw herself into affairs every other week. Is she stable? Is she happy? . . . And yet she's someone, who on the face of it, she's got a career, she might have a child later on, she spent six months in Switzerland with her job, you know she goes on holiday to Singapore

and Shanghai and you name it and you think, "This is the person that I am supposed to look up to." And then she rings me up and says, "Oh, I don't know what's happening with my husband, we haven't slept together for three years, I'm having a fling with someone."

Much of Sonya's story is a dialogue between two parts of herself. One voice speaks of the contradictory models she feels society is holding up to her as a guide for how to live her life: on the one hand, the full-time mother who provides hugs, does the ironing, makes jam, offers constant intellectual stimulation to her child, and goes to mother and baby groups; on the other hand, the woman who does it all and fits it all in, the high-powered career, marriage, and motherhood. Sonya scrutinizes her friends and acquaintances, and part of her believes that these women are living out these ideals. Another part of her constantly questions how realistic these models are and whether living your life according to these cultural scripts will necessarily bring satisfaction, contentment, or happiness.

SANDRA

Like Sonya, Sandra is still in the middle of her depression. She too is trying to hear her own voice amid the pressures she feels from her husband, her family, and the surrounding culture. Unlike Sonya, however, Sandra has gone back to work for financial reasons but wants to be at home with her daughter, Alice. Together, Sonya and Sandra's stories illustrate well how postpartum depression is linked, not so much to whether a mother is in paid work or stays at home with her children, but rather to the dissonance between what a woman wants for herself and what she feels she has to or should do as a mother.

Sandra, thirty-five, works full-time as a nurse. Her daughter, Alice, age two and a half, was a planned and much-wanted child, conceived after two years of trying to get pregnant. Sandra's depression started soon after the birth and is connected, in part, to her conflicted feelings about combining motherhood with paid work. Sandra's husband, Bob, runs his own business but the income it generates is low. Sandra therefore had to return to work full-time when Alice was four months old. She speaks of feeling disappointed and angry that she has to work against her wishes. She had always aspired to being a full-time mother at home with her child. Nonetheless, she also realizes that, intellectually, she needs to work, and that Alice has benefited socially from being cared for by other people. Ideally, Sandra would work part-time, which would enable her to spend more time with Alice, but also keep her career going. Financial pressures, however, have made part-time work impossible. One of Sandra's struggles is that she feels pressured to care for and entertain Alice as she believes mothers at home do, even though she works full-time and does not enjoy or feel gifted at children's activities:

> It tends to be the mothers who are at home that seem to go everywhere with the kids, go swimming, go to ballet classes, do this, do that and are baking and that's what I feel I should be doing. I should be sewing and baking and cooking and going swimming with her. And I mean that's cloud cuckoo land. I'm not very good at sewing anyway. I don't particularly like baking. So it's probably better that I am at work, you know, 'cos I wouldn't be, I suppose I wouldn't be fulfilled with being at home and cooking and baking, it's just having a happy medium.

Although Sandra questions the model of motherhood to which she aspires, she feels pressure to conform to it, and in the process finds it more and more difficult to cope:

> I think I've found that the hardest—having to assume *as well* as working that I should do everything else that mums at home do, you know, I should bake and clean and whatever. And you can't, it's just impossible . . . But I went on doing it. I just made myself . . . And I found that really hard to cope with. I couldn't work out how you were supposed to deal with the baby and do everything else as well which you can't . . . The psychiatrist said I had very high standards of myself, you know, I would try to keep everything going and to a degree it is impossible practically to do that. But I was trying to achieve everything.

Sandra describes herself as constantly striving to be the mother she believes she ought to be rather than the mother that the reality of her own situation requires. As she says, "I'd set myself these goals which were impossible . . . I was just working on my own perception of what I should do and what I should be." When Sandra found it impossible to be the perfect mother, she blamed herself for what she regarded as a personal failure. For example, even though she recognized that all children can be difficult and go through difficult stages, she nevertheless felt responsible when Alice struggled with what are normal, expected developmental transitions:

She throws tantrums or I think, "That's your own personal perception," if you ask it'll be, "Oh well, she's two and a half, of course she's gonna sit in the middle of the room and scream and hit me. That's what two-and-a-half-year-olds do." And you think, "Well, my two-and-a-half-year-old shouldn't do that. If I was a good mum they wouldn't." But that's the wrong way.

Sandra has conflicting feelings about how well she bonded with Alice at birth, and she continues to feel guilty about this. In the following passage, we hear how she shifts viewpoints, not knowing what to think or believe, as she struggles to come to terms with the fact that she had to think not only about her baby but also about herself. She wanted to be with Alice after the birth, but she also needed time to recover from the trauma and exhaustion of childbirth. We also hear how Sandra has been influenced by Bob's words, which echo more widespread cultural messages about mothers and how they should feel and behave. Sandra picks up on these voices and starts to tell me that, as a mother, she should be able to be selfless, forget about her own needs, and devote herself fully to her child:

> I held Alice and then Bob held her while I was being stitched. And he said he really found it hard why I didn't want to hold Alice then. But I think people are different. I was absolutely worn out. Also I think in my mind I thought, "Right, I've done my bit, it's somebody else's turn now. I've produced this normal little girl," you know. But I think from that minute you should just devote yourself to the child. I think that's the only way. You should hold them and forget about yourself. But you're in such a mess. You're covered in water and blood and God knows what. All you want to do is, they stitch you up and then you have a bath and a cup of tea. So once they'd stitched me up and I'd had a bath I was able to cope with her. But initially when she was just born I wanted somebody else to hold her. I didn't want to hold her straight away 'cos I felt in such a mess. I don't know if you understand that, which I think Bob found hard. He couldn't understand why I didn't want to cuddle Alice straight away. I mean I did, but why I handed her over when I was being stitched up . . . I just thought, "Thank God she's out and thank God she's okay" . . . I think you feel guilty about that.

Listening to Sandra, we begin to understand more about the expectations that women have of themselves, where they come from, and why women feel compelled to live up to them. Sandra explains that, even though the voices she feels surrounded by contradict her lived reality of motherhood, she finds it difficult to escape their influence, partly because they reinforce her own expectations of herself. Furthermore, she and other mothers explain that even when partners, relatives, friends, or healthcare professionals encouraged them to let go of their ideals, something within them resisted. During the depression, they felt locked into particular expectations of themselves and perceptions of the world around them from which they could not break free.

The mothers I interviewed talked about several sources for their romantic expectations of motherhood. In particular, they blamed prenatal classes for idealizing motherhood and failing to provide realistic information, including the possibility that some women may experience negative feelings or even postpartum depression. Many said the prenatal classes concentrated mainly on labor rather than on life after the birth. Indeed, British, North American, and Canadian commentators have noted that though prenatal classes tend to prepare parents for the birth, they devote relatively little time to the postnatal period and how to care for an infant.[14] Whenever life with a young baby was discussed, the women said, the emphasis was placed on the practical and mostly positive aspects of parenting. Motherhood was discussed in idealized terms. Those who attended classes designed for women who already had children commented on the more realistic depictions within these classes compared with those for first-time mothers. Caroline explains:

> I'd been to antenatal NCT classes, and they're very good, but I think they make it all sound a bit too ideal . . . The classes do perhaps present a rather unrealistic picture because the second-time classes that we went to, we'd all had varying experiences and so we weren't going to take any of the sort of nonsense that perhaps had been thrown at us in the first classes.

The biggest criticism of prenatal classes was that the emotional and psychological dimensions of motherhood, in particular feelings of ambivalence, were not addressed in sufficient depth. As a result, Louise felt totally unprepared for her emotional reactions to motherhood:

> The classes were all . . . about the practical aspects. It was "what's going to happen in labor" and "how you're gonna cope with it," and pain-relief techniques, and then once the baby's born, breast-feeding, bottle-feeding, whichever you choose . . . Your *feelings* really were never discussed . . . Nobody ever told me or indicated how you might feel after it,

that you might feel that things weren't going well, that you might feel a failure.

The women complained that the only discussion of the emotional and difficult aspects of having a baby concerned the baby blues. They felt that postpartum depression should have been openly discussed in the same way the baby blues were, as Dawn explains when asked if she knew about postnatal depression:

> *No,* this is one of the *grave* mistakes that health visitors *and* midwives make—you go to antenatal, they teach you *everything* about labor and pain relief and a little about when baby's born but they *never, ever* mentioned how *awful* you can feel, how really tired you can feel. They have these mums come in with their babies and they always talk about the birth and how wonderful things is but it was *such a shock.* They covered the baby blues, that's what they did . . . It was very *briefly* covered but there was *no* mention of "it could take a few weeks, months before you could start to be Jekyll and Hyde," or anything like that. And there was nothing like "if you're having trouble come back and see us" . . . And you think the health visitor must see *hundreds* of women who have postnatal depression and yet they still don't mention it . . . It's a very untalked-about subject and it's almost taboo. 'Cos it's *mental* I think it carries this really awful stigma. Nobody wants to know about it and nobody wants to say anything about it so it's all kept very quiet . . . It really is a very taboo illness, very misunderstood.

The mothers commented that open discussions of postpartum depression might help reduce the stigma associated with it. Indeed, a few women specifically said they did not feel any shame attached to having the baby blues, perhaps because the blues are now widely accepted and freely discussed.

Celia highlighted particularly well how more information would have enabled her to recognize her feelings and seek help earlier than she did:

> I think it can be mentioned by people at antenatal clinics without worrying it's going to become a big problem . . . It'd be nice to know, if you felt like that afterwards, that it struck a chord, and you'd think, "Ah, it's not strange to feel like this, I'm not failing as a mother . . . The midwife did say this could happen"—and then you'd probably feel happier and more confident to go to the doctor and say, "I'm experiencing this."

Many of the mothers felt that the healthcare professionals running prenatal classes were reluctant to address difficult issues because they feared that talking about postpartum depression would upset women and predispose them to becoming depressed.[15] As Petra explained, "They say, 'We don't want to frighten you, we don't want to give you too much knowledge, you've got enough to think about.'" Celia, who experienced postpartum depression after the birth of her first child, tried to raise PPD as an issue in the classes she attended when pregnant with her second daughter. She believed it was better to inform women about the possibility that they might feel low after the birth rather than to ignore the issue altogether, as the healthcare professionals were doing:

> When I first mentioned it when I was having Melissa you know it was obviously a real taboo subject. The midwife did not want it to be discussed. There were new mothers there and it was like you know, "Let's not be doom and gloom" . . . It was "Oh we're not going to have that, are we?" and that was it. And it was like "We don't want to put these girls off. You know let them go through the birth first" . . . I can understand to a certain point don't be doom and gloom when they're looking forward to this, but I think because you are on such a high you do look forward to this really momentous thing and then you can't cope with it . . . But really the medical staff were you know, "Shut up, you in the corner," you know basically "We don't want to talk about things like that," which is very unrealistic.

Louise pointed out that discussing postpartum depression "presents a slightly obviously negative view of being a mother, and I don't think that's promoted an awful lot." Other British and North American studies show that parents criticize prenatal classes for "avoiding or glossing over negative feelings or difficult experiences."[16] It appears that little time is spent on the emotional aspects of parenthood because healthcare professionals experience a "fear of teaching negative or difficult issues."[17] In fact, women say that they are not upset by this information; indeed, most want this information, and research shows that providing it can reduce the risk of postpartum depression.[18]

One of the difficulties with discussing PPD before the birth is that most women believe it will not happen to them; they expect their experiences to be, as they themselves point out, "normal" in every respect, conforming to an ideal of motherhood: they will have a "normal," uncomplicated delivery; a "normal" baby who feeds well, sleeps, and does not cry; and "normal" happy feelings rather than feelings of low mood, ambivalence, or depression. Sonya explains that she did not take in much about postpartum depression because she believed it could not happen to her:

> I read up quite a lot about maternity and pregnancy and . . . there might have been a little paragraph saying some people have postnatal depression, but I never ever thought it would happen to me, you know, I never thought, well, there's a danger. I got the baby blues but I thought postnatal depression was sort of like, I thought it was more like maybe 1 in 100 you know, that it was just those well, I can't say that it would be oddballs, but in your mind you think well, it's like looking at the alternative questions of an exam paper, you think, "Well, I'm doing this, I'm not doing that bit."

Betty, who set up the postpartum depression support group I attended in the United States, echoed these feelings. As part of her work, she contacts prenatal classes and offers to talk and provide information about postpartum depression and sources of support. She talks about encountering resistance from healthcare professionals:

> I have contacted prenatal classes many times about speaking for five minutes at the childbirth classes, and they don't want us to do that because they feel that (1) the women might get postpartum depression, which is really foolish, but (2) they say, "You're going to have 20 couples sitting in the class and they're going to go, 'Postpartum depression. We're not going to get that. Don't even bother.' They're going to turn a deaf ear." Just like they say, when one of us gets up and talks about cesarean sections, people go, 'Oh, that's not going to happen to me.' They don't think that they're going to get it. They think that they're going to have the perfect labor and everything, especially if it's their first baby. You know, so they don't even bother. But what I say is, if they have the information and they have a face to connect with it, even if the woman doesn't realize it at the time, the husband might say, "Wasn't there a girl that came to our class and talked about funny feelings after a baby's born? Don't you have some information? Or, can't you call your doctor." You know, and I think the sooner that they're going to get help, the sooner they're going to feel better. It's just so awful that they don't talk about it for such a long time that they just get worse and worse and worse.

Given that women find it difficult to imagine themselves needing help after the birth, perhaps this information might be more effectively received if it is delivered both before and after the birth, for example, within the context of postnatal groups or classes. The question arises again as to whether mothers who are feeling down or depressed would attend these postnatal groups. Clearly, finding accessible and non-threatening ways of discussing feelings of ambivalence or depression raises emotional and practical dilemmas, which Petra reflects on here:

> Perhaps you should know more about postnatal depression when you get pregnant . . . But then in saying that, if you've not been there you probably don't understand it anyway. So I can imagine that it is quite awkward to get it right, you know, how much do you want to know at that time when you're not experiencing it? Perhaps they should run a group that you all go to with your babies . . . But then if you're feeling awful would you go? I don't know.

Despite these dilemmas, information about negative or ambivalent feelings, and about postpartum depression, is likely to help mothers in a number of ways. Even if women do not process the information because of their preoccupation with labor, their partners may well take note of it. Discussion of women's emotional responses to motherhood would help mothers and their partners identify the nature of their feelings and realize they might need help. Providing contacts and sources of professional and lay support may help women seek and secure help earlier than they otherwise would. Most important, open discussion of postpartum depression would reduce the stigma attached to it and encourage women to talk about their feelings early on within a supportive and accepting environment.[19]

The women whose stories appear in this chapter questioned and internally resisted ideals of motherhood, but they still found it difficult to accept the evidence of their own everyday lives as mothers, and use this as a basis for their mothering. Instead, they blamed and condemned themselves. They wanted to change who they were to fit a particular mold. As Adrienne Rich writes about her own experience of motherhood:

> I was haunted by the stereotype of the mother whose love is "unconditional," and by the visual and literary images of motherhood as single-minded identity. If I knew parts of myself existed that would never cohere to those images, weren't those parts then abnormal, monstrous?[20]

Why, despite everyday evidence of the reality of motherhood, did these women continue to believe in the fantasy of the perfect mother? Shirley Prendergast and Alan Prout suggest that women have difficulty building realistic expectations of their lives as mothers because of the ideas they had about motherhood as young girls. In a study of fifteen-year-old girls, Prendergast and Prout found that when asked to describe what it is like to be a mother, the girls drew on observations of their own mothers, sisters, friends, and neighbors with children, as well as their own experiences babysitting younger siblings or other children. They spoke of the isolation, boredom, and exhaustion of motherhood and said that feeling "fed up," "down," and low was the norm among the mothers they knew. Yet when these girls spoke about their own futures as parents, they did not draw on what Prendergast and Prout call this "illegitimate" knowledge of motherhood. Instead, they drew on stereotypical knowledge and presented their own futures as positive, ideal, and very different from the experiences of the mothers in their lives. Prendergast and Prout suggest that this is the case because the girls regarded the experiences of the mothers around them as unusual compared with those of most other (unknown, "abstract") mothers. Their own experiences and observations therefore did not count as legitimate knowledge. Realistic knowledge, Prendergast and Prout suggest, existed in a parallel but repressed relationship to widely available, social knowledge about how mothers ought to feel and behave. They argue that the lack of discussion of real as opposed to idealized models of motherhood actively represses and denies children's firsthand knowledge. They note that "the implicit assumptions underlying the sentimental model have come to carry the legitimacy of *naturalness*. Being 'natural' they are therefore unquestioned and unquestionable at the individual level."[21]

It seems likely, then, that within Western societies at least, most women's expectations of motherhood are to some degree idealized, romantic, and unrealistic. It follows that the majority of mothers will experience some conflict between their expectations and their actual experiences of motherhood. Why, then, do some mothers become depressed while others do not? Dana Breen's study of first-time British mothers offers some clues to this question. Her work indicates that there are differences between the ways in which what she terms, "ill-adjusted" and "well-adjusted" mothers construct and interpret the mothering role, and in how they resolve the conflict between their expectations and their experiences of motherhood. She notes that

> the most striking feature amongst the women who experienced most difficulties, was the split between a very idealized picture of what they felt a mother should be like . . . and the way in which they saw themselves, af-

ter the birth of the baby. Although this same picture was at times present in well-adjusted women during pregnancy, they generally modified their picture of the good mother after the birth of the baby to a more realistic one with which they were no longer at odds . . . [The ill-adjusted women] had a stricter idea of what they should or should not be like and . . . what they should be like was more unattainable than the other women . . . They seemed . . . to be stuck with the negative experience, as opposed to the well-adjusted women who were more flexible and able to maintain an openness to other experiences.[22]

Thus women who are able to let go of their ideals and accept themselves, their experiences, and their feelings are less likely to become depressed than those who cannot. Their ability to do so is directly linked to their individual circumstances, and also partly to broader structural opportunities and constraints. Indeed, this is what Anna, who was introduced in Chapter 2, expressed when she said that in order to avoid depression "you have to have room for your feelings" and not "pretend that you don't feel those feelings." Similarly, the women who recovered from their depression said that the key to feeling better was learning to accept themselves and their children for who they were (see Chapter 8).

All new mothers sort through, interpret, and respond to cultural messages surrounding parenting. In her book *The Cultural Contradictions of Motherhood,* the sociologist Sharon Hays notes that, in doing so, individual women reshape the social ideology of appropriate childrearing and thus develop a unique understanding of mothering. However, there are also underlying similarities in women's beliefs insofar as all mothers confront and respond to a shared and dominant ideology of childrearing.[23] This kind of analysis of the interplay between mothers' beliefs and cultural ideals is invaluable to an understanding of postpartum depression, yet it is sadly lacking in at least some feminist accounts of PPD. Such accounts have tended to portray women as passively absorbing, or conforming to, a fixed set of oppressive ideals and social structures. They emphasize women's lack of control and the structural conditions that are deemed responsible for rendering women helpless.[24]

The difficulty with these arguments is their assumption that cultural ideals are fixed and influence women in a uniform way. They also emphasize structural and ideological constraints at the expense of women's agency. The individual stories of the women in my study make clear that neither cultural representations, nor social conditions of motherhood, nor women's interpretations of these are uniform. The women responded to their particular circumstances in different ways, constructing individual ideas about what it means to be a good mother. They did not passively accept the dominant ideology of motherhood. Rather, they actively negotiated it, trying to conform to the ideal while at the same time questioning and resisting it. In this sense, as Verta Taylor points out, postpartum depression can become a site of resistance to gender rules.[25] As I discuss further in Chapter 8, and as Taylor's research demonstrates, by confirming that mothers' feelings of distress are not abnormal or unique, postpartum depression support groups allow women to transform their individual and silent resistance to cultural ideals of motherhood into a more open, public, and therefore political, form of resistance.

keeping up appearances

Romanticized ideals of good mothers and good babies were common among the first-time mothers who experienced postpartum depression. This makes sense given that in the transition to motherhood a woman first becomes sensitive to the "interpretive schemes of the culture."[1] Society's expectations of mothers come to impinge on a woman's thinking, perceptions, and judgments, defining "the right way" for a mother to feel, think, and behave. As Dana Jack points out, with the birth of a first child "a woman encounters the commands of the authorities telling her what she must do to be a perfect mother in their eyes."[2]

The women in my study who became depressed after a second or third child knew from their own experiences the reality of motherhood. They understood that there is no such thing as the perfect mother or the perfect child. Like the first-time mothers, they also had certain expectations of themselves that in their eyes they failed to meet. They felt they had disappointed themselves and others by having successfully coped with a previous child or children but not with this new one. In writing about her own experience of postpartum depression after the birth of her second child, Vivienne Welburn articulates how women's expectations of motherhood can vary depending on whether they are expecting a first or subsequent child:

> Whilst I don't see this internal idealized picture of the perfect mother as part of my own depression, I do believe the effect of false expectations

can be devastating. I certainly expected myself to be able to cope with two children as easily as I had with one. In fact I expected more of myself as an "experienced" mother than I had as an inexperienced one.[3]

Six women in my study became depressed after a second or third baby. I was struck by how often they, like the first-time mothers, used the expression "to cope." How were women using this term, I wondered, and what did they mean by it?

The women defined coping as dealing with their difficulties, needs, and feelings on their own without help. As mothers and mature adults, they felt pressure from themselves, others, and society to be self-sufficient, self-reliant, and independent. This echoes Rozsika Parker's comment that mothers are seen as "icons of maturity" and self-sufficiency.[4] The psychoanalyst Jessica Benjamin also writes that

> the ideal of self-sufficiency goes unquestioned, as it did for the mother who, when asked what care and support *mothers* need, could not understand the question and finally replied, "Someone taking care of *me?* . . . *I'm* the mother, *I'm* the one, I take care of *him!*"[5]

Although the women struggled with the emotional and physical demands of motherhood, they felt constrained by this ethic of self-sufficiency. They needed help but wanted others to believe they were coping. They would not admit their needs and vulnerabilities to themselves, let alone to other people. Such an admission, they said, would be shameful, a sign of weakness and failure. As the sociologist Hilary Graham points out, the most damning indictment you can pass on a mother is to suggest that she cannot cope.[6] Such an admission threatened the women's moral identities and reputations and their images of themselves as individuals who had never needed, asked for, or relied on others for help. In their study of family life in Britain, Janet Finch and Jennifer Mason observed that people's identities as moral beings are bound up in familial exchanges of support and the processes through which they are negotiated. In particular, people try to avoid relying on relatives for help, or showing they need help, and they will go to great lengths to ensure that they do not become dependent on this support. Individuals' help-seeking and help-giving behaviors are shaped by the desire to protect and preserve their moral identities and reputations.[7] As Marcia admits, "I'm not one of those who doesn't [cope]. I'm one of those people that does." Similarly, Tina says, "We've always been a very . . . strong . . . capable, coping family." Vera explains, "I've always been . . . quite self-sufficient and not needed any sort of help." And Celia describes herself as "a very independent person. I don't rely on anybody really for any help." The need for help conflicted with the women's expectations and images of themselves. The pressure to cope led them to withdraw from their relationships, leaving them feeling lonely, isolated, and cut off from the world.

TINA

Tina, thirty-six, lives in subsidized housing. Before having children she had been a secretary; her husband, Gary, works in a nearby factory. They married when they were twenty-two and now have three children, ages ten, eight, and two. Tina became depressed after the birth of her third child, Emily. At the time of our meeting, Tina is not in paid employment but is heavily involved in volunteer work. She runs a crèche, works at a local playgroup, and participates in a community support network for mothers. She never wanted to go back to work after she had children, and she enjoys the freedom and flexibility of motherhood.

Tina describes her first two experiences of motherhood, which were both planned, as a blissful time in her life:

> It was wonderful and *all* that I'd ever wanted. And I really sort of took it on board wholeheartedly and went to mother-and-toddler groups, did everything that was available at the time and loved it, *absolutely loved it,* the whole thing. It was wonderful.

Although her third child, Emily, was not planned, the birth and the first six weeks after were an equally "elevated time" of happiness, until depression set in. Although Tina had experienced emotional difficulties in the past and had tried to commit suicide when she was nineteen, she was surprised by her feelings of depression after Emily's birth:

> I just wanted to sit down all day . . . The room, the walls would appear very white and very glary. Everything was sort of, I can only describe it when you're *extremely* tired, everything sort of looks more brilliant . . . I felt tense all the time, like "don't let go," keeping on top of everything, you know, "just in case I can't do it," "just in case," "just in case." "I better do the washing up now just in case." And then I'd sit down . . . and sort of stare at things . . . It was a feeling of hopelessness because it's never going to go away, you're never going to feel better . . . And when

Gary came home it was sort of like a relief that if anything happened to me at least there'd be somebody there. And . . . when he used to go out to meetings in the evening, I could feel panic again because you're on your own and plus you've got the two big [children] upstairs in bed and "what . . . if something happened to them" . . . I never felt like killing Emily, I never felt like killing anybody . . . It wasn't like an anger, it was like I had to keep going, you know, I had to keep being there because what happens if something happened to me, you know, what would happen to the kids. It was this real feeling of just having so much pressures, the responsibility, it was really weird.

The recurring themes in Tina's account of her year-long depression are her sense of isolation, the belief that she must cope on her own, an overwhelming pressure and responsibility, and her own need to be mothered. Unlike that of the first-time mothers, Tina's depression had less to do with motherhood than with other events in her life: the loss of her mother before Emily's birth and difficulties in her relationship with her husband. Emily, she says, "wasn't the problem, d'you see? I didn't see her as being the problem. It wasn't her I wanted to get away from, it was all the other buggers [laughs]." Like the first-time mothers, Tina felt unable and unwilling to disclose her distress, and as a result felt isolated, lonely, and depressed:

I have this theory about postnatal depression, and my theory is that it's a woman's cry for help . . . well it was my cry for help. I'm a very coping, very capable person and to actually admit that I can't cope, or even to know what not being able to cope is like, I wouldn't know. So I think . . . that's how depression set in, and it was like "Look, I can't cope but I can't tell anybody" type of thing.

Even though Tina had three close friends at the time of her depression, two of whom had children, she felt she could not confide in them. She was surrounded by people, but "there was nobody that was close, you know, that knew about anything." She felt terribly alone because nobody really knew how she felt:

If I were to look back and to have one word that described my period of depression then I would come up with the word *isolation*. I think that would be the one word that would describe that period now, you know, as I look back, I think really that sums it up.

Tina found it difficult to reach out and ask for help because she had always been able to cope with difficult situations and had seen herself as independent. But this was the first time in her life that she did not have her mother's help and support. This loss, coupled with her husband's inability to support her in the way she wanted and needed, precipitated her feelings of not being able to cope.

MARCIA

Marcia, thirty-six, has two children, ages seven and four. She experienced depression in her early twenties and then again after the birth of her son Jack. It was a "mild" though distressing episode that lasted just six weeks. In the three and a half hours that we spent talking together, Marcia returned repeatedly to the isolation and loneliness she felt in the weeks after Jack's birth. In the immediate aftermath of the birth, Marcia had a lot of visitors and support. Her mother, who lives in a nearby town, spent the first week with her and then both her parents visited frequently for the first few weeks. Her husband had a week off from work. Her brother visited from abroad and stayed three weeks. It was about a month after the birth, when her husband returned to work, her brother left, and her parents stopped visiting so regularly, that Marcia began to feel depressed. After weeks of support and company, she felt abandoned and at a loss as to what to do with her two children:

> Everyone was gone and there was just me, and the baby, and the three-year-old. I can remember some days, walking downstairs, getting up, going downstairs and thinking "I can't go on with this. I cannot cope with it. I don't know how I'm going to deal with these two children all day." And it sort of loomed ahead of me, the time, until someone else would appear. And that's really unusual for me to feel that I can't deal with things. So I knew there was something wrong, the very fact that I was thinking that I can't cope.

Jack was born during the summer, when there was no school, no playgroups, and few activities that Marcia could attend with the children. This isolation, coupled with the fact that she had not yet returned to work, compounded her sense of loneliness. Marcia explains: "[I felt] trapped in my house with these two prisoners and I was never ever going to get out." She found it more and more difficult to cope and manage on her own, which in turn made her increasingly guilty and ashamed. While one part of her recognized what she was going through and validated her feelings, another part judged, criticized, and condemned her for being "weak" and unable to cope:

> I could see myself not being able to deal with it, and I was quite removed from it in a way, and I was constantly telling myself to pull up my socks and stop being so bloody silly, but it didn't actually work. I couldn't pull up my socks and I couldn't make myself . . . There was these little voices at the back of my head saying, "Of course you can do it," and it was like schizophrenia . . . It was like, on the one hand, there was me sort of "I can't cope with this, I can't deal with it, how am I going to manage for a whole day, what time's he [her husband] going to come home" . . . and, on the other hand, there was me saying to myself, "For heavens sake, it's only two children, some people have four . . . you've got everything that you need to deal with them, it isn't a big problem, you can handle them, you've handled much worse than this in your life . . . two bloody kids, really, it's not a big deal." And so there was this constant battle going on in my head the whole time.

Marcia's biggest hurdle was asking for help. She has always perceived herself as independent and self-reliant. To need—never mind ask for —help was, in her eyes, not only a sign of weakness but also an indication that she was failing as a mother. She told no one about her feelings:

> I couldn't admit it to anyone, I guess. I didn't want to. I didn't want to say to anyone other than myself that I couldn't deal with it because I've always been able to do everything. You know, I'm not one of those who doesn't. I'm one of those people that does . . . I don't think that I actually talked to anybody during the time that I didn't think that I could cope with it for the simple reason that I was trying to convince myself I could.

When asked why she found it so difficult to admit that she was having trouble, Marcia replied:

> I guess because I was scared to admit I was a failure. I don't know, I didn't want anyone to see my weakness as I've said because I've always been able to deal with things or to cope with things. I've never had to call on outside help or that's what I felt, and why should that occasion be any different from any other in my life?

More than anything else, this reluctance to admit her difficulties made Marcia feel lonely, isolated, and depressed.

FRANCES

Frances, whom we met in Chapter 2, became depressed after the birth of her third child, Mathilda. She believes her depression partly represents the accumulation of a series of bereavements and losses throughout her life. She is convinced that PPD is the result of various events in life that, on top of the vulnerability women can experience after they have a baby, can "trigger off" a depression. Because of the losses she has experienced, Frances was in a perpetual state of fear after Mathilda's birth that her family might be struck by another tragedy:

> Depression feel likes being in a box really, too frightened to open the lid. Everything I did I thought, "Should I do that, should I not do that." Indecisive, *fear, total fear* the whole time of what's going to go wrong today. It's a very odd feeling, feeling of being frightened continuously, you know, frightened to do anything. It's almost indescribable really. I think Celia had the fear of things going wrong in the world, didn't she.[8] Well I didn't so much have the feeling of things going wrong in the world whereas in my own family, in the people that I loved because . . . terrible things seemed to have happened to them all.

Frances also talks about her particular circumstances at the time of Mathilda's birth, which seem to have contributed to her depression. She had two young children and ran a livery business. Her husband worked long hours and was regularly on-call. Frances feels she took on too much after Mathilda was born. She explains, "I tried overdoing it . . . You think you can carry on doing exactly the same as you did." However, having Mathilda in addition to her other responsibilities was "too much" for her to deal with on her own. Yet she was reluctant to ask family and friends for help for fear that this would be a sign of weakness and would bring shame on her:

> I'm my own worst enemy in a way because . . . I'm quite independent really. I depend on my sister perhaps but I'm quite independent apart from that, and I like to get on and get back into the routine. I just like to think and show people that I can cope and perhaps I couldn't at the time. I think I just tried to carry on . . . You feel stupid and you want to get over it in your own way. I think you don't want to almost reveal the fact that you feel that you're totally going round the bend, you know, that you've got all these terrible fears and problems and you feel that really that you're going to be laughed at . . . I don't suppose I wanted to admit the

fact that I knew that I had gone a bit screwy and I didn't think people would understand.

Frances felt ashamed at being depressed. Several years after the fact, she still feels that her depression is "a black mark" on her. She found it very difficult to talk about her feelings even though she was "*really* crying out for help.*" She knows that silence only made it worse. Had she confided in somebody earlier, she admits, she would have recovered from her depression sooner. At the time, she felt so ashamed that she masked her depression: "You sort of put on a face to other people but inside you're absolutely screwed up." When she told her friends about her feelings years later, they said:

> "Oh, I'd never have known," and that's how it was with me. You see I could be *perfectly normal* to you or anyone else I was talking with. No one would ever know until I got back here and then I felt almost imprisoned.

Frances feels strongly that women need to be provided with supportive environments and encouraged to discuss their feelings:

> That is what's so funny about postnatal depression, you don't want to show it. And I think that's half the problem, I didn't want to broadcast it. Perhaps if I'd broadcast it, perhaps I'd have got over it a lot better. So I think that it would be a good idea if people were made more aware of the fact that if they felt that they were even just feeling a little odd in their feelings that the best thing to do is to talk about it straight away and not to worry about it. I'm sure that if people were only aware of the situation, to talk about how they feel, and not to feel stupid whatever their fears or anxieties were, I'm sure that there'd be a lot less problems in the end.

For women like Frances, who had one or two children already, there seemed to be an added stigma attached to admitting their needs and asking for help. As she says, "I thought, I suppose, I've gone through two other children and I wasn't going to let myself down by admitting the fact that perhaps I couldn't cope." Frances did not want to tell other people about her feelings, partly because she was trying to deny them to herself:

> Trouble is, you want to hide it . . . you want to keep it to the back of your mind really. I think you don't want to actually admit to *anybody* how you're feeling . . . I think you just feel that you hope it's going to go

away and you can cope with it. Well, that's me and I think that was Celia as well, 'cos otherwise why didn't we tell each other. It seems silly not to but we're both strong, both of us really, we don't want to admit that we've failed in a way, although it's not failing at all . . . Even now it's like a brick wall talking about it, you don't *really* want to go *back into* it to knock a hole through and let it all out. Somehow you want to keep it away . . . You want to talk to people about it but something stops you.

Frances describes a double reality in which she strongly adheres to certain beliefs while simultaneously challenging them. She feels a sense of failure and weakness because she needed help and because she became depressed. Nonetheless, she questions this belief. She talks about how she both does and does not understand why women get depressed:

This is when you feel bad about it 'cos I mean basically I'm jolly lucky. I've got a lovely home, lovely kids, you know horses out there, a car of my own. Why do you get depressed, you know? It's silly isn't it, when people are actually financially terribly badly off, you know, it's strange, isn't it really? But I mean I can see why they get depressed really.

This dual perspective on their feelings was a recurring theme within the women's stories: intellectually they understood that motherhood is a difficult task that can leave anyone feeling low, but at the same time, they could not reconcile the reality of their daily lives with how they believed they should be feeling.

LOUISE

I traveled across England to interview Louise. She read about my research in the Cry-sis newsletter (see Appendix 2) and was eager to talk to me.[9] She invited me to spend the day with her and her eighteen-month-old son, Seamus. Her husband was away on a business trip that day. At lunchtime I arrived at her home in a housing development outside a large town. She had moved into this newly built house a few weeks before her son's birth. As we ate lunch, Louise told me about her life as a mother and her eleven-month depression.

Louise felt unprepared for the reality of motherhood and for the depression that descended on her three to four weeks after her son's birth. She was thirty-two when she had Seamus, a planned and much-wanted baby, but she found him difficult and different from what she had expected:

> I think I'd been fooled a little by this sort of myth that's perpetrated by magazines and things, that you know, you feed the baby, you pop it in its cradle, you sit and smile at it, it goes to sleep, you do your housework, it wakes in four hours' time, you feed it again, you pop it back and you know the same again. And with Seamus, he didn't sleep during the day at all . . . He'd only sleep for about half an hour at a time, and he needed almost constant feeding as well for the first two or three months.

Confronted with the realization that motherhood was not "the peaceful, charming little experience" she had pictured, Louise struggled to let go of her expectations. She blamed herself for failing in her new role. "The reason I felt so bad," she says, "was because of the crying, I did feel a failure with him. I felt I couldn't do a thing with him some days and there was nobody to help me." Even though she criticizes the media for portraying motherhood unrealistically, she also blames herself for believing these representations:

> I think partly I was to blame by being taken in by the way it's portrayed in the media. I mean I was sort of slightly gullible thinking that you would just sit in a chair and smile at this little cradle. And there's a lot of horrible parts to it and nobody tells you that . . . I think I had very high expectations and I realize now that was part of my downfall. I expected a lot of myself. I expected a lot of him . . . A lot of it is probably my own fault. Nobody really could have prepared me for what it was going to be like . . . I was still trying to keep a perfect house as well as look after him, and I perhaps made it a little bit difficult for myself at times with these high expectations.

Failure is a recurring theme in Louise's story. She left college before finishing her degree, and she has continued to feel a deep sense of failure ever since. When she found Seamus and motherhood difficult to cope with, it brought back these feelings:

> I've always loved children and babies you see, even though I didn't have any until I was thirty-two . . . So you know I always had this in my mind that "Oh well, I'll carry on working but I'm really going to come into my own when I have a family." And of course as soon as I had one I didn't feel like I was a success at all. I thought, "Oh God, it's another thing I've failed at." And I felt like I was a failure to my parents as well, 'cos when I was eighteen I went to university to study languages and I packed it in in my first term . . . And I had this thing with Seamus, "Oh,

another thing I can't do, another thing I've failed at, another thing people can *see* I'm not coping with very well."

Whether or not individual women become mothers, motherhood is socially constructed as central to a woman's identity, and as the ultimate source of personal fulfillment. As Louise explains, disappointment in the experience of motherhood can threaten a woman's sense of self. She found this so disturbing that she struggled to "keep up appearances" with other people:

> I didn't tell people either. I think if you'd met me then you wouldn't have known. I managed to put on this cheerful front all the time to other people . . . In the early days of motherhood you know you do want to be seen to be coping, you don't want to be seen to be struggling and getting upset about things. You want to present this calm and serene appearance to everybody.

Louise concealed her vulnerabilities from her husband but was more open with her parents. By seeking their help, however, she felt she was disappointing her husband, not living up to the kind of mother she wanted to be for herself and for him:

> I used to . . . go to my mum and dad's . . . but I didn't want to be seen to my husband "I'm going home to mother" sort of thing. But I find my parental home quite a little cocoon you know. I feel very safe when I'm there, even at my great age you know . . . so I did take him and we often stayed the night there and just having other people around was quite supportive.

Louise was aware of her needs and feelings, but she was reluctant to reveal them because asking for help was a moral issue for her. When at her wits end one morning she did turn to her neighbor, her feelings of failure were compounded:

> My neighbor actually offered to have [Seamus] but again there was this thing about "I must be seen to be coping, I can't possibly be seen to be running round next door you know every time I want somebody to hold the baby" . . . There's one Friday morning when I just ran round in desperation with him. He was just screaming, couldn't shut him up and I was in a *terrible* state . . . I just said, "Look"—I really was upset— "would you just come round and have a cup of tea with me. I feel very lonely and isolated here," and she did, you know, and she took the baby off me. She's a big sort of matronly lady, big bosom, she just popped him on, you know, just stood like this and about two minutes later he was

fast asleep and I just couldn't do a thing with him you know. So then you don't know whether to feel pleased or to feel even more of a failure that someone else has succeeded where you couldn't [laughs]. I can laugh about it now but it wasn't funny at the time, it was soul-destroying really.

Louise felt added pressure to cope because, as "an older mother," she believed she should be mature enough to deal with her situation without help:

I was bound by this fact that I was thirty-two years old, intelligent, articulate, I *should* be able to *handle* it you know. I *shouldn't* have to be calling on these people all the time. I was desperately trying not to, I suppose.

These multiple pressures constrained Louise in asking for help and left her feeling ashamed when she did seek support.

HELEN

I visited Helen on two occasions and we spent a total of four hours talking together in her small terraced house ten minutes walk from the city center. Her fourteen-month-old son, Ben, was very active and demanding, and spent the entire length of both interviews racing around the kitchen and sitting room. Helen, thirty-four, and her partner, Simon, twenty-nine, had always wanted to have children, and after ten years together they decided to have Ben. Helen's pregnancy was "wonderful." Her problems began with a difficult birth and a catalogue of interventions that she experienced as traumatic. She was induced, her water was broken, she had an epidural, she was in labor for twenty-four hours, and eventually she had an emergency cesarean. A week after the birth she returned to the hospital because her stitches burst open, something she attributes to the inadequate treatment she received. Helen then had difficulty breast-feeding. Ben had sleeping problems and screamed for the first four weeks until Helen went on a dairy-free diet. Then, shortly after she went back to work part-time when Ben was five and a half months, she became very ill and was bed-ridden for six weeks.

Helen has felt very vulnerable since becoming a mother. The traumatic operation, the overwhelming responsibility of caring for another human being, the complications she experienced, and the lack of support left her feeling very low. She has been disappointed by many aspects of her life as a mother, though not with her son. Motherhood, she said, was a "complete nightmare" and totally different from what she had expected:

> You think you'll have, you know, these young babies—they're supposed to sleep all the time, aren't they? They feed, they sleep, they wake up a bit in the early days, they go back to sleep, you know. It's not true, it doesn't happen. Well it certainly didn't in my case . . . So I think, you know, you do have this misconception really that babies sleep and you can do things. I mean no doubt some people's babies do sleep a lot of the time during the day, but I think in fact it's a minority. I think the majority of babies are very wakeful. And again that's a misconception, isn't it? . . . I felt there was a lot of pressure on me right from the word go for not picking up this baby when he cried, you know, "You should leave him to cry . . . you'll spoil him, why are you feeding him so often, you know you should only feed every four hours."

Helen's idealized expectations of motherhood are similar to those of the other first-time mothers. But they are particularly surprising given that Helen is a visiting nurse and has spent many years providing healthcare for mothers in their homes and seeing for herself the reality of motherhood. Despite extensive experience, she is unable to apply her professional knowledge to her own situation. Like the other women I spoke to, she too felt a sense of failure:

> In the first month . . . I remember feeling very concerned that I wasn't this good mother, you know, and that I should be able to be. 'Cos he was screaming all the time and I thought, "Well, I should be able to do this for you, you know. I've got gallons of milk here and I can cuddle you and I love you."

Helen's job as a visiting nurse has hindered rather than helped her. Being perceived as someone who knows about pregnancy, childbirth, and motherhood has compounded the expectation that she should be able to cope on her own. She feels a lack of support from Simon, relatives, friends, and healthcare professionals. She is caught in a vicious circle that makes it difficult for her to get help. When she tries to seek support, she feels she is treated unsympathetically. At the same time, no one offers help or asks how she feels. "I felt that was the one thing that was missing out of anything that happened to me is no one actually asked me how I felt," she says. This apparent lack of care and concern makes it difficult for her to ask for help. How can she continue to voice her needs and feelings, she says, when those around her persistently fail to acknowledge, recognize, or validate them? For example, when she tried to tell her mother-in-law about her difficult birth, she received the following response:

> "Well, everyone has a cesarean section nowadays," and so as far as I was concerned . . . there was no room for discussion or negotiation . . . The help wasn't there, that wasn't for negotiation 'cos she'd told me that you know, okay, cesarean sections nowadays is like vaginal deliveries, so talking to her wasn't any longer an option.

Helen feels that neither her mother-in-law nor her own mother has listened when she has tried to talk about her experiences. She believes they ignore her feelings and pleas for support, and this increases her sense of helplessness, frustration, anger, and depression:

> Simon's mum and dad . . . have been *so amazingly blinkered* at everything . . . When I said, you know, how miserable I was feeling at one point to them, you know, she says, "How well you look," you know. There I am feeling really pissed off with life and looking miserable and she says, "How well you look this week, Helen!" and I sort of [said], "Well no, actually, I'm really depressed," and so she changed the subject. And . . . the same thing happened to my mum as well . . . I said, you know, "I feel really depressed and I've been to my doctor," and all this sort of business and then she just changed the subject, you know . . . She's never asked me since . . . I think a lot of it is that . . . *I* am very bad at asking for help but I suspect most people are, I don't think there are many people who ask for help readily . . . I mean I think the thing I felt was when I did ask for help it wasn't given anyway.

Helen describes herself as "the sort of person who just gets on with things. I find it very difficult asking for help." This, coupled with the failure of Helen's relatives to recognize what she is going through, leave her feeling abandoned and alone. She further explains that the pressure mothers feel not to speak out, and the lack of help and support they receive, cannot be separated from societal expectations and constructions of mothers. She describes the pervasive notion that "as a mother you're expected to cope." If a mother asks for help "it's seen as very negative by everybody," she continues, because there is "this sort of feeling which, 'Well, you should get on with it anyway, you know it's no big deal, you've had a baby, that's all you've had.'"

According to Hilary Graham, this "ideology of coping" lies at the heart of how motherhood is constructed and experienced within Western societies. She writes:

> To cope, according to the dictionary, means to "contend quietly" and to "grapple successfully." To cope is to handle the vicissitudes of your daily life with equanimity and efficiency. This ideal of unobtrusive competence appears to express the essence of what it means and what it is to be a mother. Mothers are copers: they are individuals who can handle the pressures of their life calmly and effectively.[10]

She points out that coping implies that a mother should carry out her duties in silence. "The best mother is one who is seen but not heard," she writes.[11] Graham further notes that coping equals self-effacement and that the concept of coping "sensitizes us to the way in which women's roles are so constructed that their successful enactment commits the woman to a life of self-negation."[12] Graham emphasizes the ways in which mothers are expected to be selfless creatures who tend to the needs of others but have no needs of their own.

Graham's work was written in the context of coping with domestic and motherly duties. Many of the women I spoke to experienced a dual burden of having to cope with paid work as well as domestic and childcare responsibilities. Listening to these women recount their stories draws attention to the relational dimensions and implications of coping. For many of the women, coping meant acting as if they were on their own and not actively involved in a web of relationships. Coping required them to deal with their needs, feelings, and vulnerabilities single-handedly. It meant absenting themselves from their relationships and aspiring to be independent, self-reliant, and self-sufficient, characteristics that in the West are taken as hallmarks of strength, maturity, and health.[13] For example, Irene Stiver and Jean Baker Miller point to the tendency in American culture "to admire and value more stoical responses and to devalue intense open expressions of sadness and grief."[14] Also writing about the United States, the relational therapist Judith Jordan notes that the open expression of needs is seen as weak while silence, stoicism, and a denial of feeling are regarded as strengths:

> We live in a cultural milieu that does not respect helpseeking and that tends to scorn the vulnerability implicit in our inevitable need for sup-

port. The ethic of individuality and self-sufficiency still takes precedence over an ethic of mutuality.[15]

The women I spoke to said that trying to conform to the ethic of individuality and self-sufficiency left them feeling depressed because coping precluded the possibility of mutual relationships. Although both men and women may feel the pressure to cope, the Western notion that mothers are ultimately responsible for all aspects of their children's care means that women in particular feel they must conceal their needs and feelings. In the following chapters, I look at how this ideal of self-sufficiency was often reinforced within women's personal relationships.

mothers and daughters

Mothers were central figures in women's stories of depression, whether these relationships were absent, ambivalent, difficult, or positive.[1] As noted, the loss of her mother had a profound influence on Tina's experience of motherhood the third time around. Tina had always enjoyed a close relationship with her mother and relied on her company and support in bringing up her own family. The gap left by her mother's death was accentuated after Emily's birth, when, for the first time, Tina had to mother her new child without being mothered herself.

Tina was the only woman whose mother was no longer alive at the time of the interview. When the other women spoke about the mother-daughter relationship, they frequently referred to the fear of disappointing their mothers. Many felt they were not living up to their mothers' standards and expectations. They saw mothers as "icons of maturity" and often equated motherhood with the attainment of adulthood.[2] Many believed that as mothers themselves they should no longer need their own mothers (or fathers, for that matter). They felt a need to prove they were independent, separate, and autonomous adults. Turning to their mothers for help and support left many with a sense of shame.

Fears about disappointing their mothers were stronger for some women than for others. For example, two women were not even willing to "test" their relationships with their mothers by telling them about their depression. Sonya, for example, assumes that her mother cannot support her emotionally:

> I don't feel particularly close to my mother . . . I wouldn't ring her up and pour out all this that I'm telling you. I've never told her that I've got it. I don't know if she'd understand it really. So sometimes I think, why can't I have a mother like other people who would come for a walk with Suzie and listen to me and I could confide in her, and it's just not worked out that I have that kind of mother.

Celia, whom we first met in Chapter 2, feels more positive about her relationship with her mother. Now that she has recovered from her depression she feels motherhood has brought her closer to her parents; they now share an understanding of the impact children have on their parents' lives. When she was depressed, however, she felt unable to confide in her parents for fear of upsetting or burdening them. She also feared disappointing her mother and her mother-in-law by not living up to their expectations:

> I mainly didn't say anything, partly because I didn't want to upset them, partly because I felt they wouldn't understand. 'Cos my mother never mentioned that she'd had any experience, my mother had been a very natural mother . . . and . . . I knew that I wasn't just going to be better overnight so I was sort of protecting them. I didn't want them to have unnecessary worries that they couldn't really do anything about. And I wanted them to believe that I was coping, so it was more my decision to keep them at a distance rather than the fact that they didn't care or anything. And it's especially hard when your mother-in-law's had nine children to start, after your first child, to say you don't feel right [laughs]. You know it's quite something to live up to.

Other women also resisted asking for help initially, but when they did, their mothers responded warmly and sympathetically. Vera found it difficult to manage on her own, physically and emotionally, after Felix's birth. Her parents and in-laws lived close by and were very supportive: "My parents and my in-laws were ever so good. They'd come round, they didn't understand at all, you know, but they were just kind. None of them sort of said 'snap out of it.'" Nevertheless, for a long time, Vera resisted asking for help because she saw it as a weakness. "I was ashamed," she says. "I'd always got on with things. I'd never needed any help from anybody. I'm quite a private person, I didn't want people knowing, you know . . . I was ashamed 'cos I'd always coped with everything before with no trouble." Vera believed that as a mother she was morally responsible for looking after herself and her son without relying on other people. In practice, she often stayed with her parents when her husband worked night shifts in a factory. By seeking parental company and support, she felt she was failing as a mother. "I felt I shouldn't be doing this," she said. "I felt like 'This isn't right. I should not be doing this. I shouldn't be needing this help.'"

Vera was fortunate to have understanding parents. Other women had difficult, ambivalent, or unsupportive relationships with their mothers. They felt their mothers were imposing their own standards and values on them without acknowledging that childcare practices may have changed since they themselves had raised children, or that their daughters might have different ideas and views, or that the mothers' practices might not be appropriate in the context of the daughters' lives and circumstances, particularly in cases where they were combining motherhood with paid work.

Many women also felt that their mothers failed to acknowledge or listen to their feelings and needs when they tried to express them and did not offer practical or emotional support. This lack of support left them feeling hurt and isolated. It also reinforced their moral beliefs that they should be able to cope on their own. These difficult relationships often led the women to withdraw further not only from their mothers but also from other people in their lives.

SANDRA

In Chapter 3 Sandra talked about her high expectations of herself and how, by trying to live up to them, she became increasingly depressed. For Sandra, as for some of the other women, these standards and ideals in part came from, and were reinforced by, her own mother. When her daughter Alice was a baby, she used to sleep for four hours in the morning after her feed. Instead of having a rest herself, Sandra would "race round the house trying to get the house done." When I asked her whether she had very high standards for the house, and if so, where these came from, she said:

> I did have. I mean I'm letting them go. I've learnt, you know, that's stu-
> pid, you know, I'm not spending time with the child and you've got to

enjoy them, and that took a long time for that to sink in because of my mother. I was brought up to think that "cleanliness is next to godliness" and . . . you know you're on top of yourself if you've done everything.

Sandra feels her mother expects too much of her and makes her feel inadequate for not living up to her own high standards. Her mother helps her practically but Sandra feels watched and criticized. Six weeks after Alice was born, her mother came to stay for a few days. Their standards regarding housework and childcare, including sleeping and feeding routines, clashed. For example, Sandra adopts a flexible approach to childcare and does not like being tied to rigid routines. Her mother, however, used strict routines in bringing up her own children: "Mum always said to me, 'If only Alice was, you know, six, ten, two, and six your life would be [easier].'" Sandra describes other sources of tension in their relationship:

Mum used to keep coming up and saying, "You're not doing it properly, you *can't* be doing it properly, this baby shouldn't be feeding this much, why don't you go on the bottle?" which in hindsight I should have done, but I was told that if I tried and if I worked hard enough at it I could do it and I said, "I want to do what's best for Alice, if I can I want to breast-feed her, I don't want to give up."

Later she continues:

I had to take Alice to hospital on that first Friday that mum came to stay to have Alice's hip checked, and when I got back my mum said, "I've washed your kitchen floors." I said, "Ooh, great," and she said, "Well you do do it every day, don't you?" It was like a weekend like that, you know, "And when are you going to have her christened. And where. And who are you going to invite. And who's going to be godparents?" it was sort of "You've had a month now, you've got this baby sorted" . . . but I just couldn't take it on board. So when she went on the Sunday, I mean, I was snapping at her by the end of it and she went away and she never spoke to me for about four months.

After this four-month silence, Sandra's relationship with her mother improved. However, she continues to feel a lack of support and understanding from her mother, as well as from her father, her husband, and her in-laws. She struggles with their assumption that, as a mother, she should take sole responsibility for looking after Alice. She had expected her husband and relatives to take an active part in Alice's upbringing:

As soon as I had her . . . I thought, "Well, I've done my bit, this is now somebody else's problem." Of course it wasn't, it was the start of *my* problem. I assumed it would be . . . a universal thing . . . everybody would take part in bringing her up, and other people didn't look on it like that, you know, it was my role now, "You're mum, you do this, this and this." So yes, I suppose I had the wrong ideas, I assumed that if I couldn't cope then other people . . . would take over . . . but it didn't work out like that.

Sandra feels that since she became a mother, other people's perceptions of her, and therefore her relationships with them, have changed in that friends and family expect her to be a caregiver with no needs of her own:

I think everybody is just assuming I'll be here and . . . all the things will be done . . . and I find that hard. I think they assume if I've got a problem coming up I'll make my own arrangements. I don't know quite what they think I'm supposed to do in these situations.

When Sandra struggles to cope on her own and tries to voice her feelings and ask for help, she feels that her words fall on deaf ears. Nobody appears willing to help her, reinforcing the idea that she should be self-reliant. "I very much feel that a lot of it is coming in on me," she says, "and I've got nowhere to let rip and give my side of it, and if I do, you know, if I don't just plough the line then I'm being awkward or difficult."

Sandra believes that her ambivalent relationship with her mother stems from her mother's disappointment that she has not turned out to be the perfect daughter, and mother, she expected her to be. Throughout her childhood, Sandra was the model child and daughter. Her sister was the "bad" daughter who got pregnant at nineteen, whereas Sandra was the "good" daughter who always did what she was told, behaved as expected, went to college, and got married. Sandra feels that by becoming depressed she has shattered her mother's illusions and expectations. Consequently, her mother finds it difficult to respond emotionally to her difficulties. This causes Sandra a great deal of pain and leaves her feeling emotionally isolated:

I assumed that this was just another up and down and I'd get through it . . . I would be strong, and cope, and perhaps the hardest thing for everybody else is this time, I didn't. Thinking about it, I think that's probably the crux of it. This time *I cracked,* I just sort of said, "That's enough, that's it, I've had it," and threw an absolute wobbly . . . [My parents] . . . just can't cope with me going a bit funny . . . They can't understand it if I get tired or upset or something . . . I think [my mother] feels disappointed that I can't cope . . . You see, I wasn't the person she knew, because I'd been through all this and I wasn't coping, but she couldn't take that on board really, and even now, she can't really.

She adds:

If you're upset she can't cope . . . I think I've just come to terms with that, but it's still hard, I still get cross with her at not being able to just put her arms around me and say, "Look, it's all right, you know, calm down, just go and sit down and have a cup of coffee." But as soon as there is a problem she exacerbates it by saying, you know, "You're not to do that, you know, you're not to react like that."

Because she cannot find in her parents the accepting, caring, and responsive relationships she is looking for, Sandra has withdrawn from them and feels isolated as a result. She feels "a bit lost" as to whom to turn to "if things really do go wrong":

I think the main problem is . . . I haven't got one main person I can really go to . . . if I'm really in difficulty . . . I'd have to think about where I would go for help. If I was really stuck, then I'd go to mum and dad because I know they wouldn't let me down . . . but I couldn't really break down on them . . . let go, or really have a good holler.

Interestingly, her mother's reactions to her are remarkably similar to Sandra's own reactions to herself. Both mother and daughter find it difficult to acknowledge and accept the daughter's feelings. Both want perfection from her. And like the daughter, the mother is trying to deny that this is the case. This pattern of repetition or continuity between mother and daughter was most clearly articulated by Sandra, although it was present to lesser degrees in the other mothers' stories. Sandra is aware of this cycle of repetition, however, and is trying to break out of it with her own daughter. She wants to be able to comfort, support, and accept her daughter in an unconditional way. She wants Alice to feel she can be open and honest with her about her feelings of vulnerability, knowing that her mother will be there for her:

I'm hoping that when she grows up I'll be able to talk, I won't say, "Go away, I can't cope with you throwing a wobbly." I hope I'll be able to, but you tend to react as your mother does, but hopefully you learn from experience . . . I'm hoping that'll be a positive thing to come out of it.

PETRA

Petra, twenty-seven, first became depressed in pregnancy. She was still depressed when I met her twenty-one months after her son Joshua's birth. Her depression was unlike any other experience she had been through:

> It's like the end of the world, really. You've got nothing to live for, that's what it's like. I mean even though I've got Joshua, I have to keep telling myself I've got Joshua. You have to keep reminding yourself that's why you're here because you feel like, it's a bit like you're just stuck in this room and you can't get out, and there's nothing for you, and it doesn't matter how many things you think about that are good, they don't feel good. It doesn't create any feeling inside you, it's just like you've died inside . . . It seems that everything that they're here for is gone for some reason . . . all your emotions have gone.

Joshua was a planned baby, though Petra got pregnant sooner than she wanted and felt unprepared for his arrival. Her depression in pregnancy gradually worsened after the birth. She experienced panic attacks and felt alienated from her husband, family, and friends. She found it difficult to talk about her feelings, and when she tried she felt silenced and rejected. Her husband was very supportive and understanding, but she rejected all physical and sexual contact with him. Throughout the first twelve months of her depression she knew that "something was wrong." She could not talk to anyone about her feelings, even though she "*desperately* needed someone to talk to." Her words paint a picture of one hand struggling to reach out for help while the other holds it back:

> When you're depressed, it's the one thing you can't do, and that's the trouble, you can't keep in contact with people. And there doesn't seem to be enough people out there that bother, you know. You need somebody, a very very good friend that really bothers about you, that has to keep ringing you 'cos you want people to ring you, and you want people to come to you, to show they care, but there's no way that you can go to them and that's the trouble. So a lot of people just don't bother and you never see anybody.

Why did Petra find it so difficult to express her feelings? What was holding her back from confiding in her husband, her mother, or her friends? Looking back to the time when her depression was at its worst, and knowing now what she does about postpartum depression, it seems obvious to her that she was suffering from PPD. Yet at the time, she found it difficult to make sense of her feelings. She wondered whether she was simply experiencing the reality of motherhood. She also questioned this idea and believed that something was wrong: "I just thought I was a bad mother and I couldn't cope with it all," she says. "Nobody tells you what to look out for." Petra was unable to identify the nature of her feelings because of a lack of information about postpartum depression, particularly in her prenatal classes. She also feared revealing her feelings and being criticized and judged by others. The result was silence and withdrawal:

> You sort of hear generally people say, "Oh well, you get the baby blues and people are tearful or they feel down or depressed or unhappy," you know, it just wasn't like I expected at all. Not that they tell you about it anyway . . . And . . . nobody likes to admit they're depressed. And a lot of people say, "Well, you cover it up well," and I thought well, I wasn't even trying, I wasn't trying to cover it up. I suppose I covered it up in the way that I didn't go and say sit down with someone and say, "Look, I can't cope," but on the other hand I thought I didn't know really what it was exactly was wrong and I wouldn't have known where to start. You know, I thought I was just being lazy really, just letting my husband do all the work. I used to wonder why I was being like that, I used to think, "What's the matter with me," but I certainly wasn't going to ring someone up and say, "Oh look at me, I don't do anything all day, I wait for my husband to come home from work."

Petra feared that her sisters would not understand her feelings and that her mother would simply tell her to pull herself together. It was above all her sense of failure as a mother, and her shame, that prevented her from talking about her feelings. She felt guilty about being depressed because she had "a good husband, a nice house, and a good baby." She wanted to be seen as having succeeded in motherhood. Disclosing her depression would shatter her own and others' expectations of her as a mother:

> I felt I couldn't tell anybody even though I was sort of glad that they knew what was the matter, I couldn't tell anybody because I felt like I'd let everyone down. I wanted to do really well and for everyone to think, "Isn't she doing well and isn't she wonderful and isn't the baby wonderful" . . . I suppose it was sort of my one chance to achieve something, and I felt I'd let everyone down and I still feel that a bit, you know I

haven't sort of told everybody. I mean most people like my family know now but I still feel that I'm a failure 'cos I couldn't do it, you know, I sort of gave into this, if you like, it got hold of me and I was weak.

Petra tried to confide in her mother, but her lack of understanding compounded her feelings of shame:

> I was trying to tell my mum how I was feeling, from inside of me, telling her all my feelings and that I didn't want to go out and I didn't want to stay home. I found it hard and our whole family was there and she said, "You don't want to go out, you don't want to stay in, what *do* you want to do?" in a loud voice in front of everybody. And I thought, "Oh my God." I felt awful and I said, "All right, mum, I said I just told you that in confidence," and she sort of shut up then . . . I think I cried when I got home but I didn't cry there.

Her mother's response led Petra to withdraw from her emotionally. Petra also criticized her mother for not giving her enough practical support:

> She was here but I still felt as if I was left alone with this baby and I didn't want to be. I mean I know, looking back, I think my mum thought that she was doing the best, you know. She wasn't to interfere, it was my baby but on the other hand I wanted someone to help me and tell me if I was doing it right or to show me what to do . . . I still look for someone's approval whether I'm doing it right or wrong. I know that she would have had to have been careful because obviously she can't just barge in and tell me how to do it when it's my baby. I mean I understand that. But on the other hand I really wanted her to help me with the baby. Whereas she was quite good, she cleaned my house and cooked me dinners you know, but whereas when it came to the baby she just left me alone, which would probably have been great for some people, I suppose, but it just wasn't what I needed at the time.

Petra's experience differs from that of Sandra, who felt that her mother's practical help was one more standard to which she could not live up. These two contrasting accounts illustrate the dilemmas mothers may face in trying to help their daughters. Do they give their daughters practical help and risk being seen as intrusive and interfering mothers who have a definite way of doing things? Or do they take their cue from their daughters, wait to be asked for help, and risk being seen as unhelpful and unsupportive? This is the fine balance many mothers face when their daughters (and daughters-in-law) become mothers. Mothers who have their own jobs or careers may face further complications. Petra, for example, felt totally abandoned by her mother when she was at work during the week:

> I blamed my mum at first when I was very depressed. I thought it was all my mum's fault because she hadn't been there for me, and I thought that was the whole reason I was the way I was. But that was just one of the things you know . . . She used to have Thursday afternoons off and she came over on Thursday afternoon, otherwise she never came again. She never came here at all and it was like, I was just here five days a week and I didn't have anybody, no one. I think if I'd have got a sister that had had children—neither of my sisters have got children, you see—so I didn't really have anyone. It was only really my mum that could have helped me.

Even though her mother worked, Petra felt she *should* be there for her. Whereas Sandra believed that her mother was projecting her own standards onto her daughter, Petra's expectations of her mother mirror her expectations of herself. She wants her mother to be there for her, to put her own needs to one side so that she can selflessly attend to her daughter. Interestingly, Petra expected the same from herself when it came to caring for her son, Joshua. For a long time she wouldn't leave him with anyone because she believed that, as his mother, she was solely responsible for looking after him:

> I never went out, you see, never went out in the evenings. I never had anyone look after Joshua. I felt I couldn't leave him, I felt guilty. I felt that . . . I'd taken on this baby and I should be there no matter what, and it just sort of got ridiculous in the end . . . I just got obsessed with not going out and, on the other hand, nobody sort of said, "Go out, let me look after him . . . for a day while you go out or something." Nobody said that.

Petra's situation illustrates what happens when women, as well as partners and family members, internalize cultural norms that place ultimate responsibility for children on mothers' shoulders, while fathers and relatives are assumed and expected to play a more minor role.

HELEN

Helen, whom we met in the previous chapter, feared that her mother would interfere, criticize her, and impose her own standards on her daughter's life. Her fears were so great that she decided not to ask her mother to come and stay with her after Ben was born. However, Helen's worst fears were not realized. Her mother was extremely supportive and has helped her without being overbearing:

> My mother was terribly supportive . . . She didn't interfere. My worst fears were never founded with her . . . I thought that she would be very critical and tell me that I was doing this wrong and that wrong but in fact she was never like that.

Although Helen appreciates her mother's practical help, she resents her lack of understanding of her life as a mother and her depression. Throughout her depression, Helen has tried to share her feelings with her mother. Like Sandra and Petra, she feels her mother cannot accept that she is struggling with ambivalent feelings about motherhood. Her mother seems more concerned about how Helen is progressing with her part-time doctoral studies than she is about her depression:

> She thinks postnatal depression is something of, you know, a fad . . . I mean I did say to mum how I felt last November and, which is when I really hit rock bottom, and . . . she keeps going on about this *bloody* thesis. It means a lot to her for one reason or another me doing this *sodding* thesis. And . . . so she keeps going on about it, "Have you done work tonight on it?" . . . And I say, "Mum," you know, "I feel *really* low. I'm so fed up I don't know what to do with myself," and the next day she'd phone up and say, "Have you done any work on your thesis?" She had no acknowledgment at all for what you'd just said. So you know there was no support there either.

This lack of understanding has exacerbated Helen's feelings of loneliness.

The experiences of Sandra, Petra, and Helen illustrate how some mother-daughter dynamics can intensify women's feelings of isolation. Some women have high, perhaps unrealistic, expectations of their mothers, reflecting their expectations of themselves. Others feel unsupported by their mothers. And, in some cases, mothers appeared to have difficulty accepting their daughters when they failed to live up to the standards they had set for them.

MONICA

I met Monica through a mother and toddler group. She was twenty, had been married to Carlo for three years, and had two children. Her first child, Kevin, was born when she was seventeen, and her second child, Beth, when she was eighteen. They lived in a two-bedroom house in a housing development. Although Carlo is a qualified chef, he was unemployed at the time and had been for several months. Monica was not in paid work either. She first became depressed when she accidentally got pregnant with her second child, Beth, two months after Kevin's birth. When Beth was born she had very little interest in her. Her mother-in-law offered to take Beth in, and Monica saw her every day. After three months, she gradually grew to love her daughter and became increasingly distraught that Beth seemed not to realize that Monica was her "real" mother. She wanted her daughter back, but in the intervening months her mother-in-law had grown attached to Beth. After a month of arguing, Monica eventually took Beth back but did not speak to her mother-in-law for several months.

Monica's depression during pregnancy got much worse after Beth was born. Carlo had little sympathy for her feelings. "He's a typical man," she says, "he doesn't understand what women go through. He thought I was just being stupid . . . I couldn't talk to him 'cos he didn't listen . . . When I was in tears I tried to explain to him then but he didn't have much time for it all." Monica turned to her own mother for support but found little understanding. "My mother just didn't wanna know," she says. Her mother simply urged her to get her daughter back and blamed her for having given up Beth in the first place. Monica wanted to be listened to and heard rather than told what to do. She felt rejected rather than supported by her mother, and this led her to withdraw and become more and more isolated. She hid her depression from her visiting nurse, family, and friends. "Every time somebody come round I tried and put on a front for people. As soon as they were gone, because of all the things I held back, it all came out as soon as they left," she explains. She was depressed for eighteen months, although she received no treatment during this time. She did not tell any healthcare professionals about her depression because she feared that her children might be taken away. Some months after Beth was born, she joined a local mother-and-toddler group. There she met Sophie, another mother in my study, who had also experienced postpartum depression. As their friendship grew, Monica came to trust Sophie and to confide her feelings in her. In contrast to her relationships with her husband, her mother, and her mother-in-law, she felt listened to and understood by Sophie. The strength and support she drew from this friendship helped her gradually overcome her feelings of depression and come to terms with her difficult family relationships.

The four women whose stories appear in this chapter struggled to cope with their depression single-handedly in part because of the high standards they felt their own mothers had set for them. Not only did the women feel they could not talk about their experiences with their mothers; but their sense of vulnerability was exacerbated by the belief that somehow their mothers' criticisms were well-founded and valid. Their disappointment and hurt at their mothers' inability to accept them for who they were confirmed their fear of rejection from others and made it all the more difficult for them to accept themselves. The next chapter explores how women's relationships with their partners similarly played a key role in reinforcing their ideals of motherhood, as well as their expectations and perceptions of themselves.

men, women, and relationships

Research suggests that women's relationships with their male partners are crucial to understanding postpartum depression. According to these studies, male partners are the primary sources of support in mothers' lives, and one of the main causes of postpartum depression is seen as a poor relationship in which a woman's partner fails to be sympathetic, understanding, or supportive in practical or emotional terms.[1] For example, in a review of studies on postpartum depression and the marital relationship, Ian Gotlib and his colleagues conclude that "a lack of spousal support may play an important role in the development of postpartum depression."[2] Michael Sheppard notes that "a partner prepared to listen to the woman's problems, to show some understanding of them, who shows concern when she is distressed and provides the practical and child care support where necessary probably provides the single most significant preventive factor."[3]

The women I interviewed described relationships with their partners that were far more diverse than these studies suggested. I was initially struck by the fact that of the seventeen women who were living with the father of their child at the time of their depression (all except for Sophie), only eight said their partners lacked understanding, showed little interest or involvement in the home, and failed to offer the emotional support they wanted and needed.[4] Their partners, they said, expected them to take full responsibility for housework and for the children, even when the mother was in full-time work. The fathers' lack of domestic involvement created a burden of work and responsibility that the women found physically and emotionally draining. They also felt that their partners had no understanding of their day-to-day lives as mothers. They experienced this lack of assistance as an absence of care, love, and concern, and as a result they felt emotionally detached from their partners. In many cases, the decision to have a child had been a joint one, and so the women were surprised when their partners did not share the same level of interest in their child.

When these women tried to ask for help, they felt that their partners were non-responsive. Repeated rejection led them to withdraw gradually from the relationships. Frances speaks for many when she says: "I soon learnt not to rely on my husband. I find it better, I suppose, I like to be independent." Although Frances and the other women said it was easier to withdraw than to risk rejection, they did so at great personal cost.

Several of the women said that though their partners were involved in childrearing the relationship was not one of mutuality and reciprocity. That is, the men contributed in practical and emotional ways but only when it suited them and on their own terms, regardless of the mothers' needs or wishes. These mothers experienced their partners' one-sidedness as a lack of respect and an unwillingness to work as a team.

A second group of women, nine total, said their partners supported them, practically and emotionally, in motherhood as well as throughout their depression.[5] They were satisfied with their partners' contributions to the household and childcare. Three (one in part-time and two in full-time employment during their depression) said that their partners' involvement in the home was equivalent to their own. The remaining six women (one in part-time employment and five not in paid work) said their partners were less involved in the home than they were. They took on the responsibility for housework and childcare but were satisfied with their situation. Some of these women felt that because their partners worked full-time, housework and childcare was their job. Furthermore, they did not see their partners' limited involvement in the home as a reflection of male chauvinism or traditional gender roles. Several women blamed the current work ethic and a culture of long working hours for their husband's limited domestic contributions. Others said they tended to discourage their partners' involvement in household affairs, either because they had different standards or because they wanted their partners to spend their free time with them or with the children rather than doing housework. Some women said their partners failed to see or notice what housework or childcare needed to be done. They did not experience this lack of initiative as a problem, however, because their partners had otherwise shown their care and concern. Although these men sometimes lacked initiative, they were always willing to help when asked to do so.

Despite their positive relationships, these women felt emotionally isolated from their partners. They explained that the emotional distance resulted from their own withdrawal from their loved ones. Some discouraged their partners from helping or supporting them. Some said they were reluctant to ask for help or share their feelings because they feared burdening their partners and being misunderstood. Many felt that, having experienced neither motherhood nor depression, their partners would not understand their feelings. These women said that their depression itself—and not their partners' attitude—led them to withdraw emotionally from those closest to them.

The experiences of the mothers I spoke to generally echo findings from numerous studies showing that household work still belongs largely to women. Even when women work outside the home, they remain the overall managers, planners, organizers, and supervisors of housework and childcare-related activities in the home.[6] Research suggests that the costs to women of taking primary responsibility for housework and childcare are considerable, and can include fatigue; anxiety; illness; marital conflict; a "double shift" for those in paid work; a lack of time and energy for work and a career; occupational downgrading; loss of promotions, earnings, pensions, and other benefits; lack of access to financial resources; and economic vulnerability in cases of marital breakdown and divorce.[7] Some of the women I spoke to accepted the gender division of roles and responsibilities, partly because they understood the ideological and structural constraints on men and how these can make it difficult for them to participate in the day-to-day care of their children. They spoke about the pressure to work long hours, cultural notions of fathers as providers and breadwinners, and their own difficulties letting go of the domestic domain and allowing men to take a more active role.

Categorizing women according to the quality of their partner relationships, and characterizing the differences between difficult and positive relationships, is a useful analytic strategy. However, it also obscures the subtle and evolving dynamics of individual relationships and cannot adequately capture the contradictory emotions that women may feel toward their partners—the coexistence of feelings of love, companionship, and tenderness with feelings of anger, disappointment, resentment, and frustration. The experiences of five women in my study elucidate this point.

SONYA

Sonya, whom we met in Chapter 3, has known Johnie for fifteen years and has been married to him for twelve. Until she had Suzie she concentrated on building her career, and both she and Johnie worked long hours. Johnie runs his own company, where Sonya used to work. For years they shared a lifestyle that was dominated by work.

Sonya feels conflicting emotions about Johnie. She wavers between acceptance and resentment of his lack of involvement in raising their daughter. She struggles to accept the man she married and come to terms with her feelings of hurt and disappointment. She repeatedly describes him as not being a "normal NCT husband": "He's not the textbook NCT father who becomes totally involved and as soon as he comes home from work, you know, picks up the baby." For many of the women, including Sonya, the National Childbirth Trust, or NCT, represented a set of standards to which they aspired, and therefore a powerful source of pressure. In particular, the NCT was seen to uphold the ideals of "natural" childbirth, breast-feeding, and the "new father"—an involved, caring, and attentive partner during pregnancy and the birth, and an active caregiver and father thereafter. Sonya hoped that Johnie would turn into this kind of father, even though she questions and resists this ideal. For example, she wanted Johnie to be an attentive, caring birth partner; yet she also challenges the notion that the husband is necessarily the support figure women want when they are in labor:

> You're brainwashed into thinking that the husband's got to be there and he's got to be supportive and he's got to be involved and he's got to be this and he's got to be that. But because I had a birth where I was on the bed he couldn't help a lot. He did actually go to sleep at one point. I

mean it was an eleven-hour shift for him so he did go to sleep on the camp bed [cot] and I remember feeling "Well, I'm glad he's doing that." I didn't want him to feel he just had to hover around sponging me down. I mean he was annoying me a bit in the middle of my pain, I was thinking, "Why doesn't he go away" . . . It was just the way I dealt with pain . . . I didn't go to him as the main person to give me release of the pain. It was the midwife . . . But he was fully involved and everything. I don't want to give the impression he's this sort of businessman who just comes in for his tea and pays the bills and goes away again, you know, we are very close.

As Sonya's words suggest, though she clearly feels let down by Johnie's apparent lack of involvement with Suzie, part of her tries to deny her disappointment. Indeed, her depression stems partly from the way she fights her feelings. For example, she says she was not upset by Johnie's limited involvement in the birth, his leaving the hospital with champagne as soon as Suzie was born, and his failure to take any time off from work. Beneath this denial, however, she sounds terribly hurt that he appeared not to want to spend more time with his wife and new daughter. When asked whether she would have liked Johnie to take some time off, she says:

> Yes, yes, so that he could have hands-on caring for Suzie and get to know her, if you like. But I mean the day I had Suzie he went back to work with champagne . . . I didn't mind him going back to work. I didn't feel "Oh, this is great, I've just had a baby and you're leaving me now" because, you know, I was devoting time to Suzie, and he'd done his bit. But he never thought you know, "Shall I take three or four days off." He might have taken the odd day but it wasn't a chunk of time, you know, "This is the time I'm taking to get to know Suzie." But he got to know Suzie well, I mean there's no question that I look after her and he just passes through, okay? I don't want to give that impression. I mean you know he'd do anything for her and if you like he's translating the effort of his work into care for her, do you see what I mean?

Sonya explains that having Suzie has hardly affected Johnie's lifestyle or daily routine. He leaves for work at seven o'clock, comes home at nine in the evening, and spends the weekends playing golf rather than enjoying his family. Sonya, however, has radically altered her lifestyle since becoming a mother. As noted, she felt she had to obliterate the person she once was, deny her own needs and identity, and become a selfless, self-sacrificing mother. Their different reactions to the gendered realities of parenthood have become a critical point of tension within their relationship:

> After having Suzie I think my lifestyle changed a lot more than his. And I think that was one of the main things, that I was accepting a complete obliteration of what I was doing before, you know, to care for Suzie. And Johnie was changing his behavior slightly and like being in bed with Suzie, etc., but still I mean on a Saturday morning if he wants to watch his favorite TV program he'll watch it and he still reads the paper even if we're in bed, me and Johnie and Suzie together, he still *tries* to read the paper. Whereas a mother gives up reading the paper, doesn't she? She gives up watching the TV program she wants to watch, you know. And he'll say, "Well, I want to go off and play a round of golf," and I'll think, "Well, he hasn't been with us all week. Why does he want to go and play golf?" you know, that sort of thing. He still does what he's always done.

Sonya accepts that having a child inevitably changes a couple's life-style, but while she has made an effort to retain her interest in Johnie's day-to-day life, she feels he has not shown the same level of interest or involvement in their new domestic lives and responsibilities:

> The lifestyles clash more now because I'm in a different world, you know. But . . . I have bent towards him and I have said, "Right, I'm look-ing after Suzie . . . I'll try and make a bit of money on the side . . . I'll come back to work and make money" . . . I tried to make sure that I didn't slip into sort of telling him how many nappies she'd filled when he came home. So I was trying to keep myself up-to-date . . . trying to keep some interest in the business . . . But I just feel that there's not the same reciprocal "Okay, I'll try and be home at seven two nights a week," you know, because if he makes those promises they'll always be broken by other people. It's not necessarily him, it's other people exploit his time . . . It's like the total unbending nature of it, you know, that he doesn't say, "We need the money, I need to work hard, but if I could get home an hour earlier it relieves you a bit."

Sonya's feelings about Johnie's behavior as a father are mixed. She expected that he would not be a very involved father, and this was partly why she put off having children for many years:

> I knew in my heart of hearts that Johnie wouldn't be the sort of type who would take over completely, I suppose. I think that's why I put it off for so long. I used to say to him, "I'm *not* having a baby and bringing it up on my own." I used to say those words to him . . . I projected and thought that's what it's going to be like and I'm not prepared to do it.

Later, she repeats, "I know him. I accept that [work ethic] in him because I married him." Johnie has always worked hard. Sonya also recognizes that he has had to work long hours partly because this is the nature of running your own business, and partly because the recession of the early 1990s put extra pressure on the company. She nevertheless struggles to accept Johnie's lifestyle. She feels that he could reduce his hours if he really wanted to:

> I was getting annoyed about it and saying, "Look, this is not on. You've got to come back at seven o'clock. This is not living, this is just sort of existing." And he said, "Well, you know how it is with the business," and you know, "I've got to earn the money and you and Suzie have got to be provided for and therefore if I come home early I'm not going to be doing my job correctly," which is not necessarily true because a workaholic fills the time available.

Later in the interview she draws a link between her depression and Johnie's long working hours:

> When I was first ill, part of the thing going on in my mind is that if you like, he let down his part of the bargain slightly. Because I had Suzie, I was, you know, going to do the best I could, but some of the time I believed I was working in an impossible environment . . . Maybe that's why at six months it started happening because . . . my job seemed to be an endurance test, if you like, because this baby was relying on me. And . . . I started thinking, "Well I'm filling in the day because I know Johnie isn't going to be back till a certain time," if you like. I was sort of trying to be super-active and maybe the best thing would have been for me to stay home and do the ironing or sit down with a cup of tea. But I felt I had to make the days pass because the last bit at night was so hard . . . I'd come away from afternoons where we'd had cups of tea and seen everybody's babies . . . and then as I'd come home in the car at five o'clock I'd think, right, it's only five now but that's fine, you know, then I'd change Suzie, feed her and stuff, then it'd be six o'clock and then I'd think, "Okay, isn't this the bit where the father comes in now and picks up Suzie and plays with her for an hour and bathes her and you know generally gets to know her and I'm looking on as the proud mother" . . . and she's getting a balanced caring whereas me, you know, I'd been ground down a bit . . . yeah, I feel I was left on my own too much by my husband.

Sonya feels that by working long hours Johnie fails to appreciate what it is like to look after a young child all day. He does not see that she, too, needs a break and some time to herself. As shown, Sonya was very influenced by cultural ideals of motherhood, and she had rigid ideas about how she should behave as a mother. She believed she should be a full-time, devoted mother who gives up her self (and her life) in order to look after her child. Although she questions this ideal, she also feels compelled to live up to it, and Johnie's behavior reinforces her belief. His attitude makes it that much more difficult for her to resist these cultural expectations:

> I had a baby under a hard regime, you know, because the day is long anyway, to add three hours at the end of it is almost like the final crunch. And I said to Johnie recently that the time I hate is between six and nine o'clock because . . . he isn't home from work until nine o'clock and then I start cooking, you see. So I have to rally all my energies then to get up and *cook* for the last part of the evening . . . It's partly my fault because I like this time when I don't have to do anything else, but if I was efficient with time I'd be getting things ready at six so that when he came in at nine it was on the table. I mean I accept that I'm probably being a bit lazy and . . . I don't *like* myself because I *allow* myself to fall into a sloth . . . and watch TV and just let the world go by and let Suzie do her own thing and not sit with her and read a book, or I just think, well, go away for a minute. But in reality that six o'clock time is if the husband was coming in then this would be my sort of "Right-she's-yours-I'm-going-to-watch-news-at-6-*next-door*" time, do you see what I mean?

Later she continues:

> He's *never* actually taken her out in the buggy or the pram on his own away from me . . . But I think what put extra pressure on me was the responsibility was *mine* twenty-four hours a day, day in and day out . . . I think psychologically you *know* that yours is the responsibility at the end of the day. But if you just have that hour where you trick yourself into thinking this is a complete break . . . I mean we love Suzie dearly, but like me and Johnie, we don't want to be with each other all day, do we? And even with a baby there's got to be that sort of "Right, you're separate to me" . . . I've always longed for that time when I can say to Johnie, "Here's Suzie," I hate the expression "I've had the baby all day" 'cos it sounds as if you can't wait to get rid of them, but you've got to be realistic and think well, what if the baby's been crying or grizzly and you've been giving them a lot of support and tenderness and you're a bit sort of worn out now, and it's your turn to give them this support and tenderness. But I could never say, "Here is Suzie," you know, "I'm *me*, I'm *me* for an hour. I'm going to sit in the bath, here she is." I've never done that with him and I think that did put pressure on me to get obsessive about "I'm the only one that looks after her," you know, I think that

did make it hard . . . It just loaded the dice a bit more, you know, on me feeling run down, utterly depended on . . . I'd wake up at seven in the morning and think, "Well, Johnie will be home at eight tonight so I'm filling the time for thirteen hours, just me and Suzie."

Sonya struggles to convince herself that although she has a child she still is, and is entitled to be, a separate person. In her account, Johnie's attitude and unchanging daily habits and rituals make it difficult for her to validate this point of view. His prolonged absences from home during the day and on the weekends leave her confused about what she can realistically and legitimately expect of herself and him.

Johnie's long working hours have affected not only his ability to help Sonya in practical terms, but also the amount of emotional support he is able to give her. She explains that he comes home exhausted in the evening, and the last thing he wants to hear about are her feelings of depression. She has tried to confide in him but feels he does not listen to her:

He comes home, he's tired, he's been bombarded all day by other people wanting him to solve their problems and I say, "I've had a terrible day. I feel ill. It's never going to end," you know, and he says, "Look, I don't want to hear all this. Everybody else is asking me for answers" . . . So what I do then is say . . . "Okay, let's not talk about it." I'd do the dinner dutifully. He'd fall asleep. I'd make sure Suzie was all right. I'd clean my teeth, get into bed and go to sleep. So I hadn't shared it with him 'cos he hasn't got the capacity to share it 'cos he's got too many other things to think of. So all the time there was that little unresolved bit at the end of the day. I wanted to put out what I'd felt but it was negative, therefore it was just yet one other negative thing that was coming at him when he was tired and just wanted to have a whisky and sit down and have a meal and go to bed.

Johnie's reaction when Sonya tries to talk about her feelings reinforces other people's message that she should not feel the way she does. One day Sonya tells her mother-in-law on the phone, "You've gotta come here now, I just can't handle this, you've gotta come now." She tells her sister-in-law, "I've taken these tablets [antidepressants]." She tells her friend, "I feel terrible." She tells her husband, "I feel ill." She tells her visiting nurse, "This is happening to me and I don't know what to do about it." She tells the doctor, "I . . . feel bad." But the responses she receives leave Sonya feeling alone and misunderstood. Her mother-in-law says, "Pull yourself together" and gives her sunflower seeds and vitamins to take. Her sister-in-law tells her to "chuck the tablets" that the doctor has prescribed for her. Her friend says, "You need to go back to work." Her husband says, "I don't want to hear all this." The visiting nurse says, "I'll get you to the doctor." The doctor says, "Keep on the tablets."

Sonya desperately wants to speak about her feelings, but she is surrounded by individuals who are concerned with taking her feelings away rather than taking them in. Perhaps this is because women's feelings of ambivalence and depression are deeply unsettling at both a personal and a cultural level. They speak to the unrealistic nature as well as to the damaging effects of cultural ideals, norms, and expectations of motherhood. Postpartum depression questions and unsettles deeply ingrained myths of motherhood and threatens the ideal in which many women and men have invested.

Sonya struggles to negotiate a "new order" with Johnie but he is not receptive. One of their problems is that they have not reconfigured their roles since becoming parents. Johnie's life has remained the same while Sonya has taken on a new identity, a new work load, and new responsibilities. Sonya and Johnie's parenting practices reflect stereotypical notions about the roles of men and women in the family: women are expected to give up their own lives when they become mothers, whereas men's lives, work, and interests are expected to continue unchanged.[8]

SANDRA

Sandra, whose ideals of motherhood were earlier shown to be sustained and reinforced by her mother, also had to contend with her husband's expectations of her. Sandra married Bob when she was twenty-four. Their marriage has been a difficult one, plagued by financial problems and arguments. Over the years, Sandra has suggested that they see a marriage counselor, but Bob has always refused, claiming that she is the source of their marital difficulties.

Compared with Sonya's husband, Bob has been more involved in household activities and particularly in looking after Alice. "He's quite a practical person," Sandra says. "He's good at cooking, ironing, sewing, knitting [laughs]. He can do all the things a lady ought to do." Many of the difficulties within their relationship stem from Bob's expectation that Sandra should be the strong partner who can cope with difficult situations without relying on him. For example, Sandra feels that Bob fails to recognize that she sometimes feels vulnerable, low, and in need of a break from the pressures and strains of combining full-time work with motherhood:

> I don't get a break. I don't get the space to unwind. I think that's what I find the hardest thing of all to come to terms with. There's nobody around really to give me a break. It seems he needs it more than I do so it's more me having to give up the time than him . . . Unless I can be strong and work through it when I'm feeling vulnerable and can't cope with it, that's when he finds it hard . . . I think the problems started again when I had Alice and . . . the realization that suddenly I was very much, you know, having to be a strong part in this marriage and work because without working everything seemed to collapse. He doesn't feel in any way that I have a right . . . to stay at home with Alice any more than he did. It was nobody's right. It wasn't the mother's right or the father's. It could be either one . . . I had always assumed when we got married, perhaps we didn't talk about it enough, that when I had a baby I would not work 'cos he'd always seemed to have a fairly reasonable job.

As Sandra suggests, another source of tension within their relationship is that Sandra assumed they would follow a traditional gendered division of male breadwinner and female caregiver, while Bob challenged this model. Both feel entitled to stay home to look after Alice, and neither feels they should be the main breadwinner. For the first two years of Alice's life, Bob worked from home four days a week. On those days, Alice went to a registered childcare provider for half a day and Bob took care of her the rest of the day. He enjoyed his time with Alice and his close relationship with her. For financial reasons, he had to give up working from home six months ago and took a factory job in a nearby city. Sandra had to return to work full-time four months after the birth to improve their financial situation. Bob misses his time at home with Alice, and Sandra also resents that she has to work full-time. When asked if Bob would like to stay at home with Alice rather than work, Sandra replies:

> Yes, I think this is the root of it. He very much enjoyed it when he was at home with her . . . And that was discussed, you know, that he stay at home and I work but I've never earned enough for that to be viable . . . I mean at the end of the day I don't really want to split up with him. We've been through so much and I do underneath it all care for him, but there's been a lot of outside problems, you know, coming in on us and

not being able to communicate and make proper decisions together and probably him never feeling that he should take on board the responsibility of being the breadwinner.

Despite Bob's desire to spend more time looking after Alice, Sandra finds it difficult to secure his help and support when she needs it. She describes one occasion when she wanted to attend a doctor's appointment on her own, but neither Bob nor her parents were willing to look after Alice. Frustrated by her family's apparent unwillingness to support her or to take care of Alice, and their failure to realize that this practical help was emotionally important to her, Sandra withdrew from her family:

> I got really cross about it and I said, "Well, just forget it, the lot of you. I'll take Alice with me to the hospital, which is not really what I want to do, I want to go there *on my own* and have that time to myself."

Eventually Bob took time off, but only "after a lot of hassling and saying, 'This is *one thing I want, I want that hour of that day to me* and I want somebody to look after Alice—will somebody please help?'" Sandra struggles with motherhood because she feels she shoulders the burden of care for Alice and is not seen as having any legitimate needs of her own. "You ask for help sometimes," she says, "but it doesn't get taken on board, as you're screaming out to say, '*Please* will somebody do this.'" As a result of this lack of support, Sandra has increasingly withdrawn from Bob and her parents. She finds it easier to live as if she is on her own, so that her hopes and expectations will not be disappointed:

> As time goes on, it gets easier 'cos you just come to the conclusion that . . . it's better to just get on and do it yourself. But it doesn't make for a close relationship, does it, 'cos you become isolated . . . You go off and do your own thing and I find that hard to cope with.

Sandra feels that she has no choice but to withdraw a part of herself from her husband and her family in order to maintain even a semblance of relationship with them. In doing so, however, she effectively loses these relationships, leaving her feeling isolated, alone, and depressed.

Although Sandra and Bob have known each other for sixteen years, have been married for eleven, and are discussing having a second child, their relationship has deteriorated to such an extent since Alice was born that Sandra is doubtful whether the marriage will survive.

HELEN

As discussed in earlier chapters, Helen finds motherhood physically exhausting. Her life has become much more hectic since she returned to work as a visiting nurse when Ben was five and a half months old. Although she feels she is on a treadmill, she values the intellectual and financial rewards of work and believes that Ben benefits socially from attending daycare. Unlike Sandra, Helen does not find working itself a problem. Like Sandra and Sonya, she has struggled physically and emotionally with her partner's lack of involvement in household activities, and in taking care of Ben. Helen tells me that Simon fails to see how he can help her in practical terms, nor does he understand that helping her practically supports her emotionally. Looking after Ben is "one big bone of contention" within their relationship. Ben goes to daycare five days a week, even though Helen only works four days. The fifth day is her day off, to herself, and she often spends it working on her doctorate. Simon works as a nurse five days a week. He works shifts, which means he often starts at noon and has to work on the weekends. He has never spent his days off looking after Ben, a fact that Helen finds very difficult to accept. She does not understand why Simon appears not to want to spend time with their son. She also feels that because he has never looked after Ben for a whole day, he has no understanding of her life or of what it is like spending an entire day caring for an energetic and active toddler:

> Simon has never had Ben for a whole day on his own, never . . . out of choice. In the early days he said, "We're paying so much for this nursery place that I'm blown if I'm gonna, you know, he can go to nursery." My own feeling is that I actually want to spend more time with Ben. So if I had a day off during the week . . . I'd spend it with Ben 'cos I want to spend it with Ben . . . I have suggested it but there becomes a point where it's not actually worth discussing it any longer, and it's something that I want Simon to have but Simon doesn't want to have it with Ben . . . I never have a day where I don't have Ben except for my Friday whereas Simon *always* has two days off . . . and he never ever has had a day of sole charge of Ben. He's had hours you know a few hours here and there but never a whole day. And I feel that he doesn't really understand how

exhausting it is having this child all the time, entertaining them . . . I just find it amazing that he doesn't want to spend more time with Ben . . . this child that we both wanted.

Another point of tension is who takes Ben to and from daycare. Traveling from home to the daycare center and then on to work is a twenty-five-mile trip Helen makes twice a day. Ben hates the car and screams most of the way. Making this trip, day in day out, is beginning to wear her down. What she finds most difficult, however, is that on the days when Simon begins work at noon it does not occur to him to offer to take Ben to daycare so that she can have a break from her stressful routine:

> If for instance Simon was on a late [shift] on Thursday, so that means he doesn't have to get to work until one, if I was Simon I'd say, "I'll take Ben up to nursery, you have a lie-in." Oh no, I have to ask him to take Ben to the nursery on the Thursday. And I'm not sure how much of that is *him* or how much that is a man and just not seeing that these sort of things need doing, you know, or that it would be nice to give me a break. He never offers, I always have to ask.

When I ask Helen whether she feels Simon supports her emotionally, she says that he does. He is a very caring and loving partner, but he does not realize that practical help can be as emotionally supportive as expressing concern:

> He's very supportive . . . He often doesn't again see things. It takes quite a long while for things to click, but then when he does see things, he's supportive. But then he doesn't see that things do get you emotionally wound up, like this business of taking Ben to nursery on a Thursday morning if he's around. That actually gets me emotionally wound up rather than physically wound up, but he can't actually see it. But no, he is very supportive, he's very caring and loving . . . there's no two-ways about that, and he's very good with Ben.
> Natasha: So when you were feeling emotionally low, and during the particularly bad bits, he was very much there, was he?
> Yes, but I'd still have to ask him to get breakfast or he was still *there,* he was there and does, "I worry about you," and all this sort of business but wouldn't actually see that a help to that would be physical effort.

Helen reiterates this point when she talks about how she struggles, emotionally, with the fact that she and her partner now care for their child on a rotating basis, with the two of them taking turns. This system was instituted partly as a way of increasing Simon's involvement, and partly as a way of giving Helen a break. Despite this arrangement, she still has to remind Simon of his responsibility. Her feelings of frustration and hurt that caring for their child should be reduced to a strict schedule have led her gradually to give up on the system and accept the inevitable—that household chores and Ben's care have become principally her responsibility:

> We used to have this [system] to get up and feed Ben so the other person could have another sort of half an hour lie-in. But even though we knew what the rota was I was still having to remind Simon that it was time to get up and give Ben breakfast. So it's just not worth it to me anymore, I just get up. It's not worth asking . . . In the past month I've just changed. I've decided it's not worth it and Simon has got up sometimes in that time when I haven't asked but certainly not on the [rotating] basis. So that's been quite hard work. I think it's the *amazement* that he just doesn't see or doesn't appear to see. I mean you know we've discussed it a lot . . . and he says, "Well honestly, I'll do it, course I'll do it" if I ask him. Well, I mean by asking it's actually easier to do it yourself than asking, isn't it?

Helen continues:

> The problem is we've got into this terrible palaver of everything needing to take turns, and I don't know how we've got into it. "Well it's your turn to do the bath tonight because I did it last night," and all this sort of business. And again that's stopped in the past month 'cos I've just decided, you know, this is *our child* we're talking about. Before that it almost seemed that it was a point of issue that I was determined not to because I *know* that as soon as I do it, life, things, will change, I'll always do it, Simon will never see that it needs doing . . . Anyway, now I just do it and if Simon takes him up for his bath then that's a bonus . . . Silly really because if I'd thought about it I've always had to ask him to do things. Things have never been done with him seeing that they needed to get done.

As with Sonya's husband, Simon's life appears to have remained largely unchanged since he became a father. Before they had Ben, Helen was primarily responsible for the shopping, washing, cooking, and cleaning. Like Sonya, Helen expected fatherhood to change Simon. Both expected and hoped that their partners would actually *want* to be involved in childcare and domestic life. After having their children, they also believed that their partners would see how exhausting caring for a young child can be and want to give their partners a break. As mothers, Sonya and Helen have undergone dramatic lifestyle changes, partly out of necessity and partly out of choice. What amazes and disappoints them is that although they and their partners wanted a child, their partners appear unwilling to change their lives or reevaluate their priorities.

Helen's gradual emotional withdrawal from Simon echoes Sonya's experience with her husband. Having tried and failed so many times to involve Simon in caring for Ben, Helen has slowly given up the fight because it is emotionally too costly. She has reached a point where she feels it is not worth discussing these issues with Simon any longer because "it's quicker to do it than ask. Well, it's not quicker to do it than ask, obviously, but it's quicker on the emotions."

TINA

When I began the first interview with Tina I asked her to tell me about her experience of motherhood and why she thought she became depressed. Her opening words were about her mother's illness, the twelve months she spent nursing her, and the subsequent death of her mother—events that happened two years before her third child, Emily, was born. As discussed, Tina attributes her depression in part to this loss and to how it changed the dynamics of her relationship with her husband, Gary. When Tina had her first two children her mother was a great source of emotional and practical support. Being mothered, Tina explains, helped her to mother her own children.

When Emily was born, Tina experienced additional demands and pressures and a major lack of support with the loss of her mother. She turned to Gary for help, but he was unable to fulfill her needs and help her adapt to the new situation. Tina and Gary had a relationship in which she was the mother and he was the child. Caring for Tina was a role Gary could not fulfill or was not used to fulfilling:

> I needed somebody to look after me, bearing in mind that I hadn't got my mum. So I didn't have anybody for me, right, and when I wanted to let go and say, "Right, come on, I can't cope" type of thing, I'd *never say it* but all the hints were "Well, I'm going to sit down now." My husband *really* couldn't handle [it] . . . and I thought, you know, "God, I haven't got anybody, I'm having to cope with this all on my own."

Gary was very practically and emotionally supportive, Tina explains, but "at a cost"; she saw him as another child who was dependent on her:

> He'd run around with cups of tea keeping me happy . . . To everybody else, I mean *very good* husband, but at what cost, do you see? You know, he would do things for me but, in a way, I was then expected to be there for him all the time, emotionally, and I don't know, giving, well everything, every bloody everything . . . And through the depression, through when I had Emily what I needed from him then was to be a good father to both me and my baby and perhaps take her in his arms and say, "Oh, don't cry now" type of thing . . . So looking back really actually I had a tiny baby who needed me, obviously, 'cos I was feeding. I had two kids who needed me because there was a baby in the family that everybody was looking at. My husband . . . because I was so needed by others, he needed me more.

Although Tina blames Gary for not caring for her in the way she needed and wanted, she also acknowledges that she needed to change and stop playing the role of mother that she had adopted with him:

> You see, as much as he needed me to do it, it was a need for me to do it, and so now I just let go . . . Some days I'm better, or some weeks I'm better than others and I can like trust him to be able to do things for himself, to be able to be emotionally supportive to me, you know.

Later in the interview she talks about the value of the couple's counseling she and her husband received as well as the individual counseling she had. Through these sessions she learned a lot: "It wasn't *me* that was at fault, it was Gary, *but,* you know, obviously it was our relationship."

Tina acknowledges that her behavior contributed to the problems in her marriage. Relationships are between two people, and in order to understand the nature of marital difficulties it is critical to look at both parties. Yet the research studies that have examined the marital relationships of women with postpartum depression tend to focus exclusively on the male partner and his behavior. As a result, these relationships and the problems within them have often been misunderstood.[9] Celia's story illustrates the importance of looking not only at the father's behavior but also at the mother's if we are to understand the full range and complexity of the troubled relationships that women with postpartum depression experience.

CELIA

Celia was one of the women who described a positive and supportive relationship with her partner. Celia and Robert, thirty-one, have two daughters: Katie, who is six, and Melissa, who is three. Celia has not returned to her career in public relations since she had her children. Although she and Robert shared household tasks before their daughters were born, now that she is home-based and Robert still works full-time Celia takes primary responsibility for running the home, though Robert is involved. In the early days, he used to get up in the night to see to the children, and when he is home he contributes to their domestic life without having to be asked. Celia says she is happy taking responsibility for the house and the children because she enjoys it, does not work outside the home, and sees it as a job. She has even at times discouraged Robert from helping her. What seems important to her is that Robert does not hold traditional views of male-versus-female roles and does not expect her to be responsible for all domestic activities.

Celia's description of Robert is different from how Sonya, Sandra, Helen, and Tina talk about their partners. Celia feels practically and emotionally supported by her husband in a way that the other women do not. Robert takes a more active role in the household than does Johnie, Simon, or Bob. As Celia says, "If he's around he will look after the children just as much as me. He's not 'Oh, I'm just the breadwinner' and off he goes and comes back and waits for his tea." He cooks, is a do-it-yourselfer when it comes to tasks around the house, and irons his shirts. Sonya, by contrast, said of Johnie: "He'll do his own shirt if I'm really tired and it's Sunday night and he hasn't got one for Monday morning . . . but it's not his job to make sure he's got his shirts ironed." Robert also wants to spend time on the weekends with his children. He responds when Celia asks him to do things, and, unlike Helen, Celia does not mind asking her husband for help.

Like the other women, however, Celia has had a troubled relationship with her husband. One difficult area was their sexual relationship. After Katie was born, Celia shied away from sex and could not bear any kind of physical contact with Robert. This was partly due to the physical and psychological effects of motherhood—the birth and its aftermath; the change in her body; exhaustion; breast-feeding; and her overwhelming sense of responsibility for her new baby. Loss of sexual desire is also a symptom and side effect of depression. It was two years before Celia and Robert resumed sexual relations.

For a long time Robert did not know why Celia was feeling low and had lost all sexual and physical interest in him. Although he could see that she was not her usual self, it was months before he knew she was depressed because Celia concealed her feelings from him. She felt guilty and ashamed for being unhappy:

> I didn't tell anybody 'cos I think I felt a failure and I didn't really want to talk about it really. I only started to tell people when I was getting better. I'd say, "Oh well, I've just felt like this the last few months," you know. So I think if somebody had known, I would have got support and I wouldn't have felt so poorly. I mean they were supporting me as friends, as family, supportive of me in who I am, but not supportive because they knew I had postnatal depression.

In a moving passage Celia explains why it was difficult to articulate her feelings to Robert, and she describes his reaction when he found out the extent of her depression:

> Natasha: One thing I'm wondering about is the role of your husband in all this and where he fits in?
> He's very supportive and we've always been good friends . . . After a while he did say that he noticed that I wasn't myself . . . But on the whole I don't think he ever realized my true feelings about it all because I was so good at creating this impression of coping and I didn't really express how I really felt . . . It was only when I was asked to give a talk . . . at a befriending scheme . . . it was the first time I sat down and wrote down sort of chronologically what had happened. It was a really hard thing to do and I got quite upset doing it, but in one way it was very therapeutic. It sort of got it out. And when I'd done it Robert said to me that he'd like to read it and it made him cry 'cos he said, you know, I never knew how you felt, and he said you know, why didn't you say this before . . . He said I just never knew that you felt like this and it really upset him.

Many of the women who had supportive partners said they simply did not tell them about their feelings. They felt ashamed and did not want to reveal their emotions to the world. Articulating their feelings to others would mean admitting them to themselves, and many wanted to deny that the depression was happening to them. Some women said they did not want to burden their partners because they had stressful jobs, or they had financial problems, or they were coping with relatives who had serious illnesses. Others said they felt that, as men, their partners could not possibly understand the emotions women experience when they have a child and become depressed. Women like Celia said that because they had very little knowledge of postpartum depression, in the early stages of their depression it was difficult to identify their feelings *as* depression. They themselves struggled to make sense of their emotions. Celia gives a clear account of why she found it difficult to put what she was experiencing into words:

> Natasha: Why do you think you didn't talk to him about it? I mean, do you usually talk about things quite a lot?
>
> Oh yes, we do. Well I think initially because you didn't realize what was wrong . . . And I suppose because the sort of day-to-day caring of the baby sort of took over, you just sort of get on with things . . . Because I mean with my sort of depression it sort of built up so there was no moment when you sort of felt "Oh, I've got depression, I better talk about it," you know. Part of it is realizing . . . you don't realize what's happening . . . I think part of it with me is . . . it was like saying I couldn't cope . . . I mean I could cope physically but I couldn't cope mentally. And I'm a quite sort of proud person, I think . . . I tend to be the sort of person that goes and helps other people but I'm not very good at accepting help. As I said, people had put me on a bit of a pedestal thinking I was coping really well. It's very hard to suddenly start saying to people, "Well, I don't feel right" and then . . . I didn't really know anything about it, you know, it's my first child, you know, they hadn't mentioned it really at the clinic, or the hospital . . . at the NCT antenatal class . . . it was extremely hard to talk about it . . . you know. It's like you're uncovering some terrible secret and it's like sort of saying to yourself there is something wrong with me. I think part of it is you don't want to admit it to yourself. You want to sort of pretend and just hope it goes away.

Celia's experiences are not unique. Many of the women with supportive, caring, and understanding partners found it difficult to confide in them.

The women in this study describe a complex and sophisticated world of relationships. Their stories tell us that women who experience postpartum depression do not necessarily have unsupportive, unhelpful, or uncaring partners. While half the women I interviewed complained that their partners lacked interest and involvement in the home and failed to provide emotional support, the other half described their relationships as positive and supportive. The latter came to feel emotionally isolated from their partners mainly because they actively withdrew from them and did not share their feelings with them. They found it difficult to express what they were experiencing, felt ashamed, and believed their partners would not be able to help them. Their relationships changed and became less close because of their silence and withdrawal.

Current research on postpartum depression tends to focus exclusively on the male partner and his deficiencies. Because relationships are between two people with different perspectives and expectations, however, we need to look at both parties. The stories in this chapter point not only to the effects of lack of support, but also to the psychological benefits of participating in relationships.[10] The women spoke about withdrawing themselves and losing their sense of self because they felt they could not participate fully in their relationships. For some, voicing their needs and feelings led to conflict. Others feared burdening their partners. Many believed that their needs and feelings were not legitimate—their partners, and the broader culture, made them feel that their needs were less worthy than those of others. The difficulties they experienced in voicing their feelings, even in the presence of supportive loved ones, tell us that though the importance of strong, mutual relationships cannot be underestimated, the creation of an accepting, understanding, and non-judgmental broader cultural context in which women can speak their feelings of ambivalence and depression without shame or stigma is equally critical.

Why have the complex dynamics of women's relationships with their partners failed to be discussed within existing research in the area? I would suggest that this is due to theoretical and methodological limitations of this work. Much current research makes a number of theoretical assumptions that find their way into study designs. Take, for example, the study conducted by the psychologist Lois Wandersman and her colleagues on social support in the transition to parenthood.[11] These researchers explored the importance of different types of support to the adjustment of first-time parents in the postpartum period, including, among others, practical support. In order to measure the frequency of practical support that husbands offered their wives three months after the birth, measurements were made of the degree to which husbands participated in laundry, housecleaning, cooking, and shopping. The frequency of practical support offered by wives was measured as the degree to which they participated in finances and repairs.

Inherent within this study are traditional assumptions concerning gender roles and divisions of household work. If an individual or couple has gender-stereotyped roles, the work they do within their gender-specified category—for example, the woman's doing the laundry and the man's doing the finances—is not counted as support. According to these methods of assessment, then, the couples that appear most supportive of each other are those in which traditional gender roles are reversed; and the couples that appear least supportive of each other are those in which tasks are divided along traditional gender lines. The researchers also assume that participating in the spouse's tasks necessarily counts as support, while non-participation counts as a lack of support—for example, the man's doing the cooking is defined as support, while his failure to do so qualifies him as unsupportive. Using such methods, the majority of male partners are likely to be shown to offer poor support, because women today still continue to assume the major responsibility for housework and childcare, even in dual-earner households.[12]

To what extent, then, does such a study reflect how couples actually feel about the support they offer to each other? If a man takes care of all household finances and repairs and the woman shops, cooks, and cleans, who is to say that they do not feel supported by each other? Does a woman necessarily feel unsupported if her husband does not do the laundry? The laundry might be a household task she enjoys. And will she necessarily feel supported if her husband does the cooking? Again, she might find this a particularly agreeable and relaxing activity. Finally, if a partner does not participate in certain tasks, is this necessarily because he is unsupportive and unwilling to do so? As we have seen in this chapter, there are multiple reasons for partners' limited involvement in the home.

The fundamental problem with this kind of research method is that assumptions are being made about what men and women want, do, and feel—assumptions that are compounded by the fact that the men and women concerned are not given the opportunity to express their own views. Questions such as how the tasks are divided between individual partners, how partners define "participation" and "support," and how they feel about each other's contributions are not addressed. Failure to elicit women's (and men's) views regarding these issues has meant that the ways in which depressed mothers influence the support they receive or do not receive have been overlooked.

In order to understand better the dynamics of women's relationships and how they relate to their feelings of depression, we need to pay close attention to what women (and men) have to say about their lives. The active part mothers play in their relationships can only become apparent if women are given a voice within the research and an opportunity to express their own perceptions and feelings. Research would clearly equally benefit if men's experiences and accounts were solicited, especially in light of evidence suggesting how distressing it is for partners to watch women suffer through postpartum depression.[13]

mother to mother

One of the more unexpected findings to come out of my research was the importance of relationships with other mothers to the women's psychological and emotional well-being. When the women described the early stages of their depression they often spoke about feeling different and isolated from other mothers. Conversely, they linked their journeys out of depression to their identification with, and ability and willingness to talk to, other mothers.

This aspect of the women's stories surprised me because I had come across few studies exploring the importance of relationships between mothers in understanding postpartum depression. As noted, there has been a tendency for research on PPD to emphasize male partners to the exclusion of other relationships. Carolyn Cutrona's study is a notable exception.[1] She found that the strongest predictor of postpartum depression was the availability of companionship and feelings of belonging to a group of similar others, rather than the quality of intimacy with the husband.[2] In general, however, there is a pervasive assumption among researchers that relationships with male partners are more conducive to women's happiness and well-being than are other relationships. Friends tend to be seen as secondary to spousal support and, in some cases, only as back-up support should a partner be unavailable.[3]

With the important exception of Verta Taylor's work on postpartum depression support groups, few feminist social scientists have explored relationships between mothers.[4] This is partly because they tend to view motherhood as isolating, confining, and restricting women's contacts and activities outside the home.[5] As Linda Bell and Jane Ribbens point out, "mothers are frequently viewed as 'house-wives,' often portrayed as isolated within their own four walls, with paid employment as the only possible escape."[6] The tendency among many feminists to view mothers' lives in terms of a home/work split neglects women's involvement in maternal, community, and other networks and friendships that transcend these boundaries.[7]

The women in my research, however, spoke at length about the importance of relationships with other mothers with young children, and particularly with other mothers who had also felt depressed. Unlike male partners, they said, other mothers could understand their feelings because they shared the experiences of motherhood and depression.[8] Penny said that though her husband could not have been more supportive, she still felt that "another mother . . . whose children are the same age, going through the same feelings as you, gives you someone to talk to." Rachel valued the friendship of other mothers because she wanted "to be with people that you trust . . . People that'll let you say whatever you're feeling . . . other women that are feeling similar things." Women described other mothers as crucial to their journeys out of depression. For many, talking openly to another mother and having their feelings validated was the first step in the recovery process.

Yet women also said that other mothers could exacerbate their feelings of depression in cases in which they compared themselves to them and felt lacking and inadequate. This left the women with a sense of psychological isolation and difference. Many spoke about disclosing their difficulties only to find they were not echoed by other mothers. This led them to withdraw. They projected the image of the perfect, happy, all-loving, all-giving, self-sacrificing mother onto other mothers, and believed they were alone in their feelings of unhappiness and inadequacy.

Paradoxically, then, interactions with other mothers had the capacity to both precipitate women into, and retrieve them from, deep feelings of despair. Rachel articulates this paradox when she comments that, while "the best sort of support would be with other mothers with children . . . on the other hand, it's really awful being with other women that look as if they're coping. That's just as bad as being with nobody." Rozsika Parker comments on the ways in which other mothers can be both a source of negative comparison and a source of reassurance. Mothers look to each other for confirmation that they are getting it right in the face of fears that they are getting it wrong. Yet as Parker notes, for many women other mothers do not give comfort or reassurance in part because the mirrors provided by them are distorted by personal projections or elided with cultural expectations.[9]

First-time mothers in particular described feeling physically isolated from other mothers. Most of the women who became depressed after a subsequent child were already involved in networks of other mothers. After having children, the first-time mothers found that their existing friendships could not meet their new needs. Whether or not they were in paid work, mothers sought the company of other mothers with young children. They were looking for relationships with women who shared the joys and constraints of motherhood. As Penny said: "Before, it was all the fashion-conscious . . . have-a-good-time-friends where now it's the mumsy-we-love-our-children-we-want-the-best-for-our-children friends."

These women spoke about obstacles to meeting other mothers, such as the lack of a community center or a central area where they might meet other mothers out for a walk with their babies. This problem was described by urban and rural mothers alike. Although all but two of the women had use of a car, all wanted access to local places they could get to on foot.

Helen, who lives in the center of town, found it difficult to meet other mothers after Ben was born. She had Ben when she was thirty-three and until then had always worked full-time. Most of her friends at work did not have children, and she felt they lost interest in her once she had a child. Several of her long-standing friends did have children, but they lived in different parts of the country. Although she had lived in her current house for some years, she hardly knew her neighbors and local community because she was away during the day. Helen particularly missed having a local meeting place where she could gather with other mothers who lived in her neighborhood.

Helen's difficulty making the transition from paid employment to motherhood was shared by other first-time mothers who, like her, had been away at work during the day and so had limited opportunities to form relationships with people living in their neighborhood. During their maternity leave, and in subsequent months for the women who did not go back to work or returned to work part-time, they found themselves spending time at home and in their local community during the day. Many felt lonely and isolated, and their depression made it even more difficult for them to contact other people.

The mothers who returned to work following the birth also found that their day-time employment restricted their opportunities to take part in activities with other mothers, which took place mainly during working hours. Some women felt alienated from colleagues who disapproved of working mothers, and this loss of social ties in their local community as well as at work led them to feel doubly isolated. Other women like Helen found their work colleagues very supportive of their return to paid employment and the challenges of combining motherhood with paid work. Helen felt that it was mothers who had not returned to paid work who were most disapproving of her:

> When you go back to work . . . your whole social network is again completely different. You then stop any real social contact and you in fact lose very quickly, lose the contacts that you've made. The people that I met through the NCT I was very friendly with, and really enjoyed their company, but I was made to feel really much of a second-class citizen when I went back to work, you know, and they were very critical, a lot of them were very critical of me going back to work.

Despite describing the obstacles to meeting other mothers, the women did come in contact with other mothers during the first few weeks and months following the birth. Some had a neighbor, friend, sister, or other female relative who also had young children. Many first-time mothers met other women through hospital-based or local prenatal classes, and continued to see these women after the birth. Several mothers also attended postnatal or mother-and-baby groups. One mother said she felt "bogged down with invitations" to coffee.

In these initial contacts, women spoke about "checking out" their feelings with other mothers and inquiring about their experiences of the birth, feeding the baby, feelings about the child, the child's behavior, and so on. Many felt their own experiences were not reflected in those of other mothers, and this left them feeling different, alone, and isolated.

Vera was depressed for eight months after Felix's birth, which had been difficult. She felt emotionally numb when he was born, and she struggled with breast-feeding. She gave him a pacifier and felt a sense of failure as a result. She was disappointed in herself as a mother. She and her husband, Matt, lived in a small one-bedroom flat, which made it impossible to get away from Felix when he was crying. They had financial problems. Their flat was on the third floor, and Vera felt she was constantly struggling to climb the stairs with the baby, the carriage, and the shopping. The days felt long and lonely because Matt worked long hours. When working dayshifts at the factory, he left the house at six in the morning and returned at seven in the evening.

Vera attended various events for new mothers but felt different from the other women she met:

> I remember going there . . . and I sort of thought, you know, you shouldn't be here. I just felt everyone else seemed so happy and so really pleased with their labors, and I remember saying to one girl, "How did you find it?" and [she said], "I found it really much easier than I thought," and I burst into tears on the spot, so I didn't go there again. I just felt really different and I felt that people could see I wasn't, although I *was* coping, that I wasn't coping really and I wasn't enjoying it at all.

Many of the women recounted similar experiences of going to a mother-and-baby gathering, feeling different and ashamed, and sometimes fleeing, never to return. Many spoke about feeling like an "alien" and a "freak" because other mothers seemed to be happy and coping while they were not.

Louise, whose story was first told in Chapter 4, had a cousin who had a fourth baby a week after Seamus was born. While Louise struggled with breast-feeding, with Seamus's crying, and with his sleeplessness, her cousin seemed to have an easy baby and no difficulties. Louise could not help comparing herself with her cousin, and this became a great source of pressure:

> This baby of hers, you know it was one of these that sleeps all day. And so there were stories coming back through the family you know "Oh, Pat's got this baby" and "Oh, she doesn't know she's got him. He just sleeps all the time." And I used to sort of say, "Well, I know I've got mine," you know, "he doesn't sleep any of the time" . . . So I felt under pressure from that time from that point of view, you know, that someone quite close had got this easy baby.

Louise constantly compared herself with other mothers, and younger mothers in particular. She was thirty-two when she had Seamus and felt that, as an "older mother," she should be able to cope better than younger mothers. She describes attending a postnatal support meeting on a day when everything seemed to go wrong. Her feelings of shame were so intense that she fled the meeting in tears:

> I had a horrible experience. I went to a postnatal support group. He must have been about twelve weeks old or so. Oh it was dreadful. He just screamed from the moment we walked in, dreadful, and they were doing all about weaning . . . and because he was crying so much I couldn't take part in it properly and I was totally frustrated. And these other babies were just like in their baby chairs looking around, or so it seemed. It probably wasn't quite as cut and dried as that. And eventually I just scooped him up, put him in his car seat, and just more or less ran out in tears. Plus he'd dirtied his nappy and it was all running out. You could see it seeping through his [sleeper]. It was just a *nightmare* experience.

Louise realized she was projecting an illusion of the happy, coping mother and the quiet, content baby onto other mothers and their babies. Yet she could not help feeling that they were coping better and that they were happier than she was, even though some of the mothers from the group later telephoned to support and reassure her:

> When I got home a couple of the people rang me up and said, "Oh, you know, I know how you feel. It's awful some days, isn't it?" you know. But when we were all sitting there at the postnatal group, everybody's you know grinning and beaming and "Aren't the babies lovely" sort of thing . . . Plus I was nearly thirty-two when I had Seamus and a lot of people at the group were a lot younger than me and I felt added pressure from that. I felt because I was older and supposedly more mature I ought to be able to cope with it a lot better than other people. But the younger ones just seemed, nothing seemed to bother them . . . And I felt they must be laughing up their sleeves at me you know thinking, "Oh, she's older, look what a mess she's making of it all." I'm sure that wasn't the case at all 'cos I've spoken to some of them later on. They've said, you know, how sympathetic they felt.

Although mothers are potentially a valuable source of support for each other, they can also be a distressing source of comparison. Many of the women stressed how important it was to be seen by other mothers to be coping, to avoid being shown up in public by their children.

Louise and other mothers felt that people would laugh at them if they appeared to be struggling. Louise describes another traumatic afternoon she spent with an acquaintance she met through a postnatal support group. She was struggling to breast-feed Seamus while visiting this woman and felt deeply ashamed that she was seen to be struggling and getting upset:

> When he was ten weeks old I had an almighty scene. I'd had a *really* dreadful day with him, *absolutely* terrible. He'd started the crying you know almost as soon as he woke up and I struggled through the day . . . A contact in the NCT locally had rung me up and said why don't you pop round one afternoon for a cup of tea, and so I said I would. And she was a mother of two and she was a really nice person, but the thing was I had to feed Seamus while I was there . . . And I had an awful scene trying to feed him *in front* of this woman and it really upset me and I was sort of almost in tears myself.

Louise realized she was not alone in struggling with motherhood and that all mothers have good and bad days, but during her depression she felt her experiences were unique and shameful. Like Louise, Vera could not help comparing herself with other mothers:

> I was always comparing myself to somebody else and how bad, you know, how I was not coping, you know. Like there was this girl who had like a five-year-old and three-year-old and she just had twins and you know she was tired obviously but she was coping. I thought, *why am I not coping?* Sixteen-year-olds have babies and why am I not coping.

By comparing themselves to other mothers, and projecting images of happiness and perfection onto them, the women reinforced their own culturally derived ideals of motherhood. Their perceptions of other mothers gave rise to, confirmed, and fueled their perceptions of themselves as bad mothers who were failing at motherhood. This led them to withdraw from other mothers and become increasingly attuned to the moral voices of the surrounding culture. For many, this loss of open dialogue and disclosure with other mothers seems to have been linked to the onset or exacerbation of their feelings of depression.

Fear of criticism, rejection, and condemnation led most women to conceal their feelings and withdraw from other mothers (and people more generally). Many spoke about putting on an act, pretending to be the happy mother. Although Sonya wanted to confide in her best friend, Clare, her fear of rejection prevented her from doing so:

> I'd love to sit [Clare] down here and tell her the whole lot, and then, if you like, in my book, I'd expect her to walk out and say, "You're a terrible person, I never want to see you again." But she won't do that, but that's what my brain is telling me people will do, that they'll say, "My God, we thought you were okay, but you know you're telling us all this now." But people are not like that, are they, they don't say, "You are dysfunctional therefore we don't want to know you," but that's how I feel inside . . . If you like, if I open up and show them that core in the middle, are they going to stab it and say, "Ugh" . . . They're not going to say, "Well fine, you're still you, this is part of you, this is an experience you're going through"—yes, it's the fear of rejection when they know the full story.

Sonya also fears what will happen if she tells other mothers at the National Childbirth Trust postnatal group about her feelings:

> If . . . I'd given myself to them and said, "Look folks, you knew me as I was but I really feel bad now," you know, would they have all rallied round and hugged me and said, "No, it's fine," you know, etcetera, or would they have felt a bit embarrassed and thought, "Oh God," you know, "What do we say now," you know. I think I didn't want to try that out in case it went the wrong way, you know, but it's me not being very confident in human nature though.

Sonya feels constrained talking about her feelings because she expects other people to respond negatively. This is not surprising given that, as we saw in Chapter 6, her husband, Johnie, silences her when she tries to share her feelings with him. Sonya also realizes, however, that to some extent she is projecting negative words and thoughts onto other people:

> I grind myself down before I go to things . . . I'm putting words in people's mouths, and putting thoughts in their heads that are not there. But I'm doing it to myself, but I don't know why I do this . . . If I walked in and just felt that there were good feelings coming towards me, then I'd be fine. But I just walk in and think, "God, they think I'm a terrible person" . . . This mind thing, it's sort of, how do you find a solution to changing your mind's attitude? It's like, if I say to you, "I'm not going to see so and so this afternoon, 'cos I don't think they'll be glad to see me," that reality is only mine, but you can't convince me that it is.

Sonya has changed her public persona in order to conform to what she believes others want and expect of her. She wears a mask and disguises her feelings. She talks about "being able to convince friends that I was all right." "To 97 percent of the world I was a very strong, confident person"; "I can act, if you like, I can appear okay to the outside world even though, you know, I feel terrible inside." This act also consumes her energy and leaves her feeling exhausted:

> If I had been out with a group of friends and I'd been able to convince them that I was all right, you know, it took such a toll on me I'd come home and collapse because I was acting out a role *so much*.

This outward presentation of herself is driven by her fear that if other people find out that she is depressed, they will judge, criticize, and ultimately reject her. Although she wants to be able to tell people, "this is how I am, take me or leave me," she fears that if she does "none of these people will want to know me when I'm really well because they've seen me so bad." She fears that by being herself she will lose the friendship and respect of others. Paradoxically, then, Sonya disguises her thoughts and feelings to gain approval and maintain a semblance of normality with other people. This leaves her feeling alone and disconnected from her world, from other people, and from herself. As she says, "I feel imprisoned in my own prison."

While some mothers, like Sonya, went to great lengths to continue attending mother-and-baby groups despite their feelings of despair, other women, like Vera, simply withdrew from other mothers altogether and from any further opportunities at meeting these women. By cutting off ties with other mothers and no longer discussing their thoughts and feelings, they left few opportunities in which these very thoughts and feelings might be contradicted by other mothers. As they retreated into silence, their knowledge of the experiences of other mothers came to be based on their observations and perceptions of these women. It is interesting to note that, as they described their move into silence, they used visual metaphors when they talked about other mothers. They spoke about "seeing," "looking," and "impressions," as they came under the illusion that all other mothers were coping and happy. As they withdrew, the gap between their own experiences and those of other mothers seemed to them to become wider and wider. The women's illusions and isolation were maintained by the fact that they were watching, looking, and seeing other mothers but not talking to them. Although in retrospect they knew that sharing their experiences with other mothers would probably have broken their isolation, during the depths of their depression they felt unable or unwilling to do so.

Talking to another mother was, for many, the key to moving out of depression. For more than two-thirds of the women, the most valuable kind of help they either wanted or received came in the form of talking to another mother about their feelings. These women turned to female relatives or friends to whom they had previously felt unwilling or unable to talk. Alternatively, they formed new relationships with other mothers whom they met through informal channels such as postpartum depression support groups, lay organizations, or mother-and-baby groups. Others found it helpful to talk to healthcare professionals who also happened to be mothers themselves.

Women wanted above all to talk to other mothers who had experienced similar difficulties with their babies or similar feelings of depression. For some, it was important that the women shared similar fears and anxieties in looking after their babies. For others, it was the difficulties of tending to two young children close in age that was critical. For others, it was finding another mother for whom loving her child did not come "naturally" or "instinctively." Most also wanted to talk to other mothers who had experienced postpartum depression. Talking to another mother was a turning point in the recovery process, even for those who felt supported by partners, relatives, friends, or healthcare professionals.

The turning point in Penny's depression came when she had an honest and open discussion with a friend whose child was similar in age to Adam. As we saw in Chapter 3, Penny's experience of motherhood was dominated by her fear that her son would die in her care, and this led her to return to her full-time job. Discovering that her friend shared similar fears over her child's welfare was a huge source of relief:

> I never told anybody any of this, and then I told my friend once, you know, we had a real heart-to-heart . . . and that's when I started feeling better . . . 'Cos I daren't even mention cot deaths to anyone, not even my husband. And I just mentioned it to her and she said she did that . . . I'll never forget her when she said every morning she stood at her son's door and she'd take a deep breath and she'd say, "Is he gonna be dead today?" and she went in. And I thought I was the only person who thought like that, and then I found out she did as well. So then I talked

to other mums and then I found out 95 percent of the mums all felt the same. So I wasn't an incapable mother . . . it wasn't just *me,* you know. Every other mother had the same thoughts as I did so I wasn't a useless mother . . . And it was talking to my friend that really . . . made me decide to give up work, you know, suddenly I wasn't frightened anymore because I'd bottled it all up. You need someone to talk to, I think.

For Penny, who was embarrassed and ashamed to tell her family how she felt, having "someone else to talk to who was going through the same emotions" gave her support and confidence in herself. Talking to her friend, giving up work, and becoming integrated into a network of other mothers marked the beginning of Penny's journey out of her year-long depression:

> Now I'm just one of the mumsy crowd and it's great because I've got someone to talk to . . . I really regret that year, you know, just being too frightened to look after my son basically, you know, and where other mothers all feel the same way but because you've got someone to go round and talk to about it, it felt better.

It is often argued, explicitly or implicitly, that returning to paid work is the solution to the isolation and depression experienced by mothers who stay at home to care for their children.[10] Penny's story, however, suggests that this issue may be more complicated, as mothers who do return to work can also experience depression, guilt, rejection from other mothers, and a sense of isolation. Women like Penny who are able to confide in other mothers may well find that these relationships are as critical to their sense of emotional well-being as paid work is for other women.

In retrospect Penny feels that if she had talked about her feelings much earlier perhaps she would have got over her depression sooner. She has learned that talking is the best cure when you are feeling down and depressed:

> I know if I was gonna get depressed, then I'd know what to do about it, you know, go and talk to someone . . . There are people there to help you if you need help, and none of these people have had their children [taken] away from them. So I know, you know, you don't have to be scared about telling somebody if you're not feeling how you're supposed to.

Like Penny, Louise found that one of the most valuable sources of support in helping her overcome her depression was another mother she happened to meet at the health center who had a child of a similar age:

> I said something like, "Oh, I nearly didn't come today because," I said, "Oh, I had a right to-do with this little one here." I was trying to make a joke of it but I was aware that she was looking at me quite closely. I said, "Oh, you know, I've had a little cry before I came here," you know, and she could tell I had. And she sort of took my hand—I didn't know her— and she just sort of said, "Oh, I *really do* know what it's like," she says, "my little girl's got colic all the time. I'm up all night with her. I know how you feel. It's really difficult, isn't it." And she wrote her number down on a piece of paper and she said, "If you're feeling down, please why don't you give me a ring, you know, I'll come round and we can have a cup of tea." And that was the beginning of a really good friendship . . . But that was really good that I met somebody like Judy . . . someone who was prepared to be honest about their feelings . . . If I find somebody who is receptive, you know, I don't mind telling them exactly how I feel about things. And we've always been like that, Judy and I. She's one person I can talk to and say exactly how I've been feeling and not think, "Oh, she must think I'm a dreadful mother." We appeal to each other because we're both very honest and we're very open and we just say how we feel and we don't judge each other at all . . . That's one friendship that is very very valuable because it was somebody else who was prepared to admit that they were having trouble.

Louise has known Judy for a year, and they continue to be close friends. Louise's description of her friendship with Judy illustrates the qualities in these relationships that the women find so valuable. In particular she highlights her ability to be honest about her feelings— honesty that, ultimately, broke down the silent isolation of her depression partly because it also broke down the idealized versions of motherhood that are implicit in women's silence. Many women, by their refusal to speak out about the hardships of motherhood, are complicit in projecting an idealized image of themselves and of motherhood, which can be very alienating to other women. Their silence is understandable given their fears of exposing themselves and their vulnerabilities, but it also contributes to creating a judgmental, antagonistic culture of competition, rivalry, and potential failure.

All but two of the women in my study either attended, or wanted to attend, a postpartum depression support group. They saw such groups as offering a safe, accepting environment in which they could disclose their feelings. As Celia says, "You need to speak to like-minded people or to people who know *exactly* what you're talking about because they've been through it . . . Unless anyone's gone through depression they've no idea what it's like." She continues:

> You really want people who understand and know that it's not something that you've created yourself or you're not a particular type of person who's prone to feeling sorry for themselves . . . I think definitely to know of a group or somewhere they can contact and have a talk, somebody to tell them, you know, "It's all right to feel like that," and you know, "a lot of people feel like that and you're not on your own."

Petra has been depressed for the twenty-one months since her son, Joshua, was born. A few months into her depression she realized she needed help but could not bring herself to admit her feelings. As we saw in Chapter 5, she has a difficult relationship with her mother but enjoys a close relationship with her husband, Marc. Marc has been supportive and caring, but Petra did not tell him about her feelings because she felt he would not understand:

> I could tell him. It's just that I think he'd never been depressed. He didn't understand depression, and I think a lot of men are probably like that because they don't even have to suffer with PMTs like we do.[11] But I mean he even said, he admitted that he's never understood people being depressed. He can't understand why they're depressed. So I knew it was hard for him. So I mean he probably wasn't as understanding as someone that has been depressed would be.

For the past four months, Petra has been attending a postpartum depression support group that Dawn, another mother I interviewed, set up in the village where they both live. The group meets once every two weeks, and it has been Petra's lifeline:

> I find it helpful because it's just that you can go there and tell people and they'll listen. Nobody listens to you, that's the trouble. Nobody wants to know. You can't really sort of sit and tell people what it's like or what's happened or how you're feeling 'cos you know they're not listening or they talk about themselves. And you could go there and you could talk and everyone would listen or someone else would talk and you'd think, "Well, that's how I felt," and you don't feel so sort of isolated. And it's nice to know that it's not you going mad. 'Cos you do tend to think that it's all your fault.

In voicing their difficult feelings, and in coming to realize that such feelings were shared by others, the women felt liberated from their isolation. Talking to her friend Judy as well as to mothers she met through Cry-sis, the voluntary organization that provides support for parents of crying babies, Louise gained the reassurance that she was not alone in her depression. She contacted Cry-sis seven weeks after Seamus was born and found this organization to be a great help. Although the women she got to know as a result had not necessarily experienced depression, they did understand how debilitating it can be to have a demanding child. Louise felt she needed "this sort of peer group of support and people to empathize with." She explained:

> Cry-sis was very helpful because the whole emphasis is on talking to somebody who's been through it themselves and is able to reassure you a little bit that you're probably not doing anything wrong, it's just the way the baby is. And really that helped me a great deal. And through getting involved with them I've realized that what I was going through is something that lots of people go through. But at the time I felt like a freak, like I was the only one in the world who couldn't cope with their baby and that, you know, the only one who felt so miserable about it all. And I've since met a lot of people and I realize what I was going through was really quite normal, certainly not abnormal.

In her classic text about the experience and institution of motherhood, *Of Woman Born,* Adrienne Rich writes about her own experience as a mother:

> Slowly I came to understand the paradox contained in "my" experience of motherhood; that, although different from many other women's experiences it was not unique; and that only in shedding the illusion of my uniqueness could I hope as a woman, to have any authentic life at all.[12]

"Shedding the illusion of their uniqueness" is precisely what enabled Louise and others to re-evaluate their moral worth as mothers. Once they realized their own experiences were not unique, they were able to feel good about themselves as mothers. They knew they were not the incapable, useless, terrible mothers they had thought they were. As Rozsika Parker has pointed out, mothers look to each other to find absolution for negative or ambivalent emotions about motherhood that the surrounding culture renders unacceptable and that mothers themselves experience as both painful and unforgivable.[13] Talking openly to other mothers led them to rethink their ideas about how mothers and children should behave. They questioned cultural representations of motherhood, re-evaluated their perceptions of other mothers, and modified their expectations of themselves and their children. Indeed, the developmental psychologist Cathy Urwin has highlighted how mothers' friendships with one another can lead women to resist normative images presented in the childcare literature.[14]

Sonya, who was only just emerging from her depression at the time I met her, was beginning to realize that her ability to look at mothers without preconceived notions of them as perfect would help her overcome her feelings of depression. "Instead of being hard on myself," she said, "I should think, 'Well, look at her. She looks fine but you know maybe she's got problems.' And I think this is part of the recovery process, being able to do that." The mothers who had recovered spoke about moving beyond their projected and idealized images of motherhood and being able to build more realistic expectations of themselves and their children, as well as more realistic ideas about how other mothers cope. As Louise explained: "It wasn't the sort of peaceful, charming, little experience that you see pictured, and I've since realized, by talking to other people, that it's not really like that for anybody." Many also said they now understood that appearances—whether media images or their perceptions of, and projections onto, other mothers—can hide a very different reality. Vera realized this after her visiting nurse told her about an acquaintance of hers who was also experiencing depression:

> I remember the health visitor saying she'd been looking after a girl who also lived in [the town]. It was her third child and she'd had [postpartum depression] quite badly . . . And I'd look at her and I'd think, "God!" I could never believe it . . . 'cos she seemed so happy . . . she seemed such a sane person. But I've since learned that appearances are very deceptive.

The women also came to appreciate that all mothers, all children, and indeed all people are individuals whose experiences may be different from but not necessarily better or worse than anyone else's.

At this point it is important to ask whether talking to other mothers with similar feelings earlier on may have prevented some of the women from becoming depressed in the first place. Research studies and anecdotal accounts suggest that support groups that enable women to talk to one another, and that allow them to express negative or ambivalence feelings, can prevent postpartum depression.[15] This kind of evidence points to the role of prenatal classes in providing a forum in which mothers can talk to and learn from one another, as well as form friendships that might continue into the postnatal period. Prenatal classes can also inform women that sharing their feelings with other mothers can provide reassurance that they are not bad or exceptional because they have negative feelings. Extending prenatal classes into the postpartum period would also provide important continuity in the women's relationships with other mothers and with the healthcare professionals running the groups. Indeed, by discussing their feelings as they experience them in a non-judgmental setting, women may become more accepting of themselves and their unique experience of motherhood, thus preventing their feelings from becoming worse and turning into more severe forms of depression.

The relationships women developed with other mothers were transformative in that they had a profound effect on their thinking, feelings, and behavior. They recognized that one of the problems for new mothers is that women experiencing difficulties tend to hide their feelings from one another. Women felt determined to break this conspiracy of silence between mothers because they saw how it had isolated them and contributed to their depression. It was important for mothers to talk openly and honestly to one another, they said, about the joys and the difficulties of motherhood. Having experienced depression after her first child, Caroline now behaves differently with other mothers:

> People I've since spoken to who I was seeing at the time said they had no idea, and I think I didn't tell anyone that I had postnatal depression . . . I've never met anyone else who has admitted to having it. I always tell people now and particularly the first-time mums I've met because I'm sure that there must be an awful lot more people who suffer from it that either don't admit to it or are afraid to recognize it or can't recognize it, and no one was aware I had postnatal depression.

As a result of the difficulties they initially encountered in finding other sympathetic mothers with whom to talk, many of the women either wanted to or already had become involved in helping other mothers in a number of ways. Caroline set up a postnatal group in her village for first-time mothers. Dawn started a postpartum depression support group. Sonya and Sandra also hoped to organize such a group in their village. Sonya said her mission was to pass on information about the experience of postpartum depression, and this is why she wanted to take part in the study. She also wanted to become a counselor for women with postpartum depression. Vera was a telephone counselor for the Association for Postnatal Illness.[16] She had been counseling Sonya for the last six months and called her every week. Celia became the postpartum depression helpline counselor for her regional branch of the National Childbirth Trust. Other mothers, such as Frances and Penny, helped in more informal ways by visiting mothers they knew were having difficulties and reassuring them that their experiences were not unique. Louise joined Cry-sis and became a telephone counselor for women experiencing difficulties. She was also involved in giving talks to postnatal groups about the difficulties of dealing with a fussy baby. Louise is involved in these activities not only so that she can help other mothers, but also because volunteer work gives her a sense of worth in a work-dominated culture that de-values motherhood. Getting involved with Cry-sis "helped me a lot," she says, "'cos I'd got people ringing me up and they *valued* me, you know, people were saying, you know, we *need* you and we need you because you've got this experience of this crying baby. You're of great value. And I suppose I'd felt I wasn't of any value anymore."

journeys to recovery

Marcia's depression set in a few weeks after the birth of her second child and lasted six weeks. It was mild and short-lived thanks to her doctor, who detected her problem early on and encouraged her to talk about her feelings. Her discussion with the doctor was a turning point in her depression and helped her toward a speedy recovery. "I think if he hadn't recognized it and talked to me and seen it, then it could have got a lot, lot worse," Marcia says, "because I wouldn't have sort of asked for help, I don't think." She continues:

> The doctor didn't give me any antidepressants . . . He did say, "You've obviously got a problem and at this stage I don't want to give you drugs for it, I'd rather we tried to deal with it in a different way" . . . I think he was really wonderful. I mean he listened to me, that was what was so good. He gave me a box of tissues, sat there while I cried, and then you know, made me talk to him about it, which was really good.

Marcia also felt that her doctor's own personal experience of depression enabled him to understand and support her.

Sophie's depression after the birth of her second child was more severe than Marcia's, but it was equally short lived, also lasting six weeks. Like Marcia, Sophie had a supportive doctor and visiting nurse. Unlike Marcia, she did not have the strength to see her doctor on her own. A friend had to make the appointment and physically take her to the health center. Her doctor immediately diagnosed postpartum depression and prescribed some antidepressants. While these gave her some relief, it was really "knowing that my doctor and health visitor were there if I needed them" and their willingness to listen to her that helped Sophie the most.

Marcia and Sophie's stories were unusual in that their depression was so short-lived. The other women faced long and tortuous journeys toward recovery. For many, the process of seeking help, getting their feelings acknowledged and recognized, and securing the kind of support they wanted and needed took several months, and in some cases years. For these women the depression lasted longer than it might have had they found the right kind of support early on. Research indicates that if identified and treated at an early stage, the recovery rate for postpartum depression is over 90 percent.[1] If not, it has been shown to last up to four years.[2] Three of the women I interviewed were depressed for two to three and a half years. In six cases, the depression lasted between one and two years. Seven women were depressed for between eight months and a year. Although all the mothers said they were feeling better than they had in previous months, only eight said they had fully recovered. Six said they were still quite depressed, and four said they felt they had nearly recovered but still had days when they felt low, anxious, and prone to panic attacks.

In many cases the women's depression lasted as long as it did because they found it difficult to ask for help, and because their depression was not detected. As shown in previous chapters, feelings of guilt and shame, a sense of failure, fear of rejection, and a desire to protect their moral identities made it difficult for them to reach out to partners, relatives, or friends. They were reluctant to confide in healthcare professionals for similar reasons. Many feared that should a healthcare professional find out how they were feeling, they would be seen as unfit mothers and their children would be taken away and put into state care. Several feared they would be hospitalized in a psychiatric institution. Many women also felt that their problems were not legitimate and so they did not have the right to call upon healthcare professionals. Vera, for example, said she had "the feeling in my mind that 'you shouldn't be in there talking about this while there's other sick people.' You're not ill, you're just being useless and neurotic." Many had difficulty identifying their feelings as depression, and they admitted that they tried to deny the depression to themselves. For these reasons, recognition of their depression by a healthcare practitioner was critical because it broke the internal and external silence into which they were locked.

Penny was depressed for sixteen months. She feared that she would lose her son should a healthcare professional find out about her depression, and so she did not seek help. Penny was one of the few women, along with Fiona and Monica, who had minimal contact with healthcare providers and got through their depression largely on their own:

> You hear these things about, you know, "mothers who can't cope have their children taken away from them," so you don't go out and say to health visitors, you know, "I can't cope with my child" in case they come take him away and say, "Right, we'll take him away and when you can cope we'll bring him back" . . . Because you often read in magazines, "Social services took my child away from me because," you know, "I was ill," and things like that, and "I couldn't get him back." But they're very, very rare cases, you don't hear of all the normal cases. Magazines and papers just like the things that are going to make a big sensation, don't they? You're not logical when you're tired and depressed, though, you know, you only look at the black side of things . . . So I think I was frightened of letting anyone know anyway that I was depressed in case they come and took Adam away from me and say, you know, "You're not capable of looking after him in your state of mind," which depresses you even more, you know. I don't think they do that, I think they just give you more help and support but, you know, you think the worst. So I didn't go to see anybody about it.

Suspecting she was depressed, Penny's visiting nurse came to see her every week and spent time talking to her. Penny also had the support of her female doctor, who had recently had a baby, which made Penny feel that she had some understanding of her life and difficulties. As shown in the previous chapter, however, it was having a heart-to-heart talk with her friend that finally helped Penny overcome her feelings of depression.

Recognition of her feelings by a healthcare professional was critical for Caroline because, like Penny, she found it difficult to ask for help. She was depressed for a year after her first son, Oliver, was born. Three months into her depression, her doctor diagnosed her with postpartum depression and prescribed antidepressants, which she took for six months. Caroline explains: "Once someone had taken notice and said, you know, 'You're not very well, are you? Let me help you,' then things started to get better and I was able to cope much more." Having her feelings identified was crucial because she felt she did not have the emotional or psychological strength to ask for help herself:

> It was good that someone recognized it 'cos I didn't know, I couldn't have said or wouldn't have wanted to have said I was depressed, you know. The midwife calls on you for ten days after the baby's born, until the baby's ten days old, and then they disappear and unless you then say "help" you don't get any help.
>
> Natasha: But it's hard to say "help"?
>
> Yes, because you don't know really whether you're just being pathetic. You really don't know whether this is how it is and so therefore you have to accept it or whether there is something wrong.

Celia also spoke about the difficulties she had identifying her feelings, realizing she was depressed, and getting a healthcare professional to acknowledge what she was going through. For six months, she did not recognize that she had postpartum depression, partly, she says, because she was given too little information about PPD at the prenatal classes, and because the midwife and visiting nurse who came to see her did not mention it. "It's not something that's talked about," she says. Nobody said to her, "If you feel like this please contact us." "You're not given anything, so when it does happen," she continues, "you're not really together. The last thing you're thinking of is being logical, 'Oh, I better get a doctor.'" This silence about postpartum depression made it difficult for Celia to bring up the subject herself. Talking to the visiting nurse was also difficult because she felt that the nurse was more concerned about the baby than about her. She believed that, as the mother, she was seen only as "an appendage to the child":

> Once you've had the baby, health visitors are so concerned with the baby . . . you take very much a back stage. And I remember walking into the health center to have Katie weighed . . . and the health visitor said, "Oh hello, Mrs. Patterson, how are you? Oh, Mrs. so-and-so, how . . . ?" and she immediately turned round to somebody else. So when you feel quite vulnerable, I mean, you're not going to go up and say, "Oh, can I have a word." I mean, you feel ready to say something and the opportunity is gone and then you think, well, they don't really

want to know anyway. They're not really asking how you are, it's just a habit.

Celia's account speaks to the feelings of vulnerability a new mother can experience, and how sensitive such a vulnerable person can be to the words and behavior of those around her.

Sandra tried talking to her visiting nurse but felt neither understood nor supported. This upset her because, as a district nurse, she works closely with visiting nurses and knows how important they can be for mothers who are experiencing difficulties. She believes that if visiting nurses provide the right kind of support early on they can prevent the new mother's depression from becoming more prolonged and severe:

> The health visitor where I work says if you go every week to a mum, if you possibly can, who's suffering, if you put a lot of input in right at the beginning you can almost, you know, you can give them a lot of support then that will stop it progressing, you know, quite so badly.

Sandra continues to feel frustrated that "there's not one focal point for support." "You have to go through a very long process to get support," she says, "and in the beginning, when you're really quite ill, nobody really takes it 100 percent on board." In the two and a half years she has been depressed, she has tried antidepressants, seen her doctor, a community psychiatric nurse, and a counselor, and has been counseled by a woman from the Association for Postnatal Illness.[3] Sandra feels that she's "been depressed for a long time unnecessarily" because she has been "unable to find the right kind of support," namely, a postpartum depression support group.

As both Sophie and Sandra explained, in many cases it was partners, relatives, or friends who eventually had to physically escort the women to the doctor or contact an organization concerned with mothers and their well-being. Those women who would have liked to have gone to a postpartum depression self-help group said they did not have the courage to go to the group on their own and would have needed emotional help getting there.

One of the difficulties partners, relatives, friends, and professionals face in trying to help is that the women are unable to talk about their feelings and ask for help until the worst of the depression is over and they have started to feel better. Dawn knew this from her own experience as well as from the time she spent running a postpartum depression support group:

It shows a lot about the illness that people just do not want to come and talk about it unless they're feeling perhaps a bit better. I mean, in the depths of depression, I didn't want to talk to a soul about it. I just didn't think there was any point, but when I got slightly better that's when I was ready to talk. So you can't necessarily help people that are really, *really* badly affected by it, but you can help them when they start to come out of it.

Tina echoes Dawn's words when she explains, "I couldn't talk to family and friends until I was at a certain point in recovery." "I didn't want to," she says, "you just want to get better, and then once it started getting better, you could then, like, explain how you were feeling." Indeed, the fact that these eighteen women agreed to talk to me about their experiences is itself an indication that they were feeling better and had emerged from at least the severest part of the depression.

In a few cases partners, relatives, and friends rather than other depressed mothers were instrumental to the women's recovery. Frances was one of these women. As noted, after the birth of her third child, Mathilda, Frances was depressed for three and a half years. For much of that time she felt unable to admit her feelings. When after two years she eventually spoke to her sister, she was surprised at her reaction: "she just sat with me and listened to me." This was the turning point in her depression. It made her realize that her sister "cared enough to care . . . for me to get better." A friend in whom Frances eventually confided contacted a voluntary organization for information and support. The love and concern people showed her, despite the fact that she was depressed, contributed to her healing.

During their depression, Frances and the other mothers felt abandoned and alone. They felt unloved and unlovable. Because they condemned and disliked themselves, they expected others to feel the same way. Many did not voice their feelings because they did not want to risk rejection and condemnation. When they eventually found the courage or were encouraged by others to speak their emotions, they often encountered more support and understanding than they had anticipated. The turning point in their depression came when, having disclosed their feelings, they were neither silenced, nor judged, nor criticized, nor condemned. The terrible repercussions they had anticipated did not happen; instead, they were accepted by the friend, the sister, the mother, or the husband in whom they had confided.

Sonya called this the ability to "trust human nature." Although she can see that this trust is a critical initial step in the journey out of depression, she still cannot find it within herself:

> My psychotherapist says, "What would it hurt if you were yourself, if you slumped in the corner and said, 'Look, I'm ill, this is how I am, take me or leave me.'" I can't do that. Would that be so terrible? And in my mind, yes. I'd think—well none of those people will want to know me when I'm well because they've seen me so bad, you see? . . . which makes the illness go on longer . . . I'm accepting points now from . . . the psychotherapist. She is saying, "If you pretend it didn't happen, or just hide from it or whatever, it's not going to go away, because if you don't walk into it and accept that this is an experience that I have to face . . . then it's gonna linger on" . . . And like now, when I said to her I was feeling so much better and I want to put this under the carpet a bit, I'm already trying to do that . . . As soon as I'm well for five minutes I'm thinking, "Right, it was bad but we don't want to talk about that now." But that's denying it, d'you see? But I find it painful to say, "I've been through it, it wasn't a nice experience, but it's made me stronger." I know all those things logically, but in my heart of hearts, in a way, I wanna say, "No, that wasn't me . . . this is me," which is not positive for recovery, is it?

Sonya hides her depression from other people partly as a way of denying it to herself. She realizes that revealing her feelings and having them accepted by others will in turn help her to accept herself for who she is, despite what she sees as her imperfections. Unlike Frances, she still cannot make that leap of faith; she still cannot find within herself the confidence and trust that other people will listen to her, hear her out, and still be there for her once she has revealed her feelings.

Most of the mothers sought professional help for their depression. Twelve of the eighteen women took antidepressants. They were on them for one month to three years, with an average of eleven months. Only Sonya was still on antidepressants at the time of the interviews. On the whole, the women felt unhappy about taking medication for several reasons. They feared addiction; they felt they should be strong enough to manage without antidepressants; some mothers were unhappy about taking medication while breast-feeding; and they felt debilitated by the side effects.[4] They were particularly concerned that these side effects might affect their ability to care for their children. Despite these reservations and some resistance, most of the women eventually agreed to take antidepressants. They felt desperate to help themselves in some way and thus saw medication as a positive step toward recovery.

The mothers said that the antidepressants helped them because they lifted the depression. As Petra said, "They pull you out of a hole that's too deep for you to get out of." However, what they really wanted was to talk about their feelings.[5] Medication, they said, covered up their underlying problems whereas talking got to the root of their difficulties.

Dawn, whom we met earlier, was depressed for three and a half years. She took antidepressants for nine months but longed to be able to talk about her feelings:

> To have someone to talk to without any limits, I think that would have done more good than tablets would, actually. I think it gets to the *root* of the problem, whereas tablets just sort of cover it up. I mean they must have done some good but I still think that talking about something is a lot better way of getting it all out in the open, than to sit and fester with it and just pile more pills on.

Dawn never actually articulated to her doctor that she wanted to talk to a professional. Looking back, however, she realizes that her constant trips to her doctor's office for minor ailments such as headaches, eye problems, and chest infections were an indirect way of asking for help. Her doctor, though, did not pick up on what Dawn was trying to communicate.

Dawn had been depressed for more than two years when she saw a family therapist for her son's behavioral problems. This therapist, whom she saw every week for three months, was her "savior":

> I think she knew how I must have felt. She had two children very close together, so she's got an idea what it's like to have two little ones on your hands. She never judged me. She never looked shocked at some of the things I said. And she was always there and she was always at the end of the phone.

The difficulties Dawn encountered in trying to find support for women in her situation inspired her to set up a postpartum depression support group, which she had been running for a year when I met her.

Antidepressants, Tina believed, were just a way of silencing women. Giving medication to a depressed mother is like giving sweets to silence a child's cries, she told me: "It's a bit like . . . if a child falls over, 'Oh, here, have a sweetie,' instead of being able to take them in

your arms and let them cry and let them scream and just hold them."
When Tina's third child, Emily, was four or five months old, Tina
went to see her doctor about her depression. She went, not because
she wanted medication, but because she wanted her doctor to put her
in touch with a counselor or therapist. Tina felt angry and disappointed with her doctor's response:

> He just said, "Be grateful that we have recognized it now and you
> haven't committed suicide, like, you know, so many people did years
> ago," which is a real shitty thing to say . . . He said, "I can give you some
> tablets . . . they'll probably take a couple of weeks to work, but if you
> take these you'll be fine." And I said, "Well, I think I really need some-
> body to talk to." He said, "You've got me, you can talk to me, can't
> you?" and then he started talking to my husband about politics and the
> cuts in the health service and everything and that was it.

Tina remained on antidepressants for two years, and this was another
source of distress. She felt abandoned with medication; there was no
follow-up planned other than the doctor's asking her to come back
and see him two weeks later. But "the *last* thing I wanted to do was go
back to the doctor," she admitted. Tina was critical of a system that
relies on women returning to their health center when they are struggling with a condition like depression that is paralyzing, debilitating,
and makes them want to shut themselves away from the world. Tina
eventually returned to her health center but saw a different doctor
whose response was much more supportive than the first doctor's:

> The lady doctor, she was *really* wonderful, you know, she sat and you
> know she *talked* to me and I kept thinking, "I've gotta go now, I've got,
> you know, other patients waiting," but she sat and she actually talked,
> you know. That's *really* what was needed, somebody to be able to listen
> to you.

Like many of the mothers, Tina kept returning to a central theme
within her story—her desire to talk about her feelings and about herself to somebody who would have the time and interest to listen to her
in an accepting and non-judgmental way:

> Natasha: Looking back, what would have helped you, what would you
> have wanted?
>   I would have wanted somebody to come in and to talk to me about
> me, I think, not about Emily or about anything else. Just come in, and
> say, "Right, look, how are you *really* feeling today?" . . . If I'd gone and

the doctor had said, "Ah, yes, there's a counselor I know," you know, "specifically to deal with postnatal depression" and I'd gone to talk to somebody, it didn't matter who it was, you know, as long as it was somebody with some sort of counselling skills, I would have talked myself through it and talked myself better.

Tina eventually found this kind of support. With money her mother left to her, she was able to afford private counseling, which helped her through her depression.

Like Dawn and Tina, many of the women felt unhappy that the doctor's main role seemed to be prescribing antidepressants. While they understood the time and resource constraints under which doctors operated and knew the doctors themselves could not necessarily spend the time talking and listening to them, they felt that their physicians had two important functions to fulfill. First, they believed it was the doctor's responsibility to recognize their depression, given the difficulty many mothers have admitting their feelings. Indeed, many of the women complained that it was sometimes months before a healthcare professional detected their depression.[6] These women felt that doctors should be better informed about postpartum depression in order to recognize and respond to the mothers' needs.[7] Second, the women believed that it was the doctor's duty to suggest other kinds of help that he or she was not in a position to offer, in particular, some form of counseling. Many, however, felt very little help was offered to them. Some women admitted that they may not have clearly articulated their need for help, and consequently their healthcare providers may not have realized they needed support. Others encountered unsympathetic and unhelpful doctors who opposed their requests for counseling. This happened to Petra when, thirteen months after her son's birth, she finally went to see her doctor, who suggested she take antidepressants even though she wanted to see a counselor:

> I didn't want to go on tablets. I said I didn't need tablets, I just needed someone to talk to, that's what I thought. And the doctor actually put up a fight about giving me the counselor. It was between me and the health visitor that got the counselor. The doctor didn't want it. She just wanted to shove me on the tablets.

Petra eventually saw a counselor who was not very helpful. She also saw a community psychiatric nurse and, with her husband, a sex therapist because their sexual relationship had come to an end with the birth of their son. Petra also discovered the self-help group run by Dawn, which she found particularly helpful. When I met her, Joshua was twenty-one months old. Although she felt "much better," she was still depressed, had many "bad days," and was feeling low at the time of our interview.

Louise also knew that antidepressants would not take away her feelings. Medication helped her, especially because it conveyed to her loved ones the severity of her condition and mobilized support from family and healthcare professionals. As discussed in the previous chapter, Louise wanted above all to talk about her feelings to a trained professional who had some knowledge of postpartum depression. Her visiting nurse was supportive, but Louise felt that because she had neither personal experience of motherhood nor professional knowledge of postpartum depression, she could not understand what Louise was going through. Louise had been depressed for five months by the time she saw a community psychiatric nurse, whom she found extremely helpful. The nurse supported her by listening and enabling her to accept Seamus for the child he was:

> The community psychiatric nurse was very, very helpful in a completely non-judgmental way in that she would just let me rattle and rattle and rattle and she was very, very sympathetic, you know, but in a supportive way . . . She was excellent. She was very, very understanding, very nice but at times she could be very firm with me, you know. And she would say, you know, I would say, "Well, I take Seamus to postnatal groups, you know, and he cries and the other babies don't and I feel embarrassed 'cos he's the worst baby." And she'd pull me up and she'd say, "Stop putting that child in a mold," you know, "He's Seamus. He's who he is and you mustn't go through life comparing him with other children," and I found that, you know, that was a great help.

Louise, who saw the nurse for six months, is grateful for the support she received but still feels angry that throughout the first five months of her depression her doctor did not suggest any type of counseling:

> I think what upset me was that I had to keep asking for the help. I feel my GP . . . should have referred me to the community nurse. I don't think I should have had to ask for it . . . I really did need somebody to talk to, and if the GP can't do it she's really got to try and help me find someone who can.

Petra's and Louise's experiences with their doctors were by no means unusual. Several mothers, however, did feel supported by their doctors.[8] Marcia, Sophie, and Caroline said their doctors recognized their feelings and took them seriously. These women were able to talk to their doctors openly and felt listened to and understood. Moreover, some women said that their doctors did suggest other forms of help, sometimes asking the visiting nurse to see the mother on a more regular basis, or offering the mother the option of seeing a community psychiatric nurse, a psychiatrist, or some other type of counselor.

Given the difficulties the mothers described in identifying their feelings and in seeking help, visiting nurses were ideally placed both to recognize the women's difficulties and to bring them help.[9] As Yvonne Keeley-Robinson points out, "The health visitor is well placed to detect what might otherwise remain a hidden problem." She continues, "It is important that if the health visitor suspects that a woman is depressed, she should bring the issue into the open" because "it is not easy for mothers to freely admit that they are not coping with something they believe everyone else manages without difficulty."[10] Visiting nurses were often described by the women I interviewed as potential or actual lifelines to the outside world. Women like Sophie, who felt supported by their visiting nurses, valued them because they identified their depression, visited them on a regular basis, and gave them permission to talk about their difficulties. In other cases, however, the mothers' feelings were not picked up. Celia, for example, would have liked her nurse to recognize her feelings and put her in touch with other women experiencing the same thing. She explains:

> I would have wanted some sort of acknowledgment or recognition of it, perhaps from the health visitor initially to have said, "You've got this. Don't worry," you know, to still sort of be a positive support, saying, "You're doing really well but we need someone to recognize it and to take the burden of trying to cope with it all [yourself]" . . . To be aware of a helpline for somebody to talk to, to be aware of other mothers who had gone through it or, you know, so that I could talk about it without feeling "Oh, I'm really pathetic and you know I'm not a very good mother."

In fact, Celia's visiting nurse not only failed to detect her depression but upheld her as the model of a happy mother. The nurse's lack of perception made it harder for Celia to admit to her feelings:

Everyone was sort of complimenting me right from the beginning—
"Oh, what a marvelous mother you are"—and I think they all put me on
a pedestal. And I mean even the health visitor had me go down the
health center to give a talk . . . about motherhood and what it's like. And
she was saying, "Look, she's a really successful breast-feeder and what a
healthy child," and so I found it hard to make people realize that "well, I
know it all looks like that but I don't feel like that." I didn't want to
shatter people's illusions, I suppose, so it made it harder for me to go
and say to them, "Well, actually . . . "

Although the role of the visiting nurse is to visit mothers fairly often
during the first weeks after the birth, and then on a less regular basis,
several of the women I spoke to said their nurses had not visited them
at all. They were angry about this, although some, like Tina, admitted
that their visiting nurse may not have realized that they needed help
because they did not ask for assistance or communicate their distress:

You see, when the health visitors come round: "Any problems?" "No,
everything's fine" . . . I mean it's classic, isn't it, you get somebody coming round to visit you . . . to make sure you're healthy and your baby's
fine and "Are there any problems?" "Oh, no no no." Again it's "I can't
. . . take up your time, I'm not that important" type of thing, isn't it? It's
the attitude of women and how we've been brought up not to make a
fuss.

Helen, whose relationships with her mother, partner, and other
mothers have been discussed in previous chapters, is a visiting nurse,
and so she knows from experience how important such professionals
are to women after they give birth. Helen's own experience has influenced her practice. Now when she visits mothers in her professional
capacity, she asks them a direct question—Are you feeling low or depressed?—because she recognizes how difficult it is for women to admit their feelings.

Helen felt she had no support from her nurse, who never visited her
at home. She saw her at the postnatal clinic she attended regularly
when Ben was a baby. Although she talked about her traumatic birth
experience, her difficulty breast-feeding, and Ben's sleeping problems,
the nurse never picked up on what she was saying or on how low she
was feeling.

When Helen first went to see her doctor, he too failed to recognize
that she might be depressed. Although she described her feelings to
him, she did not fit the stereotypical image of a depressed mother.
Helen's experience warns of the dangers of drawing up categories and

trying to fit women into them rather than listening to what they say about how they feel:

> In the sort of training that you get you are told that, you know, people who have postnatal depression are people who don't want to leave the house and can't get up in the morning and that sort of thing. And I think that's just one spectrum of it . . . I mean I actually *made* myself go out every day for a long walk with Ben. I just think there's just such an enormous spectrum of this feeling of just despair after you have a baby, depression, whatever you want to call it. There's just, you know, variations upon the theme. I think that's why it's so difficult to diagnose . . . I do think that there are extremes of postnatal depression and we all don't fit nicely into the categories that the books like us to fall into . . . When I went to see my GP he said, "Oh, you're not depressed because you're not waking up early and doing all these things that you have to with depression."

Helen's depression lasted for twelve months. For much of this time she was trying to get her doctor to take her feelings seriously. It was only after she had been seeing him for eleven months that he realized how depressed she was. This acknowledgment of her feelings eventually helped her overcome her depression:

> It's not until quite recently I went to my GP 'cos I was feeling really low in November and we talked about it then and he appreciated it then, I think. He realized how I felt about it, which was good, you know, at last after I'd been going to see him for eleven months [laughs] . . . He was not reading the signals directly . . . And having seen my GP and spoken to him about it and being encouraged to go back to him when I feel low has actually made a lot of difference, just someone else acknowledging how low you feel.

Several women suggested that new mothers be given access not only to a visiting nurse but also to a professional with specialized knowledge of postpartum depression. These professionals would work alongside the nurses and would deal specifically with the emotional aspects of motherhood. Their role would be to talk to mothers and advise them to "get all the support you can and if you do start feeling down *talk* about it, *don't* . . . brush it aside," as Frances put it. They would also provide women with the names of other mothers who had experienced similar difficulties and would help them contact national and local organizations or self-help groups. The women also felt it would be important for the specialist to visit them in their homes given the difficulties they experienced in reaching out for help.[11]

Nine of the mothers saw a mental health professional either privately or free of charge through the National Health Service. These professionals included community psychiatric nurses, psychiatrists, family therapists, sex therapists, couple therapists, and private counselors or psychotherapists. On the whole, the women valued their sessions with these therapists. They felt they had time to talk in depth and unreservedly about a range of feelings and experiences, including negative ones, in the knowledge that they would be heard, listened to, understood, and accepted by someone who was non-judgmental. The therapists validated their emotions, made them feel that what they were experiencing was legitimate, and reassured them that their feelings were shared by other mothers.

For Vera, the combination of antidepressants, a postpartum depression support group, and meetings with a psychiatrist finally helped her recover. Her depression was first diagnosed by her visiting nurse, who was supportive and came to see her daily. She was prescribed antidepressants by her doctor and also saw a community psychiatric nurse, who visited her in her home every week. When Felix was six weeks old, Vera started attending a postpartum depression support group set up by her community psychiatric nurse. She valued this group because, she says, it was the only time she could talk freely. When Felix was five months old she decided to come off the antidepressants. Two weeks later she had a significant panic attack and had to go back on them. At that point she asked to see a psychiatrist. She had her first session a month later and found the doctor very easy to talk to. "The psychiatrist, he's a specialist," she tells me. "I'd had it from the sort of horse's mouth, so to speak, that I wasn't going mad, that it wasn't unusual, and that reassured me." He prescribed different antidepressants and soon, Vera says, she "was near enough back to normal." This was eight months after Felix was born. "It was at Christmas I think I really fell in love with [my son]," she says.

Sonya, too, emphasizes how much she wants and needs to talk about her feelings. As shown, Sonya has struggled to confide in her mother, her husband, and other mothers. She has been depressed and on antidepressants for a year. She finds it hard to accept that she has to take pills: "I'm the type of person that says, well, you know, if you persevere and try, you can manage without them." "It's only human nature not to want to be on tablets," she says, "to think that to make my behavior normal in inverted commas, you know, to keep myself stabilized I've gotta take something artificial." The antidepressants dull her feelings. Although she is grateful that they keep her despair and hopelessness at bay, she feels that they are not helping her toward recovery. Sonya wants to talk about what she is experiencing, but for the past few months she has struggled to find a receptive environment in which she can open up and freely discuss her disturbing thoughts and feelings.

Sonya has tried to talk to her general practitioner but feels constrained because the appointments last only ten minutes. She realizes it is difficult for the doctor to give her more time:

> The doctor's job is to give you the medication, to keep an eye on you, to listen to you every two weeks and then decide whether you're ready to . . . decrease the medication. I'm not saying she's just a pill-pusher, but I appreciate it's not the medium to talk for a long time.

Sonya is also unhappy about the lack of support she receives from her visiting nurse. During the summer, when her depression was at its worst, she felt withdrawn and isolated. She wanted to see the nurse on a regular basis, and she needed her help to find other sources of support:

> In that isolation in the summer I wasn't reaching out and that's why the health visitor was the one who'd have to come in and say, "I'll reach out for you." Do you understand? "Either I'll come myself or someone will come round and talk to you." But because you're so numbed you can't take the initiative, therefore you can't reach out yourself.

The nurse, however, rarely visited her. Four months before I met her Sonya started seeing a psychotherapist privately. She goes once a week and feels this is one of the few places she can be herself and talk openly:

> I wanted somewhere I could sit down and say, "This is how I am," and for someone to say, "Okay," you know, they wouldn't judge it, they wouldn't criticize me for maybe not trying hard enough. They would just say, "Okay, you're in it but one day it will end" . . . At the end of the day I mean I went to the psychotherapist simply because I wasn't getting any help anywhere else. I go there every Tuesday morning without Suzie. I sit and have a cup of coffee. I talk for fifty minutes, I pay £25 for that privilege and come away and, you know, feel better every time.

Although the psychotherapy is helping her, Sonya would like to attend a postpartum depression support group. Sonya and Sandra live in the same village and meet regularly to talk about their feelings, which Sonya finds helpful. Sonya is also being counseled on the telephone by Vera, which she also finds to be a great source of support. But she feels she is at the point where she needs to hear about other women's experiences and share her feelings with a wider group of mothers:

> The ultimate reason for going is not that we're all sitting there in tears, but it's like any group where everybody's got something in common—you feel that there's no holds barred, you can say, "I did this. Isn't it terrible?" and somebody else will say, "But I did *that*," you know. And it reaffirms the fact that you're not isolated and you're not alone and that's the main point of why I want to go and at this point I feel strong enough to talk. I'm still a bit scared of breaking down, you know, this thing about well, it'll be weakness but at least you'll be in a warm sympathetic response.

Sonya's psychotherapist also believes that a support group is what she needs. For several months she has been looking for a group but cannot find one. The week before I met her, the visiting nurse from a neighboring village informed her about a group that was running. (In fact, this was the group set up by Dawn.) Sonya described the relief she felt when she found out about the group:

> She said there's a meeting of people over at Milton tonight for postnatal depression, and I said to her, "Well, I should be in that, you know, I should be there." She said, "Well okay, go to the next one" . . . and in three minutes she'd given me more help than the other health visitor had given me in six months . . . The moment the health visitor said the group *existed* then I felt a hundred times better, you know it lifted, it lifted off me because there was a solution and all these months I've thought well, you know, what I want isn't there, you know, like a self-help group.

Sonya was not alone in valuing support groups as a place where she could express herself freely. As the women in the next chapter demonstrate, mothers of different cultures often find such groups an integral part of their recovery from depression.

Two mothers, Celia and Rachel, saw practitioners of alternative medicine including a homeopath, an osteopath, an herbalist, and a natural healer. Seeing a homeopath finally helped Celia out of her two years of depression. She first went to see a doctor when Katie was six months old but received no help. She returned four months later and was prescribed antidepressants. She was reluctant to take medication partly because she was still breast-feeding, and partly because she feared becoming dependent on the pills. She also had a psychological resistance to taking antidepressants: "I really felt, well, I'm a strong enough person . . . and I *should* be able just to get over it." Nonetheless, two months after they were prescribed she began to take the pills and remained on them for ten months.

Celia's doctor also suggested that she see a psychiatrist. This suggestion frightened Celia because she thought it meant that she was "going crazy." Out of desperation to get better she agreed to go. An appointment was made for three months later, leaving Celia feeling "absolutely awful . . . because I really thought, you know, I desperately need help. These people don't realize that I need help *now* . . . and that really made me feel worse, the fact that nobody realized how bad I felt." When the time for the appointment arrived, the hospital cancelled and set up another appointment for three months later. This series of events compounded Celia's feelings of isolation and loneliness, as well as her sense that "*nobody seemed to understand,* nobody was prepared to help."

When Katie was twenty months old, Celia contacted a homeopath living in her village. The homeopath invited her to visit that evening, and Celia valued this immediate response: "If you have to wait any time . . . it's very hard to face then, or to cope with, but the fact that she said come this evening, it was very positive." A week after seeing the homeopath Celia felt dramatically better. Celia links her recovery to the homeopath's validation of her as a person and of her feelings of depression. She valued the fact that there was no time limit to her visit. She felt that the homeopath was interested in her and her life and not simply in her depression: "What was good," she said, "was that as homeopaths work they need to know *everything* about you . . . they're not just treating the symptom, they treat the person and this really agreed with me. I thought, well, she wants to know about *me*." The homeopath also reassured her that other mothers experience similar feelings. Moreover, Celia felt that, with three children herself, the homeopath had some insight into her life as a mother. She gave Celia a remedy for what she described as a "weeping depression"; the "amazing thing," Celia explained, "was that a week later I felt my old self";

although "the antidepressants had got me so far, I think I needed something just to get me over the edge." When Katie was twenty-two months old, Celia came off the antidepressants. She felt so well that she and her husband decided to have another child. Melissa was born nine months later with no recurrence of the depression.

The women I interviewed followed different routes out of their depression. Some received no medical help and turned to family and friends. Others took antidepressants, saw a range of healthcare professionals, and contacted voluntary organizations for support. Some were depressed for long periods of time. Others were able to mobilize help early and recovered from their depression relatively quickly. The ability to voice their feelings was key to the recovery of all these women. Claiming a voice and talking about their difficult and ambivalent feelings, feelings they had previously kept buried, helped them overcome their depression. In her study of depression in women, Dana Jack similarly found that "the metaphor for movement out of despair becomes dialogue. Dialogue . . . provides a way to come into new forms of relation with others, with the self, and with the world beyond the self."[12] The mothers also emphasized that it was talking within a receptive, responsive, and non-judgmental context, in which their voices were heard and their feelings recognized, acknowledged, accepted, and validated, that they found particularly valuable. Being able to admit their negative and ambivalent feelings about motherhood without fear of condemnation or criticism was very healing. Having their feelings legitimized by others led the women to question cultural representations of motherhood. Those who had attempted to confide in partners, mothers, and mothers-in-law during their depression realized there were other relationships in which they could express their feelings without being silenced or blamed. The mothers who had not risked revealing their feelings to anyone came to see that their fears had been to some degree unfounded and that others *were* there for them when they asked for help. By revealing that other people could accept them for who they were, these relationships enabled the mothers to accept themselves and their children and ultimately let go of the illusion and fantasy of the perfect mother and the perfect child.

For Louise, recovery was about accepting and loving her son, Seamus, for who he was rather than struggling to turn him into the child she thought he should be. She tells of a day when her feelings of frustration with Seamus's day-long crying and screaming gave way to feelings of acceptance of him as he eventually calmed down:

> I was just crying and I don't know why I was really upset but I was sort of saying, "Oh, I don't mind, Seamus, you know, you're just the way you are and it's all right, you can be like that if you want and I don't mind. I love you just whatever you're like." And I remember just crying my eyes out 'cos I realized I loved him so much and even though he'd upset me and I don't know from that day on I felt I accepted him. I just started to accept the way he was rather than fighting against it all the time saying, "You shouldn't be like this, you should be quiet, you shouldn't be crying." I just started for some reason accepting the way he was and saying, "Well, he was just Seamus. That's just the way he was and I was just gonna make the best of it." And I feel that by accepting it that did help me to sort of overcome the feelings that I got about him.

As they recovered the women no longer saw themselves only through the eyes of others. Because they were now able to accept and love themselves for who they were, their sense of identity and moral worth was no longer tied to what others thought of them. Penny says:

> I don't worry what people think anymore. Before I had Adam, for instance, my friends used to come round, my house used to be kind of immaculate . . . I was so house-proud. But now they take me as they find me. If they don't like the way I am, they're not friends, you know. So instead of worrying what my house should look like, and what I should look like, I just enjoy myself more.

In recovering from their depression the women thought about themselves for the first time and took into account their own feelings, needs, and limitations in approaching their lives as mothers. Celia's depression helped her let go of her ideals of the perfect mother. She realized that she needed to take care of herself, and that in meeting both her own and her children's needs, she benefited not only herself but ultimately her children as well:

> I look at some mothers and I think, "Aren't they good. They do this and that with their child . . . They're totally unselfish" . . . But I think I know my own shortcomings. I know how much I can give . . . When I try to do more things, something will be compromised, and if at the end of the day, it made me short-tempered because I was trying to be here, there, and everywhere, then I think that would be a compromise for the children . . . I think at the end of the day . . . it's accepting the sort of per-

son you are and your own capabilities and not trying to be something you're not.

Celia accepts that she is not perfect. She believes that being human and imperfect provides a better, more realistic model for her children of how to be in the world, and how to relate to others. The all-giving, all-loving, happy mother is a myth. Children need to recognize that mothers have good and bad days, positive and negative feelings. Like all people, they are emotionally affected by, and not emotionally immune to, the behavior of others:

> I'm human and I'm not perfect and I will have days when the children will get the rough end, and I don't feel I get cross with myself but I don't feel ultra guilty. I think, well, that's life and they've got to find out that, you know, people are affected by people as well . . . It's only when I think I'm being quite selfish that I feel I'm not being a very good mother or perhaps that I feel I'm not doing enough with them, they're not being creative enough, you know, I'm just sort of abandoning them to a video while I get on with something. That's when I feel I'm not being a very good mother.

As Celia's words show, she still has residual feelings of guilt, feelings that most if not all mothers experience some of the time. Even though the women challenged, questioned, and resisted cultural ideals of the good mother, they still found it difficult to let go of them fully. But these ideals and feelings of guilt no longer controlled them as they had when they were in the depths of their depression. Vera, who was toward the end of her journey out of depression, explained:

> I think even now as a mother I'd always think, "Well, maybe I could do a bit more." I feel terrible guilt if I smack him . . . But I worry and I'll always worry, nothing will change me. And now I realize I accept things in myself . . . I think at the end of the day all I can do is sort of love him as much as I can, make him feel secure, cuddle him, not be cruel to him and that's all I can do and I try to be as good as I can.

The mothers did not arrive at their new understanding of themselves and others without difficulty. Some had clearly struggled to accept what felt to them like "a new self." This was particularly true of the mothers who were still emerging from their depression. For instance, Sandra, who was still depressed, said she had changed but "probably not for the better" because the depression had brought out the "bad side" in her. She added that this "is probably good in a sense," illustrating the way in which she was still ambivalent in her definitions of "good" and "bad." Despite the progress she knew she had made, an internalized moral voice still had some grasp over her. She was still involved in an ongoing struggle in which this voice told her that her emerging self was "hard," had "lost its niceness," and was a "bad" self. She illustrates this transition in progress, and how difficult and painful it was for some mothers, when I asked her if she had changed as a person since her daughter was born:

> Yes, but probably not for the better . . . I think this has actually brought out the bad side in me, which is probably good in a sense. I think I went *years* of . . . whatever I was asked to do, or people wanted me to do, I did . . . I think that's why they've all found it quite a shock because, suddenly, this nasty little beast has come out in the middle of it.

Sandra's account highlights this process of questioning and reassessing moral standards, and what is best for whom. Although the women struggled to break free of the moral voice that had dictated their lives as mothers, they were now more inclined to feel that it was better to express their needs, even if doing so resulted in conflict and appeared to others as "bad" and selfish behavior.

As they emerged from their depression, the women stopped fighting with themselves. They came to see themselves as good people, not because they had fulfilled their high standards, but because, as Sandra said, "none of us are perfect and we just do the best we can at the time." Although painful and traumatic, their experiences of depression made them better mothers and better people, they said, because they were able to recognize not only their own limitations as mothers but also the limitations of others. They became more understanding and accepting of themselves, and they said this would lead to better relationships with their children. Many felt they were more understanding of their children, and their daughters in particular, than their mothers had been of them. They were also able to be more "honest" with themselves and others. They were prepared to admit their feelings and be open about who they were and about their experiences of depression. As Louise says, "I realize there's no stigma attached to [postpartum depression]. I'm not bothered and I freely would admit that I'd had it." Vera explains: "I can be more honest to people in general, you know, talking to friends, talking about things, I can be more

honest like I can't always do this and I don't always do that . . . I think
I can maybe let things go a bit more." She says of her depression:

> It's made me realize I'm not perfect. It doesn't matter if you're not per-
> fect, people have to accept you, you know. I could admit a lot of things
> to people that I'd never admit before, like I can sort of be honest, like I
> had psychiatric care while I had him and all that, and I think, well, if
> they think, "Oh god, she's funny," that's their problem . . . I think,
> "Well, it's your loss not mine" . . . That's changed me, I'm definitely like
> that now, "It's just tough" . . . I can admit all things like that and I real-
> ize people don't sort of shrivel up and think, "Oh," you know, 'cos I
> think everybody's quite complicated in their own way.

The most important difference in the women as they recovered
from their depression was that they now felt more comfortable with
themselves as mothers and individuals, however they happened to define motherhood in our society. Dana Breen makes a similar point
when describing the mothers in her sample whom she defined as
"well-adjusted." She notes that this position "does not automatically
imply either that [the mother] must conform or that she must give up
her individual creativity or that she must fight her social environment."[13] Similarly, the mothers in my study did not simply either reject or embrace cultural ideals. Rather, they found a positive resolution of the difficulties and conflicts in their lives as mothers, ultimately
choosing a path they felt was best for them and those they loved. In
accepting themselves (and their children) for who they were, they di-
minished the conflict between their ideal and their actual self. They
reached a position in which they were at peace with themselves, and
therefore were more accepting and tolerant of others.

voices from a different culture

On the evening of October 25, 1994, Susan Smith's two sons, Michael, three, and Alexander, fourteen months, went missing in South Carolina. Susan Smith, twenty-three, told police that a black man had ordered her out of her car at gunpoint and then had taken the car with the children still in it. For nine days authorities searched for the man. Susan Smith and her estranged husband appeared at a televised press conference in a joint plea for the return of their children. The nation's attention was captured by a story that played on every parent's fear of a stranger's abducting their child. Then Susan Smith confessed. She had taken her children for a ride in the car. She drove for nearly three hours and was contemplating suicide. Michael and Alexander, she said, were asleep when she pulled up to a boat ramp by a lake just off the highway. She opened the door and stepped out of the car as it began to roll down toward the lake. The car sank in the lake, taking with it her two sons.

As this story was beginning to unfold, I had been in the United States for two months. I had come for a year to learn about American women's experiences of postpartum depression. I was planning to research postpartum depression support groups and was in the process of contacting voluntary organizations to find a group willing to let me sit in on their meetings for six months.

The Susan Smith case dominated much of the media for the year I spent in the United States. It also became an important topic of discussion within the support group meetings I attended. Media and public reactions to the case, and the reactions of women who had themselves felt close to taking their own or their children's lives, could not have been more different.

The cover of *Newsweek* carried the headline "Sins of the Mother."[1] The media portrayed Susan Smith as an evil woman who "committed an act of savagery that defies understanding."[2] She was a "murderess" and "a baby-killing bitch." Her story told of "how much evil can lurk in even a mother's heart."[3] "A town rallied for a lost child, only to see its efforts mocked by an even greater evil than it imagined."[4] Public opinion as well as residents of Union, South Carolina, where Susan Smith comes from, supported the death sentence. According to a *Newsweek* survey, 63 percent of those polled thought she should have been put to death. Even though details emerged about Susan Smith's unhappy life—parental divorce, a father who committed suicide, sexual abuse by her stepfather, attempted suicide in adolescence, an unfaithful husband—the media and the public were unforgiving.

The media placed the spotlight on Susan's sexual behavior but not on that of her ex-husband. She was described as "a promiscuous, sexually exploitative adult."[5] The killing of her children was portrayed as a reaction to the fact that the man she was currently seeing had just ended their relationship. "If a mother who deliberately drowns her children in a pique over a failed romance doesn't deserve to die, who does?" wrote *Newsweek*.[6] In July 1995, Susan Smith was charged with the murder of her children, but she was sentenced to life in prison rather than death, to the outrage of many.[7]

The tone and content of the conversations about Susan Smith that took place in the group meetings I attended during that year were quite different. The women criticized the media for sensationalizing the case, and for being selective in the information they provided about Smith's life. They spoke about Susan Smith's depression, and they speculated that she might have been depressed since the birth of her first child. These women had some understanding of what she had done. Susan Smith's story also frightened them precisely because they could identify, up to a point, with her actions. They too had had disturbing thoughts of killing their children. At the same time, they recognized that something had pushed Susan over the edge to a point they had not themselves reached. Nevertheless, in stark contrast to media and public reactions, these women showed compassion for this woman's plight. "She needed help and she didn't get it," one mother said. Another agreed: "Yeah, she could have had depression for years." And a third responded: "Sure. She could have had it from her first child or even before."

In a culture that vilifies and condemns mothers who do not show undying love, affection, devotion, and unswerving positive feelings toward their children, it is easy to understand how postpartum depression groups can provide a safe place in which mothers can talk about "unspeakable" thoughts and feelings. Here, women can discuss thoughts that are taboo within a culture which idealizes the mother-child relationship: thoughts such as not loving their children and feeling compelled to harm and kill them. Simone was able to talk about "having obsessive thoughts about harming the baby with a knife." Jill also said she "used to obsess about the knives in my kitchen. I used to just be convinced that I was going to open the kitchen drawer and take out a knife and kill my daughter." These thoughts coexisted with strong feelings of love for her daughter. "I loved her to death," she says, "I couldn't stop hugging her and kissing her." Betty felt similar contradictory feelings and asked herself, "How could I ever have those thoughts about this little baby that I love to death?" She describes her state of mind after the birth of her third daughter:

> I had Holly in a carriage at [the shopping mall], going onto the escalator, and I remember thinking, "if I let go of this carriage, she'll probably be dead at the end," and then I thought, "That's really horrible," but I remember thinking it and thinking it would really take care of all this anxiety that I'm having, because she'll be out of the picture and I won't feel this way anymore . . . And then I remember giving her a bath in the sink. And my oldest daughter came in, she was eight, and she said, "Mom, would you plug the blow dryer in." And I thought, if I just put that blow dryer in, she'll be electrocuted and that will be the end of it.

Nancy, Paula, and Annette share similar thoughts about harming their children:

> *Nancy:* I'd pick up a knife from the dish drain . . . and I'd say, "Oh, my God. I could hurt him with this." And I'm folding the blankets in his crib, same. "I could hurt him with this."
> *Paula:* Right. I had those thoughts, too. I used to live on a lake and it was like, "I could drop Jamie right in the lake and he'd be drowned."

Annette: I've thought like that too. One day, it was like I wanted to throw her against the wall . . . And then another day, it was the knives, I had my husband hide all the knives in the house. I was actually visioning these thoughts, and they were very gory. Then I thought, "Well, I'd end up in jail. That would be the last thing I'd like." Then I thought, "Well, okay, who cares? These thoughts are driving me crazy. I'd rather just get rid of them, take care of the problem."

Sharing their thoughts and feelings with one another helped these women understand the confusing nature of their emotions, and the fact that they could both love their children and at the same time have fears and compulsions about harming them. The postpartum depression group provided a supportive environment within which mothers could voice feelings of love and hate for their children, what Rozsika Parker has called "maternal ambivalence."[8] In this sense, the group provided women with the opportunity to challenge normative ideals and representations of motherhood, as well as to reconstruct motherhood in light of their own experiences. One of the reasons I was interested in attending meetings of a postpartum depression group was to understand better how sharing thoughts and feelings, which the British women also found invaluable, helped women through their depression. I was also intrigued to learn about the experience of postpartum depression within a different cultural context.

Between February and July 1995 I attended nine meetings of a group that Betty had set up and been running for six years. I found out about the group through Depression after Delivery (DAD), under whose auspices it was run. DAD is a non-profit national self-help organization of women who have experienced postpartum depression. It was founded in 1985 and has branches in the United States and in Canada. DAD is staffed by volunteers and offers support and information about postpartum depression in cooperation with healthcare professionals and researchers who have a special interest in PPD.[9]

The group I attended met twice a month, with more sporadic meetings over the summer holidays. Meetings lasted between one and a half and three hours. With each of the women's consent, I tape-recorded the meetings. My role in the group was primarily to listen to the discussion and occasionally ask questions. During the six-month period I attended the group seventeen women came. Two brought their babies and family members (including partners and parents). Betty, the group leader, said it was quite common for partners to come just once, usually the first time the mother attends the group. Betty encouraged partners to come because "then they see that they're not alone, that their wife isn't crazy, that there are a lot of other women that suffer from this, and that there is help." The mothers came at varying stages in their depression. Betty observed that in her experience the mothers whose depression included significant anxiety tended to come to the group early on in their depression. The mothers who were mostly depressed, by contrast, came only after they had been depressed for several months.

Of the seventeen women, not including the group leader, two women came regularly: Paula attended eight of the nine meetings I sat in on and Nancy came to six. Connie, the leader of a group in a neighboring state, came to two meetings. Three long-standing members who had been "regulars" in the past and had recovered came occasionally to give support. One woman came once to learn about setting up a group. Nine mothers suffering from depression came only once. The number of mothers at each meeting ranged from three to seven with an average of four. Betty explained that those who attend regularly come for six months to a year.

From talking to Betty and Connie, who have years of experience running groups, as well as from my own observations during the six months I attended group meetings, I found that there are several reasons many women come to the group just once. Some feel better after one meeting, or feel that what they have is not postpartum depression but the blues, or a crying baby, or the ordinary difficulties many mothers experience. Some simply come to get information about postpartum depression and the professional support available. For some, getting to the group is problematic either because they live some distance away or because they need and cannot receive physical and emotional help to get to the group. Other women do not feel comfortable talking about their experiences. Some women find the group and other women's stories frightening. Indeed, one of the women who came to the first group I attended never returned because she feared that by hearing about other mothers' experiences she would develop the same symptoms. However, she kept in regular telephone contact with Betty as well as with two other mothers from the group. Telephone support was an important function of the group and was invaluable both for those who came regularly and for those who came just once.

The style, membership, and emphasis of particular groups (for example, on conventional medication, alternative therapies, and so on) can be off-putting to some women. One of the mothers who came only once, and who was a practitioner of alternative medicine, told me at the end of the meeting how surprised she was that much of the group discussion had focused on medication: whether to take it, and different women's experiences of it.

The group I attended was based in a white, middle-class area and this was reflected in the group membership.[10] The group leader also influences membership. Betty was more in favor of conventional medicine than alternative approaches. She was quite explicit about the differences between her group and others. For example, she often made reference to the "muesli crunchers" and the "crunchy granolas" who lived in other areas, and to the fact that other groups adopted holistic approaches and herbal remedies. Although she accepted that different solutions work for different women, she was less sympathetic of these approaches and more in favor of conventional medication. It is important to bear in mind, then, that the issues discussed in this chapter are representative of only one postpartum depression group, based in a particular geographical location, and lead by a particular woman.

The dynamics of each group meeting depended on who was present. When the meetings consisted of mothers who attended regularly, the discussion was informal and focused on the women's day-to-day activities, events, and feelings during the two weeks since the last meeting. Whenever a new mother attended, the meeting was more formally structured, with each woman telling her story. The "telling of your story," what Verta Taylor calls "survivor narratives," was a key aspect of these meetings.[11] Listening to other women's stories enabled new mothers to see that they were not alone. This was perhaps the single greatest benefit of attending a meeting. In the following exchange, Nancy, a regular member, tells her story to Annette, a new mother:

Nancy: I have a one-year-old. And when he was about six months old, I started to have overwhelming anxiety and just not really knowing what to do with him and how to keep him happy through the day, I was very nervous, and not relaxed, and feeling unhappy and isolated and the whole nine yards. And when I look back, I think it started to creep in probably within one month after he was born. But it finally got so bad that I was having bad thoughts.

Annette: What kind of thoughts?

Nancy: Well, I was worried that I might harm my child.

Annette: I've been having homicidal ideations.

Nancy: I've heard of people having that, too.

Annette: So I'm not the only one with this.

Betty: Yeah. It's kind of common.

Annette: I've just never been through something like this. I'm glad to know, not that I would want to see someone else go through it, but I'm glad to know that other people do. So I'm not the only one. You know, I was walking around thinking I was a lunatic.

Betty: Right, right. You think you're the only person going through it.

Nancy: I did, too. I thought, "There can't be other people in existence that have had these kinds of thoughts." It just seems unbelievable at the time.

Annette: For me, it was an ongoing, twenty-four-hour-a-day thing. I was constantly repeating to my husband, "I have these gory, gory thoughts. You don't understand. They're not normal."

Betty: Yeah, yeah, we've heard this. We've heard this.

Annette: Really?

Betty: Yup, yup. You're not alone. It has happened.

Annette: Oh! Wow!

The women also valued the group because it provided them with reassurance that they would get better, that it was possible to have another child and not get depressed, and that they were not to blame for their depression. Alyse attended the support group for two years after the birth of her third child and found it very useful:

What I found most helpful about coming here was that I was not alone. There were other people in the same boat. And I just felt there was no one I could talk to. And everybody was June Cleaver, and you know, could handle it, and had their jobs and their lives and their families and just handled it without having any problem at all, and that's what I saw.

Just to know that I wasn't alone, that I would get better, that, you know, there were things I could do to help myself get better, but even if I didn't do anything, that it would end, that it had an end. And also that I didn't cause it. That it wasn't my fault. There was nothing that I did to cause it. There was nothing that I could have done to prevent it. That it was just something that happened to me.

The mothers validated each other's feelings and experiences. They also felt comfortable telling their stories in the knowledge that the other mothers would understand and support them. The group helped women realize that postpartum depression happened to ordinary people, not women who were "freaks" or "weirdoes," as Betty explains:

They can identify with the other people and they respect them. You know, like many people that come here, you know, they've been doctors, nurses, teachers, whatever. So, you know, they can see that, gee, it's not just the dregs of society or it's not, you know, it's not people with a mental illness that this happens to. It happens to everyday, normal, middle-class American people. Black, white, Chinese, you know, whatever. It happens to everybody and they're not alone. And that's where I think the support group is so helpful.

Christine attended only one group meeting. She came with her parents, her husband, and her baby. She is in her late thirties, a lawyer who worked for seventeen years before having a baby. After we had all introduced ourselves, Betty asked Paula to share her story. In the following passages we hear how Paula's story helps Christine make sense of her experience. Christine asks a lot of questions, seeking information and reassurance that she is not alone:

Paula: Well, it was after my third baby and I didn't even know what postpartum depression was.
Christine: So, you have three and the third one, it hit.
Paula: Yeah, I have a four-year-old and a three-year-old. And you know I got a little blues after that, but—
Christine: Yeah, but that's normal, right?
Paula: Right. But like the first week your adrenaline is high. "Oh, this is wonderful. I can handle everything. Life's just great." And then the second week was just like, from then on, my head just raced and raced and I thought I was gonna lose my mind.

Christine: Yeah. I mean, was it more a manic feeling or more
   depression, or?
Paula: Definitely depression, but I didn't know it was depression
   because I never suffered from depression . . . But I was home all
   summer, so, you know, I was lonely, depressed. It was just like
   being home with three babies.
Christine: So, when did it all start, though?
Paula: Oh, it started right from the beginning. See, I didn't know
   it. I thought it was my panic and anxiety, so I thought I could
   shake 'em. You know, so I wasn't telling anyone. I wasn't
   complaining to my husband . . . And like all summer a lot of
   times I didn't sleep. I couldn't eat. I never sat down. I never
   relaxed. I cleaned the whole yard. I did everything by eight
   o'clock in the morning, my kids were dressed, everything.
Christine: You sound like it's more, I mean, to me, see, I'm in a
   mode where I can't do anything.
Paula: But a lot of people are like that.
Christine: Okay.
Paula: Then by September, I started back to work and I love what I
   do. Even that wasn't making me happy. I just felt empty and
   lonely and scared.
Christine: Yep.
Paula: And I was always crying, and I just dreaded the mornings.
Christine: Yeah, that's, that's my worst—
Paula: They're tough for me.
Christine: Yeah, mornings I can't handle at all.
Paula: No, I can't either.
Christine: Right. I wake up at 5:30, and as soon as I open my eyes,
   I'm in a panic state.

Paula talks about the medication she has been taking, and Christine
asks how long it was before it started taking effect, and whether Paula
feels that it is helping her. Christine then shares her story and tells the
group about the onset of her depression. After Christine has spoken
for a while, Nancy arrives late at the meeting and Christine starts asking her about her experience—whether this is her first child, when her
depression started, whether she has gone back to work, whether she is
on medication, and whether it has helped. Nancy supports Christine
by telling her that she was at Christine's stage once, but now that her

son is eleven months old she is much better, and Christine, too, will get better. At the end of the group, Christine tells how relieved she is that other mothers have been through what she is experiencing. "It's good to know there are other people," she says, "especially when you think you're losing your mind."

The group provided a place where women gave one another permission to focus on themselves without feeling guilty. The group encouraged and supported them in thinking about their own needs and feelings, and what was good for them. Each mother reinforced this message for herself and others with expressions such as "you have to put yourself first," "you have to think of yourself," and "you have to take care of yourself."

The group meetings provided the opportunity for mothers to discuss in depth their experiences of motherhood and, importantly, to voice thoughts and feelings they could not express to family, friends, or healthcare professionals. They talked about how motherhood changed their lives, the demands and challenges of being a mother, the difficult early weeks after the birth, and the fact that mothers get neglected once the baby is born and are rarely asked how they feel. They discussed needing different types of friends once they became mothers, the challenges of having more than one child, and whether and how to combine motherhood with paid work. They spoke about how different their lives were compared with their partners'. They also spoke about their partners' need for support as a result of their depression. They spoke about their feelings of depression, anxiety, and panic, not wanting their children, not loving their children, and what they called their "obsessive-compulsive" thoughts about harming their children, thoughts and feelings they believed were unspeakable within other settings and within society more generally. At the group Annette found a safe place where she could admit her feelings about her baby and be supported by Betty:

Annette: I'm not sure about my love for her. I know I'm not
   enjoying it. And I feel bad about saying it. I feel guilty.
Betty: No. And don't ever feel bad. That's why we're here, because
   you can say any of that stuff here. You can't necessarily say that
   to your friend who's got three babies and absolutely loves it. But
   you can say that here because we've all felt the same way. We all
   lived through that.

They talked about the lack of information about postpartum depression and the difficulties some women had finding help. Healthcare professionals, hospitals, and local newspapers needed to advertise the existence of postpartum depression support groups, they said. They also discussed the cultural silence and taboo surrounding the difficulties of motherhood, a silence, they believed, that is perpetuated by mothers themselves. They spoke about women being protective of the image of blissful motherhood and presenting their experiences as unambiguously positive.

The women talked at length about the medical treatments they received and the psychiatrists and therapists they saw. As mentioned, medication was a dominant theme within all the group meetings I attended. The women discussed whether to take medication, their fears of addiction, the different types of medication, the cost and side effects, how long to take medication and how long before it worked, and their feelings of guilt about being on medication because they felt it meant they were not trying hard enough. They were concerned about the effects of their depression on their children. Would their children be damaged for life? Would they remember their mothers being depressed? Fears that they may have damaged their children lingered within some of the mothers for many years.

Much of the group discussion centered around a reframing of postpartum depression as a hormonal, societal, marital, or family problem as opposed to an individual problem to be blamed on individual women. As Betty said to one mother, "It's a whole-family issue, not 'This is your thing, honey. You've got postpartum depression. You deal with it.'" This is why Betty encouraged husbands and partners to attend at least one meeting—in order to understand how they might help mothers overcome their feelings. Betty had a particularly important role within the group because, added to her own three experiences of depression, she also had six years of experience seeing and talking to other mothers who came to the group. She was able to offer advice, anecdotes, and information based on these experiences as well as on the wide reading she had done on the subject. Importantly, she was able to emphasize that while mothers can derive a lot of support from hearing other stories, each mother and each depression is different. "Nobody's story is the same," she explains.

Postpartum depression support groups also allow women to challenge cultural assumptions and ideals of motherhood and reconstruct more realistic notions of what it means to be a mother. As Verta Taylor points out, women can openly discuss the need to replace the myth of maternal bliss with a more inclusive view of motherhood, one that is more realistic and accurate and that places emphasis on the challenges and difficulties that are intrinsic to the experience of motherhood.[12] Taylor argues that postpartum depression support groups have therefore brought women's emotional distress and suffering to the fore of public and political debates, and by doing so, they have opened up a space for new definitions of motherhood that compete with traditional models. By redefining gender roles within society, self-help groups provide not only individual support but also the basis for broader social and political reform and change.

BETTY

> Depression is to not see any good in anything. To be really, really, really sad. To not be able to laugh at a joke or a show. Just not feeling any, any joy. Not being able to feel anything. To look at my daughter and not have any feelings. That's depression. To have no feelings at all. Just to feel nothing.

Betty experienced these feelings of depression after the birth of each one of her three daughters, now ages fourteen, ten, and six. Her first depression lasted a month, her second, two months, and her third, six months. Her depression was accompanied by high levels of anxiety, especially after her third child. Her husband, Jeff, has always been very supportive physically and emotionally. Indeed, he has played an important part in helping her set up, run, and advertise the postpartum depression support group. He occasionally comes to meetings, hands out leaflets on postpartum depression at the shop where he works, and has appeared on television programs and at conferences with Betty to speak about their experiences. During her depression, however, Betty felt anger and resentment toward him because his life was less affected by parenthood than hers was, and because she felt the burden of having to take care of everyone's needs.

Unlike most of the British women, Betty does not struggle to understand her depression and why it happened to her. Having spent several years thinking about her own experience and listening to the stories of other women, she believes postpartum depression is primarily a hormonal condition that can be exacerbated by other life stresses and circumstances, by a previous history of anxiety or depression, and by a woman's upbringing and relationship with her family:

> I do think that other stresses in your life can make it worse, but I definitely think it's hormonal. I really, really do, because I don't have these feelings any other time than after the birth of a baby . . . With my pregnancies, I threw up for like five months, and that is caused by hormones . . . I definitely think it's a hormonal, biochemical imbalance, caused by, you know, the hormonal flux during the pregnancy and then with the birth of the placenta, how the hormones, you know, are practically diminished.
>
> Natasha: If it's hormonal, why do you think some women get it and others don't?
>
> Not everybody's hormones react the same way . . . Some women, you know, their hormones stay latent and then they slowly start to increase or whatever. Some women's may not start to increase, and maybe that's the reason that they . . . get the postpartum depression.

Betty believes that being a perfectionist and concealing her feelings also contributed to her depression:

> The one thing that I've noticed is that—and it has to do with not being able to reach out and ask for help—most of the women that come to my group are perfectionists. And I've noticed that with, I'd say, 95 percent of the people. I am, too. I expect to go out of the house, I want my hair to look good, I want my children to look good. I want my house in order before I leave . . . I would get up, take a shower, blow-dry my hair. I looked great. The world thought, "You know, gee, isn't Betty great? Her kids look perfect. She's doing great." But on the inside, I was just a total basket case. I couldn't eat. I couldn't really sleep. Every time I ate, I threw up or had diarrhea. I lost forty pounds in a month.

Betty talks about putting on "a perky face" because she was reluctant to admit her feelings to her mother, friends, or healthcare providers for fear of disappointing them. She felt guilty about needing her mother's help at the age of thirty-one:

> I felt like I was thirty-one and my mom was still taking care of me and my kids. That was horrible even though I needed her . . . And you don't want your mom to know how bad you feel because you don't want to feel like a failure. And even though your mother might not be judging you as you feel it, you think you're a failure so you think, then you're mom's going to think, "She can't really handle it."

When Betty eventually sought help, the support she needed and wanted was not available. This inspired her to set up the support group because she wanted above all to talk to other mothers about her feelings:

> What inspired me to set up the group was the fact that there was no help for me when I was going through the postpartum depression the third time. Because what I wanted to do more than anything was talk to other mothers that felt the same way as I did . . . My midwife was great and she listened to me, but I needed other mothers to validate me as well.

With the help of her midwife, a nurse, and another mother who had also experienced depression, Betty set up the group when her third daughter was nine months old.

Although Betty clearly believes that sharing feelings with other mothers is critical to the move out of depression, she is also convinced of the power of medication. She herself took valium for a month when she was depressed the third time. She says she would "love to see people not take medication" but believes that it is helpful. She encourages women to try it, to make sure they are on the right medication and the right amount, and to stay with it until it takes effect.

CONNIE

Connie experienced postpartum depression after the birth of her son, Patrick, and then after the birth of her twins four years later. Her depression started just a few weeks before Patrick's first birthday. Connie has a close-knit family and feels she benefited enormously from their support. She also felt physically and emotionally supported by her husband, who worked night shifts in a factory. Nonetheless, initially she felt unable to talk openly to her husband and family. She feared losing her baby and felt she was "going crazy." When she started to talk about her feelings, she learned that others also experienced similar emotions. She felt very supported by her family once they knew about her depression but nevertheless wanted medical help. However, she was disappointed by the reactions of three doctors she approached. "They didn't know anything about postpartum depression," she says, "I was told that, you know, I'd probably be okay if I went out to dinner and this type of thing." When Patrick was six months old Connie went back to work full-time as a receptionist, thinking this might help her overcome her feelings. When he was ten months old, she saw a psychiatrist who diagnosed her depression. This came as a relief to her: "It was just such a relief for me to have a medical professional diagnose me and give me a name for this illness that I was going through. I think that when I did get to that point it was like a load taken off my shoulders." The psychiatrist prescribed antidepressants and tranquilizers. Patrick was a year old when Connie felt "normal" and like her "old self" again.

It was at this point that Connie set up a postpartum depression support group. Like Betty, she was inspired to establish the group because she could not find the medical support she needed and wanted. She also felt she would have benefited from having more information about postpartum depression, which she had never heard of before she got sick. Part of the reason she wanted to set up a group was to inform parents, parents-to-be, and healthcare professionals about postpartum depression. She believes in talking about PPD in prenatal classes and letting prospective parents know about the availability of support groups and sympathetic health professionals. Although mothers might not hear or later remember what was said about it, partners and other caregivers will because they are likely to be less preoccupied with labor and childbirth.

When Patrick was three years old, Connie became pregnant with twins. She was still on antidepressants at that time. Because she was afraid of becoming depressed again she had progesterone-estrogen treatment for the first four months after the birth. When she was on the hormonal treatment she felt wonderful: "It was like night and day after having my son. I really enjoyed it." When Connie came off the hormonal treatment, she had what she describes as "PMS-type symptoms." She became depressed and called her doctor, who prescribed Prozac, which she took for two years. She tried coming off it twice but developed the symptoms again so she went back on it. Her twins are now five years old and she has since gone onto a different type of medication. Connie was initially reluctant to take antidepressants but over the years she believes they have helped her. She needs them and says that if she has to remain on them for the rest of her life she is willing to do so because she never wants to experience again the feelings she had after the birth of her children.

Like Betty, Connie also believes that her depression is hormonal because her feelings change across her menstrual cycle:

Once I started keeping track of when these things were . . . it was from the time I ovulated until the time my period was over was when I had any of this. But once my period was over until the time I ovulated again, I never had any of these symptoms. So . . . I just feel that mine was definitely a hormonal type thing. And after talking to the psychiatrist that I did go to, I mean that's what they told me also. So, I mean, that was a nice thing to hear when you are thinking that way. But when you're going through it, you don't think that way. That's the problem. Because, you know, you put the guilts on yourself. I remember at six months, going back to work to my full-time job and saying, "Maybe I wasn't made to be a mother. Maybe I should be working full-time." I mean, you just don't know what to do when you're in that state. But I think once you come out of it and you feel okay and you look back on things, that's when you realize, "You know, it wasn't my fault. This was a hormonal thing."

Connie explains that by attributing her depression to hormones, she relieves her feelings of guilt and responsibility. Because her negative feelings originate in her body, they are beyond her control.

PAULA

Paula has three children under the age of four. She was a regular member of the support group, and she spoke at great length about the stresses and strains of her life as a mother. Her depression set in a few weeks after the birth of her third child. She describes her depression in the following way:

To not have any hope . . . It's like you're suffocating or you're in a little prison . . . And to wake up and to dread the day, I think, was the most hardest for me. To get up and go, "Oh, my God, I've got to go through another day." I mean, I never thought about killing myself. I never had those thoughts. I just thought I wanted to dig a big hole and have no one ever find me . . . It's just like "Someone, take all these responsibilities. Just let me be a kid again. Let my parents take care of me." I think being depressed is the most scariest feeling in the whole world, because you do feel alone.

Paula struggles to understand why she became depressed given that marriage and motherhood were what she aspired to her whole life. Yet she speaks about many aspects of her life that contribute to her feelings. She talks about trying to do too much, not allowing herself to slow down, and neither accepting nor asking for help. Her husband, who is a joiner, went back to work five days after the birth, leaving Paula to care for three children on her own. Her third child was born in late spring and she felt very lonely and isolated during the summer, when many of the mother-and-child activities stopped running. She says that no one visited or helped her because they assumed she could manage on her own. Nor did she want to ask for help; indeed, she felt pressure to cope single-handedly even though she was actually "falling apart." She told virtually no one about her depression for fear of being judged. Later, when she began to speak about it, she found that many people were much more supportive than she had anticipated. Similarly, for a long time she resisted confiding in her mother even though she is very close to her. Like Betty, she felt ashamed that at her age she still needed her. She felt she should have outgrown what she regarded as her dependence on her mother. Much of Paula's talk is also dominated by her belief in a biochemical basis to postpartum depression, a belief that helps her cope with her feelings.

Paula did not have use of a car and found it a great strain going anywhere with three children. Her third child was "a wonderful baby" who was easy and content, making Paula feel even more guilty for being depressed. She also struggled with her husband's drinking problem and occasional violence toward her. She said they had often been on the verge of splitting up. At one of the last group meetings I attended she was very upset and cried most of the time. Her husband had become frustrated with her depression, with the fact that she was still on medication and seeing a psychiatrist, and with the cost of treatment. He became violent toward her and had taken to hiding her medication, which caused her a great deal of stress and anxiety.

Paula started coming to the group three months after the birth of her third child. She has found it invaluable. Knowing that others have experienced similar feelings and have recovered, and being able to talk to understanding women, has helped her. When she first came to the group she was very resistant to the idea of taking any kind of medication. When her baby was about seven months old, she decided to take the medication prescribed by her psychiatrist. She was given antianxiety medication to treat the panic and anxiety she has experienced since she was a teenager, and Prozac for her depression. She also started seeing a therapist. Paula now feels proud that she has stopped giving herself a hard time for taking medication. "That's the only thing I haven't done to myself is beat myself up because I've been on medication," she says, "but I could care less if I stayed on it for the rest of my life." The medication has made her feel better, and that is all that matters to her.

Although her depression has been the worst experience of her life, Paula says that she has learned from it. It has changed her as a person and influenced the way she behaves within her relationships. She tried to do too much, she says. She went back to work as a dance teacher part-time two weeks after her daughter was born: "There I am thinking I'm superwoman." Now, she is beginning to lower her standards and stop striving for perfection in everything she does:

> You beat yourself up because you want everything perfect and you want them to have fun and do everything. And it's like, that's when I just stopped doing that. Three weeks ago, I'm like, "No, I'm not doing that anymore." And I've changed my attitude. And I have to. I've gone from one extreme to the other. From ironing their clothes every day to—You know?

Paula has also given up trying to please everyone at her own expense. "I've changed my whole lifestyle," she says, "I just don't put the pressure on myself like I used to. I used to feel like I had to do everything and everything for everybody, and now if I do it, I do it, if I don't, I don't." Now she puts her children and herself first and asks for help when she needs it:

> I never, ever would have asked anybody for help. I would have never asked anyone to come over. Never in the lifetime. I never would ask my father-in-law for anything. Now, it's like, "Can you pick up Jamie from preschool." I don't even think twice about it. And I'm glad now, so maybe God tries to teach you different things in different ways, but it's like—And to show you that you can't be Wonder Woman and you can't do everything.

NANCY

Nancy's son, Craig, is nine months old and she has been coming to the group for a month when I first meet her. Motherhood was something Nancy had looked forward to for a long time. "It had been my dream to be an at-home mother," she says. "I always had this perception that I would just be this perfect mother and, you know, nothing like this would happen to Nancy." She and her husband tried to conceive for several years. Yet when she finally got pregnant, Nancy was not excited. Even after the birth she was not as happy as she had expected to be. She felt she was "faking" her joy. From the birth onward, she started to have "weird thoughts." A month after Craig was born, she began to experience anxiety. When he was six months old, her anxiety was overwhelming and she was almost constantly nervous, unable to relax, unhappy, and isolated. She feared Craig was not getting enough food. If she went out of the house, she was afraid to return and face her feelings of anxiety. Nancy never feels that she is giving her son enough and never feels comfortable with herself as a mother:

> I have really ambivalent feelings. I mean, if you're with them, you feel like you don't want to be with them. If you're not with them, you're not sure if you feel like you want to be with them, or if you don't want to be with them, why don't you want to be with them? You feel guilty. You feel as if you're a bad mother if when you're not with them, you're not pining for them.

Nancy also had "bad thoughts about harming my child." "I never harmed him and I never intended to, but I just had these horrible thoughts," she says. For six months, she was reluctant to disclose her feelings to her husband, her family, or her doctor. Although she has no previous experience of depression, there is a history of mental illness in her family, and she feared that if she revealed her feelings her child would be taken away and she would be institutionalized. She also refrained from asking for help because, she says, "I thought I was supposed to do it all on my own." At many of the meetings Nancy repeated these words: "I should have reached out a lot earlier but I thought I was supposed to do it on my own." She did not think of herself as the kind of person who needed help. She was a self-sufficient woman with a successful fifteen-year career as an administrator who had never needed to turn to other people.

When Craig was eight months old Nancy saw a psychiatrist. She was diagnosed with postpartum depression and obsessive-compulsive disorder and was prescribed medication that she was reluctant to take partly because she was breast-feeding, and partly because she feared addiction. At about the same time, she started coming to the support group and found this a great help:

> Calling Betty was a big, huge step, because you keep thinking to yourself, "How can there be other people going through this? I'm a total nut

case. How could I be having these thoughts?" To know that there are other people that go through this was such a help for me.

When I attended my last group meeting Craig was fifteen months old and Nancy described herself as "much better," although she still has bad days. The medication, which she is still taking, has helped her, but she would also like to see a therapist to talk in depth about her feelings.

DONA

Dona came to the group just once to find out about setting up a group in her area. She experienced depression after the birth of her first and only child, who is now four years old. It took her a year to conceive, and she had a "wonderful" pregnancy. "I was in a real hormonal high," she says. As the pregnancy progressed, Dona began to experience panic attacks. She realized she was completely unprepared for motherhood and looking after a young baby. "I'd never really dealt with the idea of having a real baby. I was more into being pregnant," she says. Dona had a long and difficult labor and felt very flat after the birth. As the weeks went by, she says, "I was trying to put effort into trying to be happy because everybody expects you to be happy." Inside she started regretting what she had done:

> I felt nothing toward this baby. I felt like, "I have made a mistake. Boy, have I made a mistake. And not only have I ruined my life, I have ruined my son's life. I have ruined my husband's life. I only wanted to be pregnant." I kept telling myself, "I don't want him." I was like praying for crib death. He would cough a little bit and I'd think, "Maybe he'll choke." I kept thinking, "But people say they love their own babies, they love their own kids." I wanted him out of the house. I didn't want just time off. I wanted him out of the house.

Although Dona had always been able to cope with chaos and multiple demands at her job in the media, she felt utterly helpless faced with the chaos of her life as a new mother. Like so many women, she felt she was a bad mother, the only woman in the world to feel ambivalent and even indifferent toward her child.

Dona had the support of her in-laws, her parents, her husband, and her friends, but she could not express her feelings to them. When her son was four months old she came to the group and found it helpful, though she continued to feel depressed. It was not until her son was nineteen months old that she finally sought medical help. She saw two counselors and a psychiatrist, who prescribed Prozac. Part of the reason she delayed taking medication was because she wanted to continue breast-feeding. Within days of taking the Prozac she began to feel like herself again:

> I started on Prozac and like, in days, I felt like, "Oh, gosh, I feel like singing when there's music on the radio, driving in the car." I had forgotten what that felt like. I had just so totally lost my baseline after my son was born. I think medication can be wonderful in just restoring any physical imbalances.

Now, more than two years later, Dona still takes Prozac, as well as a drug for her anxiety. She also takes sleeping pills and Ritalin for her recently diagnosed attention deficit disorder. For Dona, the medication has been "a lifeline." She believes it works because postpartum depression is a hormonal condition. "I was in hormone hell," she says when describing her depression.

Dona feels her experience of depression has changed her positively by helping her find a better way of coping with her feelings. She used to internalize her feelings, keep them to herself, and bury them. Now she has learned to voice and confront them:

> I think probably for me the biggest thing I've changed was just that it's okay to feel certain things. And I think, again, a lot of this was just the way I was brought up and the way that I've learned to cope is that everything that ever concerned me or that I was scared, frightened, or whatever about, stayed inside, so that now what I'm able to do is kind of say, "Okay, this is bothering me."

Although she has learned from her depression, Dona feels that she cannot have another child and risk experiencing depression again. She had always wanted to have two children, but when she recently got pregnant accidentally she felt ambivalent and had an abortion. The depression, she says, "almost killed me. I don't think I could have another one. I would never ever want to risk that again, ever."

PATSY

When her first son, Tyler, was eighteen months, Patsy became pregnant with her second child. She had a healthy pregnancy and a delivery free of complications. The day after the birth Patsy says she felt "funny" and "out of sorts." She returned home the following day and could not stop crying. She felt frightened and overwhelmed by the responsibility of having two children to care for. "I just got overwhelmed by the whole picture," she says, "I thought, 'Oh, my God, I've got to do this for the next eighteen years of my life.'" Three weeks later she started having panic attacks:

> I'm walking around the store, and all of a sudden . . . I got really scared, and I started getting the tingles and the sensations. A panic attack was setting in, not that I knew what it was at the time. I grabbed some lady walking by me who I didn't know from Adam but had two kids, so I figured I was safe. I said, "Please, stay with me." I said, "I think I'm going to black out." Rob was just four weeks old in the stroller, and Tyler beside me who wanted to bomb all over the place. I just sat down on the cash counter, took some deep breaths, and it finally passed . . . I just got the hell out of the store. I just went home. So, I never told anybody. And then on the Expressway, driving in the car, like they would just come out of the blue. Then, the more they came, the more anxious I got . . . I couldn't eat. I couldn't sleep. I was vomiting. I had diarrhea. I paced the house like this constantly. And that was about seven weeks post. And it progressively got worse to the point that I would not leave the house. The panic attacks were happening in the house, which is supposed to be your safety place, and it wasn't even my safety place any more. I would just feed the kids, dress the kids, put a movie in for Tyler, sit him in front of it. I would bathe Rob. I'm sitting and saying, "Why the hell is this happening to me?" I couldn't understand what it was.

Patsy found it very difficult to admit her feelings, even to her husband:

> Being stoic me, I didn't tell anybody for a long time. My husband didn't even know. He knew something was going on, but I wasn't telling him what was going on. And then I just got very reclusive. I wasn't talking on the phone to anybody . . . I wasn't talking to my mother, I wasn't talking to my sister. I wasn't talking to anybody. I just sat in the house with the kids. I wouldn't even go outside the door.

When Rob was two months old, Patsy saw a doctor who prescribed medication for her anxiety, which worsened nonetheless. When she was on her own she was fine, but her feelings of anxiety and panic overwhelmed her when she was with the children. Patsy called the doctor, who referred her to a psychiatrist and a clinical nurse specialist. Patsy also asked her mother-in-law to take the children away and look after them, which she did for several months:

> My husband packed their bags, packed their things. I had no feeling, no emotion. I was like—they left, I felt fine. It was really disgusting. I mean, I felt fine when they were gone. I was relieved. I didn't have that responsibility, which was my biggest fear on me of the children. Why I had this fear of the children, I have no idea. I love children. I've always loved children. I've wanted these kids. It took me over a year to have Tyler and over a year to have Rob. I'm like, "Why is it scaring me so much?"

Patsy saw a psychiatrist once a week who prescribed medication for her anxiety and depression, even though she was very resistant to the idea of taking medication. She also saw a counselor three times a week. However, she did not feel any better and began to have suicidal thoughts. She was frustrated with her psychiatrist because he was treating her feelings as depression rather than attributing them to the fact that she had just had a baby and had two children to look after. "He told me right off the bat he would treat this as depression but not postpartum, because it was something he just didn't see as a problem because he was a male." Her psychiatrist was "not approaching this as a female, biological-type problem. He was digging and looking for other things in my life, which there wasn't anything of." Patsy later contacted a psychiatrist who specialized in postpartum depression. This psychiatrist prescribed Prozac and also suggested that Patsy stay with her mother-in-law so that she could spend time with her children but withdraw and let her mother-in-law take over when she needed a break. Patsy did this for three weeks. Slowly she started to feel better, and she came to terms with the fact that she was on medication.

Five years later, she still takes Prozac as well as medication for her anxiety. Although she feels bad about this, she says it helps her feel like herself:

> I feel much better on it. I just, I hate to say it, but I do. I don't tell people now that I take it anymore because I just feel that five years, Patsy, come on. Postpartum depression doesn't last that long. That's not postpartum anymore. But I'm just too PMS, I get too anxious, I get too keyed up. So, I'm fine with it, and I'm just going to take it.

Her beliefs about the value of medication are connected to her understanding that postpartum depression is hormonal in origin:

I'm an extremely hormonal person. I'm an extremely premenstrual person, and I calculated on my calendar every period, and I had them all worked out. And every time I got very anxious or every time I got very keyed, I would just look and I would be ovulating. And that's why I would feel myself changing inside. The hormones would start kicking in . . . and that just shows how much it is a hormonal problem. It's not a mental disorder. This is my lecture now, to make you feel better. It's nothing you did. It's nothing anybody did. It's just hormones that are just fluctuating.

When Rob was six months old, Patsy started to come to the support group. Her husband also came and found it useful. The combination of different types of help have gotten her through her depression. She has also tried to change herself and her lifestyle, and in this respect her depression has been "a learning experience." She has learned her limitations and now knows "to give yourself a break because, you know, we can't be supermom." She has started to say "no" whereas before she was always trying to please everyone:

> I was one who was very eager always to help somebody out and always say, "Yeah, okay, sure," when I really didn't want to do it. Well, I learned to say, "No, I don't want to do that."

Patsy returned to part-time work and started looking after herself more.

The stories of these American women echo many of the themes voiced by the British women. They, too, struggled with the images, expectations, and demands of motherhood and felt compelled to be perfect wives, women, and mothers. Those who had more than one child talked about how much easier it was to let go of their high standards with a second or third child. With a first child, they said, they were more easily influenced by doctors and books. These sources of pressure and comparison reinforced their sense of inadequacy:

> *Annette:* I'm reading this book about what to expect in the first year, and every night I read this book, and I panic. If she's not doing something that it says that she should be doing, I'm thinking, "Oh, my God, we haven't been paying attention to her." Or, "She's been on the floor too often. We've got to put her on the jumper." "No, we'd better not. Hold her more often."
> *Nancy:* See, I had to stop reading so religiously because it was

making me a wreck. You know? It was just making me nuts. I had three or four books that I kept reading sections of, you know, "We're not doing enough. Or we're doing too much. It's too much attention, or it's not enough attention," and I just wasn't relaxed at all. I was just a bundle of nerves for six or seven months.

Annette: It's like I panic, thinking, "Oh, my God. I didn't start reading to her, you know, a month ago. I should have started reading to her. And I'm a terrible mother."

With a first child, the women were more likely to listen to the doctor than to other mothers who had experience with several children. Betty and Nancy talk about why they took the doctor's advice over that of other mothers:

Betty: Even if she's had ten children and they're all healthy and you admire her, you feel like you have to listen to the doctor. I think once you become a second-time mother, then you listen to what the doctor says and you say, "Oh, okay, bye," and you go home and you do whatever you want. But the first time, it's like gospel. Whatever they say, well, then you're going to listen to it.

Nancy: Yeah. When it came to things like, oh, how much milk he needs and when he should start solids and things like that, even though other people were saying to me, "Oh, he can have this," or "He can have that," I was looking at the situation and I didn't see any reason for him to be on solids, based on what the doctor said to me. And also, by so many people saying to me, "Oh, do this, do that, do this, do that," I sort of rebelled and said, "Well, I'm just going to do what the doctor said," and I just stood by it.

Betty: And don't you think there's a little part of you that might say, "Well, maybe they have been a mother three or four times, but they're not a mother to *my* baby."

Nancy: Right.

Betty: You know? And it's like, "This is my baby," and they don't know how my baby is. And I'm probably going to be a better mother than they are because they let their baby eat something at three months, and my doctor said, "No, wait until six months," so I'm going to listen to the doctor.

Nancy: And my child is going to grow up more healthy.

As the conversation between Betty and Nancy reveals, the American women, like the British mothers, compared themselves with other mothers. The former also compared themselves with their own mothers and mothers-in-law. The fact that these mother figures had had several children and seemed to breeze through motherhood was another source of pressure.

The women found it difficult to admit their feelings and ask for help. They felt constrained by the ethic of individuality, self-sufficiency, and self-reliance discussed in Chapter 4. As Nancy said, "I should have asked my family to help me but I just thought I was supposed to do it all on my own." To ask for help, even from their own mothers, was a sign of weakness. They also feared being seen as bad mothers, being institutionalized, and having their children taken away. They wanted, above all, to talk to other mothers about their feelings—women they felt they could trust, women who would understand their experiences.

Although medical health care systems differ in Britain and the United States, within both systems women found it difficult to get recognition for their problems and to secure therapy-type treatments. The changes that have taken place over the last two decades, on both sides of the Atlantic, in social policy toward mental health care have reduced provision of, and access to, out-patient and in-patient care. Moreover, the impact of Managed Care in the United States means that insurance companies are increasingly reluctant to pay for a course of therapy as opposed to medication. Many of the American women resorted to private treatment at considerable expense. This was less common among the British mothers, although in Britain, too, there is limited counseling available free of charge on the National Health Service and waiting lists are long. Difficulties accessing, and paying for, "talking treatments" were partly responsible for women's interest in postpartum depression support groups.

The American and British women differed most in their descriptions of their depression and in how they made sense of and coped with their feelings. The American women expressed more extreme and graphic thoughts of killing their children. They spoke at greater length about their overwhelming anxiety in caring for their children, their fear of hurting them, and their feelings of responsibility for their children's lives. They also described much higher levels of anxiety and panic and talked of having "obsessive-compulsive" thoughts. Indeed, there was a greater tendency among the American women to use medical terminology in describing their feelings. They talked about having "obsessive-compulsive disorder," "homicidal ideations," and "manic" feelings, terms none of the British women used.

Like the British women, however, the American mothers were relieved when they were given a label for their feelings and a medical diagnosis (see Chapter 2). Both groups of women also shared an initial resistance to taking medication. But they differed markedly in their beliefs concerning the hormonal cause of postpartum depression, in the amount of medication they took and the length of time they were on it, and in their views about the value of medication. In general, the accounts given by the American women centered far more on biological arguments and solutions—the hormonal causes of postpartum depression, the linking of their mood disturbances to their menstrual periods, and the benefits of medication. Simone, for example, ties her depression and her mood swings to hormonal influences:

> What I found is that, when you start to get really confused, that means that maybe you're going too fast. That's what I found for myself. If I'm doing things and losing things and knocking things down, then something is going off, either my hormones, either it's that time of the month, or I'm going through the beginning of menopause.

Betty often asked women whether they noticed their depression worsening around the time of their period:

> *Betty:* Now, have you noticed that sometimes the way that you feel might have to do with your menstrual cycle?
> *Annette:* Oh, yeah. I get a lot worse, a lot worse.
> *Betty:* Right, right. And a lot of women do. So we tell you to keep a chart on your calendar so that if you are starting to feel really lousy and you can't put your finger on it and he's saying, "What the heck is the matter with you? Why are you such a witch?" you can look at the calendar and say, "Oh, well, I'm due."

Their beliefs about the hormonal causes of their mood swings and depression were tied to their convictions that medication worked:

> *Patsy:* I'm just too PMS, I get too anxious, I get too keyed up. So, I'm fine with the medication, and I'm just going to take it.
> *Paula:* Then, don't you wish you took it years and years ago.

Patsy: Darn right. I probably could have used it.

Betty: Well, obviously, there's a chemical imbalance and you need to take that medication.

Compared with the British women, the Americans were more committed to the value of medication. Many more of them were on medication, they were on a greater number of different types of medication, and for longer periods of time.

Like the British mothers, several of the American women explained that it was helpful to think of postpartum depression as hormonal because this theory absolved them from feelings of blame and responsibility and protected their self-images as good mothers. As Connie explained earlier, "It wasn't my fault. This was a hormonal thing." Similarly, when talking to a new mother at one of the groups, Patsy says: "This is my lecture now, to make you feel better. It's nothing you did. It's nothing anybody did. It's just hormones that are fluctuating." It was clear that the women derived psychological comfort from a medical discourse and solution to their problems. However, are the benefits of a medical approach only short-term? Do they prevent women from addressing the more deep-rooted interpersonal or social processes that may be contributing to their depression? Does latching onto a hormonal discourse and a pharmacological resolution mean that women are less likely to confront painful issues in their lives that may require change on their part or on the part of others? Nancy's account suggests that although a medical diagnosis provided her with immediate relief, in the long term it has not prevented her from addressing other problematic issues in her life. In the early days of her depression she wanted to believe it was hormonal. Now she feels that her depression was caused by a combination of factors:

> For me, it was such a relief. I really wanted it to be a hormonal, biochemical imbalance because the only other alternative, to me, was that I was somehow causing it myself. But now, I've come to the place where I think it's a combination of hormones and lots of other stuff that's just going on with your life. Stopping work, this new child, new responsibilities, I think it's all those things tied together. The medicine gets you to a place where you can start to dig out on your own hole and use your own resources and start to put it behind. I was so relieved to hear "biochemical hormonal." But now, when I can really look at it from my own experience, I really think there's more to it than that.

Interestingly, despite the women's strong adherence to a medical, and therefore an individualized, conception of their difficulties, they nevertheless effected important changes in their lives and in their relationships. For example, they spoke about letting go of their perfectionism and high standards, challenging cultural ideals of motherhood, redefining motherhood in light of their own experiences, giving up their ethic of self-sufficiency, acknowledging their feelings, prioritizing their own needs, and renegotiating their relationships. Verta Taylor has also written about how women's views represent both a resistance to, and a reinforcement of, cultural ideals of motherhood.[13] Writing about the postpartum depression self-help movement, she highlights its contradictory nature and the way it is both supportive and subversive of gender as an institution. On the one hand, the movement challenges the meaning of motherhood in contemporary American society. On the other hand, it advances a therapeutic model that characterizes women's experiences as "illness," thus reaffirming the model of the self-sacrificing mother.

Women on both sides of the Atlantic clearly felt a degree of confusion about the advice of medical experts and a medical framing of their difficulties. Postpartum depression was a hormonal condition, they said, but it was also related to idealized images of mothers and babies, cultural pressures and expectations, gendered parenting ideologies and practices, the demands of motherhood, the fact that the burden of care and responsibility fell on women, and problematic relationships. There was also ambivalence about the benefits of medication—an initial resistance followed by capitulation. The British women remained skeptical while the American women became strong advocates of medication. Both groups of women, however, wanted some type of talking treatment, and most believed in the power of talking to other mothers.

David Karp observes that this type of confusion reflects a broader cultural struggle between professional and lay definitions of illness, reality, and self.[14] However, the greater commitment on the part of the American women, compared with their British counterparts, to a medical view of their problems also points to subtle cultural differences between these two countries in their ideals of motherhood, and in their handling of psychological and emotional distress.

From listening to both groups of mothers, it seems that the pressure on women in the United States to incorporate motherhood and a new baby into their lives, rapidly and efficiently, may be greater than it is in Britain. There was pressure on women to get on with their lives, and few allowances were made by themselves, others, or society for the fact that they had just had a baby. This pressure manifests itself in the increasing requirement for women to leave the hospital within twenty-four hours of giving birth. It is also evident in the limited parental leave offered by many companies—typically, twelve weeks. These policies encourage women (and men) to "carry on as normal," to resume their busy lives, and to return to paid work soon after childbirth. The women I spoke to said they felt they were expected to be "supermom, "wonder woman," or "superwoman." Within this hostile cultural context and climate, explaining their "failure" to live up to these ideals in bodily and biological terms represented an attractive alternative to blaming themselves. They took refuge within a biomedical view of their feelings because it allowed and validated their own experiences of motherhood and justified them on medical grounds. In this sense, women's depression, and their definition of it as an "illness," can be understood as a form of resistance, a legitimate way out of conforming to an oppressive ideal.

By virtue of the fact that they belonged to a self-help group, the American women were part of a larger movement—the postpartum depression support movement—and their accounts reflect, in part, the discourse and rhetoric of the movement more generally. One of the key features of the movement is its campaign to medicalize women's distress associated with childbirth, and convince physicians, mental health workers, and society at large to take their problems seriously by defining them as a disease. The movement is one of the principal advocates of the label and diagnostic category "postpartum depression."[15] The greater tendency of the women in the United States to use mental illness terminology to characterize their experiences reflects in part the broader campaign of the postpartum depression self-help movement to get women's feelings of depression recognized as a form of mental illness. However, the movement's medical view of postpartum conditions in turn reflects the mainstream American tendency to conceptualize problems mainly in individual and therapeutic terms, and the greater power of the medical model in explaining and defining women's emotional lives in the United States compared with Britain.

appendixes

notes

acknowledgments

index

women interviewed

Caroline. Age: 31. Education: completed secondary education; secretarial qualification. Employment: at time of depression, not in paid work; prior to motherhood, secretary; at time of interview, not in paid work. Two sons, ages 3½ and 19 weeks. Depression: onset, 6–12 weeks after birth of first child; duration, 12 months; medication, antidepressants for 6 months; health professionals seen, general practitioner.

Celia. Age: 30. Education: completed secondary education; university degree. Employment: at time of depression, not in paid work; prior to motherhood, manager for a public relations firm; at time of interview, not in paid work. Two daughters, ages 6 and 3. Depression: onset, in first 6 months after birth of first child; duration, 2 years; medication, antidepressants for 10 months; health professionals seen, general practitioner, psychiatrist, homeopath.

Dawn. Age: 25. Education: left school at 15. Employment: at time of depression, not in paid work; prior to motherhood, clerical assistant; at time of interview, not in paid work. Two children: son, 3 years, 9 months; daughter, 21 months. Depression: onset, soon after birth of first child; duration, 3½ years—still feeling depressed at time of interview; medication, antidepressants for 9 months; health professionals seen, general practitioner, family therapist; voluntary-sector support, postpartum depression support group.

Fiona. Age: 26. Education: left school at 16. Employment: at time of depression, not in paid work; prior to motherhood, typist and cleaner; at time of interview, not in paid work. Two children: daughter, 2 years, 10 months; son, 1 year, 11 months. Depression: onset, 3–4 months after birth of first child; duration, over 2 years—still feeling depressed at time of interview; medication, none; health professionals seen, general practitioner.

Frances. Age: 37. Education: completed secondary education; secretarial qualification; incomplete nursing training. Employment: at time of depression, running her own business part-time; at time of interview, part-time nurse, occasional secretarial work, running her own business. Three children: two sons, 12 and 10; daughter, 6. Depression: onset, 6 months after birth of third child; duration, three and a half years; medication, antidepressants for three months; health professionals seen, general practitioner. Previous experience of anorexia and depression as a teenager.

Helen. Age: 34. Education: completed secondary education; nursing qualification; enrolled in doctoral program. Employment: at time of depression, full-time work as visiting nurse and part-time doctoral student; at time of interview, full-time work as visiting nurse and part-time doctoral student. One son, 12 months. Depression: onset, soon after the birth; duration, 12 months; medication, progesterone; health professionals seen, general practitioner; voluntary-sector support, Cry-sis.

Louise. Age: 33. Education: completed secondary education; incomplete university degree. One son, 18 months. Employment: at time of depression, not in paid work; prior to motherhood, secretary; at time of interview, not in paid work. Depression: onset, 3–4 weeks after the birth; duration, 11 months; medication, antidepressants for 4 months; health professionals seen, general practitioner, community psychiatric nurse; voluntary-sector support, Cry-sis, Association of Postnatal Illness, Meet-a-Mum Association. Previous experience of depression in her early twenties.

Marcia. Age: 36. Education: completed secondary education; journalism qualification. Employment: at time of depression, part-time public relations officer; at time of interview, part-time public relations officer. Two children: daughter, 7; son, 4. Depression: onset, a month after birth of second child; duration, 6 weeks; medication, none; health professionals seen, general practitioner. Previous experience of depression before having children.

Monica. Age: 20. Education: left school at 15; incomplete nanny training. Employment: at time of depression, not in paid work; prior to motherhood, nanny training; at time of interview, not in paid work. Two children: son, 3 years, 4 months; daughter, 2½. Depression: onset, soon after birth of second child; duration, 18 months; medication, none; health professionals seen, general practitioner; voluntary-sector support, postpartum depression support group.

Pam. Age: 26. Education: left school at 16; certificate in social care. Employment: at time of depression, part-time childcare provider; at time of interview, part-time childcare provider. One daughter, 4. Depression: onset, soon after birth; duration, 3 years; medication, antidepressants for 3 years; health professionals seen, general practitioner, psychiatrist; voluntary-sector support, postpartum depression support group.

Penny. Age: 31. Education: left school at 17. Employment: at time of depression, full-time accounts clerk; at time of interview, part-time childcare provider. One son, 2. Depression: onset, soon after the birth; duration, 16 months; medication, none; health professionals seen, general practitioner.

Petra. Age: 27. Education: left school at 16. Employment: at time of depression, full-time work consisting of several part-time jobs (clerical work, cleaning, sales assistant); at time of interview, not in paid work. One son, 21 months. Depression: onset, in pregnancy; duration, over 2 years—still feeling depressed at time of interview; medication, antidepressants for 2 months; health professionals seen, general practitioner, community psychiatric nurse, sex therapist; voluntary-sector support, postpartum depression support group.

Rachel. Age: 29. Education: completed secondary education; university degree. Employment: at time of depression, not in paid work; prior to motherhood, book illustrator; at time of interview, not in paid work. One daughter, 2. Depression: onset, soon after the birth; duration, 12 months; medication, tranquilizers for 12 months; health professionals seen, general practitioner, osteopath, herbalist, healer.

Sandra. Age: 35. Education: completed secondary education; nursing qualification. Employment: at time of depression, full-time nurse; at time of interview, full-time nurse. One daughter, 3½. Depression: onset, soon after the birth; duration, over 3 years—still feeling depressed at time of interview; medication, antidepressants for 1 month; health professionals seen, general practitioner, community psychiatric nurse, counselor, psychiatrist; voluntary-sector support: Association for Postnatal Illness.

Sonya. Age: 39. Education: completed secondary education; incomplete university degree. Employment: at time of depression, not in paid work; prior to motherhood, secretary; at time of interview, not in paid work. One daughter, 18 months. Depression: onset, 6 months after the birth; duration, 12 months—still feeling depressed at time of interview; medication, antidepressants for 12 months; health professionals seen, general practitioner, psychotherapist; voluntary-sector support, Association for Postnatal Illness. Previous experience of depression in her early twenties.

Sophie. Age: 31. Education: left school at 17. Employment: at time of depression, not in paid work; prior to motherhood, shop assistant and home-help; at time of interview, not in paid work. Three children (by 3 different partners), 12, 6, and 2. Depression: onset, 5 months after birth of second child; duration, 6 weeks; medication, antidepressants for 2 months; health professionals seen, general practitioner.

Tina. Age: 36. Education: left school at 16; secretarial qualification; enrolled in counseling course. Employment: at time of depression, not in paid work; prior to motherhood, word processor; at time of interview, part-time crèche worker. Three children: son, 10; daughters, 8 and 2. Depression: onset, soon after birth of third child; duration, 2 years; medication, antidepressants for 2 years; health professionals seen, general practitioner, therapist, couple's therapist. Previous experience of depression as a teenager.

Vera. Age: 28. Education: completed secondary education; pre-nursing qualification. Employment: at time of depression, not in paid work; prior to motherhood, nurse; at time of interview, not in paid work. One son, 2. Depression: onset, soon after the birth; duration, 8 months; medication, antidepressants for several months (she does not recall exactly how long); health professionals seen, general practitioner, community psychiatric nurse, psychiatrist; voluntary-sector support, postpartum depression support group.

listening to women's voices

FINDING THE WOMEN

My initial strategy for finding a group of women for my British research study was to write to members of two national organizations
concerned with mothers and their well-being—the National Childbirth Trust and Cry-sis—inviting them to take part in a study of
"women's experiences of becoming a mother and the wide range of
emotions that women feel during this time." I was inundated with responses, predominantly from middle-class women whose experiences
of motherhood were largely positive and unproblematic. In order to
find women who had experienced depression, I contacted a national
organization specifically concerned with postpartum psychological
problems, the Association for Postnatal Illness, and was given contact
information for a number of women. I also approached mothers directly at sites where they were likely to congregate—a mother-and-
toddler group and a health clinic in a public housing development—
seeking women who had been or were depressed. I also used snowball
sampling and asked women I had already interviewed to suggest other
mothers who might be willing to take part in the study.[1] I explicitly
stated that the study was about postpartum depression. Although I
initially feared that this approach would be off-putting to mothers
who were experiencing difficulties, it had the opposite effect of en-
couraging them to come forward. My initial silence over postpartum
depression, and apparent collusion in the myth of happy motherhood,

made it difficult for women to break their silence. Explicitly stating that my research concerned women with depression conveyed my interest in these women and created a safe space within which they could tell their stories.

ENCOURAGING VOICES

The style of interviewing I adopted was designed to encourage women to tell their stories. I began each interview with an open question: "Perhaps you would like to begin by telling me a bit about what motherhood has been like for you?" This enabled each mother to set her own agenda (within the limits and constraints of the interview situation and relationship), and raise issues of concern to her. This question usually prompted a lengthy monologue in which I was a responsive listener. I then used an interview guide (see Appendix 3) to encourage women to further elaborate on certain issues, or to address new questions.

The interviews brought back painful and upsetting memories. Several women were brought to tears in recounting their stories. On these occasions I switched off the tape recorder and offered to end the interview, although the women always asked for the interview to be continued either later that day or some days later. It was obvious that it was both distressing and helpful for the women to talk about their experiences. Many said that it was difficult to think back to the darkest moments of their depression, but they also said that it was therapeutic to talk about their feelings. Many said they had rarely spoken in such detail and depth about their experiences because few people were interested in hearing their stories.

Within these interviews I inquired about the circumstances and decision-making processes that led up to pregnancy and childbirth, the women's experiences of pregnancy and childbirth, and their feelings during the first few days after the birth, both in the hospital and at home. I asked about their expectations and experiences of motherhood, their emotional and psychological responses to it, and their thoughts and decisions about combining motherhood with paid work. I explored their relationships with male partners, parents, other relatives, friends, other mothers, neighbors, and acquaintances. I asked about the support they received from health professionals, alternative practitioners, and voluntary support groups, the extent to which they had recovered from their depression, and how motherhood and their experience of postpartum depression had changed them as individuals, as women, and as mothers.

The forty in-depth interviews I conducted ranged from one to six hours, lasting on average three and a half hours. The longer interviews were carried out over two visits. With the women's consent, all the interviews were tape-recorded and transcribed verbatim. I interviewed the mothers in their homes. The interviews took place in kitchens, sitting rooms, dining rooms, and in one case in the attic. I was offered cups of tea, cookies, and sometimes lunch. One or more children were usually present during the interviews, and sometimes male partners appeared intermittently. These interviews had to be fitted in and around women's domestic responsibilities, paid work, and community commitments. They record women's words about their lives as well the hubbub of everyday domestic life—washing machines spinning, children crying or screaming, dogs barking, oven timers beeping, doorbells ringing, telephones ringing, and friends and neighbors popping in.

A METHOD OF LISTENING

In analyzing the interview material I collected, I was seeking to understand how the women experienced, understood, and constructed motherhood and postpartum depression. I was not aiming to test any predefined theories, nor did I wish to impose any externally derived categories onto the women's accounts. Rather, I attempted to understand the women's meanings, subjectivities, and sense-making processes and use these as a basis for constructing my own theory and understanding of postpartum depression. At the same time, my methodological and theoretical framework was that of feminist relational psychology. I was interpreting the women's accounts through this perspective, which meant that I paid particular attention to relational issues, both cultural and interpersonal (see Chapter 1).

I used a range of methods to develop this grounded understanding of their experiences of motherhood and postpartum depression.[2] First, I used a version of the "voice-centered relational method" developed by the Harvard Project on Women's Psychology and Girls' Development.[3] This method entails reading and listening to an interview transcript at least four different times and in different ways. The first reading has two components. In the first element I read the interview for the plot. I listened for the overall story; the main events of each woman's experience of motherhood; the principal areas of difficulty and stress; and the key relationships in each woman's life. I also noted the recurring words, themes, and images women used to describe their experiences, and I looked for any contradictions in their stories.

In the second "reader-response" element of this first reading I read the woman's story "on my own terms" and attended to my intellectual and emotional response to the individual woman and her story. I considered the similarities and differences between each woman and myself. I reflected on how my understanding of their lives might be affected by the fact that I was a white, middle-class woman in my mid-twenties, without children, and discussed this issue with the women during the interview. I also explored how my relational lens was influencing my interpretation of their accounts.

In the second reading of the interview text, I listened for the first-person voice, for the voice of the "I." This reading centered my attention on the active "I" telling the story. It amplified the terms in which the woman saw and presented herself; it highlighted where she might be emotionally or intellectually struggling to say something; and it identified those places where she shifted between "I," "we," and "you," signaling changes in how she perceived and experienced herself. Spending this time carefully listening to each woman was critical because it allowed me to create a space between her way of speaking and seeing and my own, discovering how each woman "speaks of herself before we speak of her."[4]

Reading for the voice of the "I" was particularly valuable in pulling out what became a central issue in my understanding of postpartum depression, namely, that the women seemed caught between two voices that articulated different viewpoints and ways of assessing their feelings and experiences. One voice, or set of voices, reflected the mothers' idealized expectations of themselves, and their interpretations of cultural norms and values surrounding motherhood. This was a moral voice. It spoke about what women should feel, think, and do: "You should breast-feed," "You should be happy," "You should not be asking for help," "You should not be depressed," "You should look after your child full-time," it said. The other voice, or set of voices, seemed to be informed by the mother's concrete and everyday experiences of mothering her particular child, in the particular circumstances in which she found herself. This experiential voice questioned the moral voices: "Maybe it is understandable that I feel depressed given the circumstances in which I had a baby," "Perhaps it is unrealistic to think I should feel happy all the time," "Maybe going back to work would suit me because I enjoy my job."

In the third reading of women's interviews I listened for how the women spoke about their interpersonal relationships, both positive relationships and relationships in which they struggled to voice their thoughts, feelings, and needs. This third reading drew my attention to the interpersonal relational difficulties experienced by the women with depression.

In the fourth reading of the interview texts I placed the women's stories within the broader social, political, cultural, and structural contexts of their lives. I listened for places where their thoughts, feelings, decisions, and choices seemed to be constrained by these contexts. I was particularly interested in the ideological context of motherhood, and I looked for instances in which the women voiced, reflected, or resisted cultural norms and expectations of motherhood. I also listened for the women's use of moral language—cases where women spoke about what they felt they "should" or "ought" to do, about what was "wrong" and "right," "good" and "bad," and about their sense of failure, weakness, and inadequacy. It has been suggested that in using this type of language individuals are silencing a part of themselves and capitulating to debilitating cultural norms and values.[5] I took the use of these moral terms to indicate places in the women's stories where they were speaking in terms of, or through, cultural imperatives and prescriptions for how mothers should feel and behave. As noted above, these moral voices often conflicted with, and constrained, the women's concrete, everyday experiences of the lived reality of motherhood.

These four different readings of each woman's interview transcript emphasize the multilayered nature of the mothers' stories and trace different voices across and within a particular transcript. This approach is fundamentally different from the thematic-organization characteristic of many methods of analyzing interview texts. The method I used emphasizes the importance of getting to know individual stories in depth rather than "coding" the contents of these stories. Tracing voices through individual interviews, as opposed to linking themes across interviews, also heightened my awareness of the differences among the women. This method enabled me to understand the similarities between women's experiences of depression as well as the details of their different pathways into and out of postpartum depression. It highlighted the underlying processes of their depression—such as the conflict between women's expectations and experiences of motherhood, and their sense of individual failure in the face of this conflict—which all the women experienced despite the differences among them.[6]

After spending several months working with individual women's interviews in this way, I searched for different and common themes across the interviews as a whole. Many of these themes and sub-themes emerged as a direct result of the intensive case-study work, and others were taken from the interview guide. For example, one of the overarching themes was the women's interpersonal relationships. A sub-theme that emerged from the case-study work was the importance of women's relationships with other mothers.

I spent a total of seventeen months making sense of the women's stories. During that time I was part of a small research group, to which I brought my interview transcripts and interpretations. The group served as an "interpretive community" where colleagues shared their interpretations of my material and pointed to where I might have missed or glossed over what they regarded as key aspects of a particular woman's story.[7] This process made me acutely aware of my own role and power in interpreting the women's stories. It highlighted the reflexive and relational nature of the act of interpreting someone else's words. In particular, I was using a relational interpretive framework to make sense of the women's stories, and in this sense the interpretations came to reflect this interplay between the women's accounts and my own understanding of their accounts.[8] Indeed, this "joint construction of knowledge" is the hallmark of qualitative research.[9]

interview guide

Can I ask you why you felt that you wanted to take part in this study?[1]

Perhaps you could begin by telling a bit about what motherhood has been like for you?

1. Background Information

   [Age of the interviewee, her husband/partner, and her child/ children]

   [Family tree: parents and siblings (ages, occupations, marital status, children, where they live, frequency of contact)]

   Did your mother work when you were a child? How did you feel about this? Who looked after you while your mother was at work? What was that like?

   How would you describe your childhood and adolescence?

   [Educational history: age at leaving school; further training/ education]

   [Marital status: length of relationship and/or marriage; how couple met; decision to marry]

2. Pregnancy

(i) Getting pregnant

   How did you feel when you first found out that you were pregnant?

How did your husband/partner feel?

Was the baby planned?

If planned Was it a joint decision? Was it an easy decision? How was the decision timed? Was it something you and your husband/partner discussed a lot?

Had you always wanted to have children? And your husband/partner?

If unplanned [Contraception at the time]

Did you want to keep the baby? What about your husband/partner?

If unwanted Why did you decide to keep the baby? Who was involved in making the decision? Did you feel pressured by anyone to keep the baby?

Any previous pregnancies: miscarriage, abortion, still birth, child who died?

(ii) Being pregnant

How did you feel during your pregnancy?

Did you feel low at any time? Why was that?

Did you have any particular physical problems?

Did you attend any antenatal classes? Did your husband/partner attend any with you?

Did you find them useful or helpful? In what ways?

3. The Birth

What was the birth like?

Was your husband/partner present? Did you find him supportive?

Was the birth something that had worried you beforehand? Was it as you had expected?

How do you think you managed the birth? Did you feel in control of what was going on?

How did you feel about the baby being a boy/girl?

Did you breast- or bottle-feed? Is this what you had intended to do? Were there any problems? How long did you breastfeed?

4. Coming Home

How did you feel when you first came home?

Did your husband/partner take some time off after the baby was born? How long?

Was it important to you that he should/should not be around?
Was anyone else around when you came out of the hospital (e.g.,
    family, friends, neighbors)?
How did you feel about the support that you were getting?

5. Mental Health

If experience of depression postpartum:

(i) Feeling depressed

When did you start feeling low/unhappy/depressed?[2]
Did you have any physical symptoms (e.g., headaches, chest pains,
    migraines, pins and needles in the limbs, panic attacks)?
Had you been expecting to feel this way?
Can you explain why you felt so upset/low/depressed?

(ii) Past psychological difficulties

Have you experienced anything like this before?

(iii) Sources of information

Did someone tell you you had postnatal depression? Who?
Did *you* think you had postnatal depression?
Did you know about postnatal depression? What did you know
    about it?
Had you read/heard much about it? Where/from whom?
Was it mentioned in the prenatal classes, by your midwife, health
    visitor, or doctor?
Had you ever known anyone who had postnatal depression?
Were you happy with the amount of information you were given/
    came across about postnatal depression?
What is your understanding of the reasons some women get
    postnatal depression?

(iv) Support

Could you talk to anyone about how you felt? (husband/partner,
    family, friends, neighbors, doctor, health visitor) If no, why not?
What sort of help did you find most useful (e.g., an "official"
    source of help such as a doctor, health visitor, psychiatrist; other
    mothers in similar situations; emotional; practical; baby-sitting;
    recognition and understanding; just someone to talk to and to

listen; books, magazine articles, TV programs about postnatal depression)?

Was there any sort of help and support you would have wanted and did not receive?

Did you speak to any other mothers suffering from postnatal depression?

Did you think about joining a group for women with postnatal depression? Would you have liked to join such a group?

Overall, who would you say has helped you the most?

(v) Encounters with healthcare professionals

Did you see a doctor about your depression? How soon was that after you started feeling unwell?

Was the doctor helpful? In what ways?

Were you prescribed any medication (e.g., antidepressants, tranquilizers, sleeping pills)? How did you feel about this? Did it make you feel better?

Did you see a psychiatrist? Was she/he helpful and understanding?

Did it make any difference to you if your doctor/psychiatrist was a woman or a man?

If no experience of depression postpartum:

Did you feel at all low during the first few days after the birth?

Was postnatal depression something that you had thought about or feared before having the baby?

Did you know much about it? Where had you heard about it? (antenatal classes, books, TV, magazines, a friend/acquaintance who had it)

Do you know anyone who has had postnatal depression?

Do you have any ideas about why some mothers get postnatal depression?

6. Being a Mother

(i) Feelings about childcare

Had you had any previous experience with babies or children?

What is it you enjoy about looking after the baby?

What is it you dislike about looking after the baby?

Have you ever thought about harming the baby?

(ii) Self as mother

Before you had your child, were you concerned at all about your
ability to be a mother?
Before you became a mother, did you have a fixed idea about what
a mother ought to be like? Where did these ideas come from?
How satisfied are you with yourself as a mother? Do you think
that you are a good mother?
Do you compare yourself with other mothers?
Are there any particular mothers you could say you admire?
(mothers you think it would be nice to be more like?)
What kind of mother does your husband/partner think you are?
Do you think you have changed a lot since you became a mother?
In what ways?
Do you feel that by becoming a mother you are fulfilling
something within yourself?

(iii) Feelings about motherhood

Has motherhood turned out to be what you expected?
Is there anything you resent about being a mother (responsibility,
loneliness, loss of freedom)?
What do you enjoy most about being a mother?

(iv) Time alone

Do you manage to find time to yourself?
Do you have as much time to yourself as you would like?
What sort of things do you enjoy doing during this time?
How important to you is it that you find time to yourself?

7. Marital Relationship

(i) Changes in the relationship

Some mothers have mentioned that they feel their relationship
with their husband/partner changed during pregnancy and then
after the birth. Have you felt this? In what ways? When did you
first feel these changes? Has this worried you?
Were you able to talk to your husband/partner about these
changes?
Do you feel that having a child has improved your relationship in
any way?

(ii) Communication and emotional support

Are you able to talk to your husband/partner about how you are
feeling and about things that might be bothering you?
Does your husband/partner give you the emotional support that
you need and want?

(iii) Division of housework and childcare

Do you divide the housework and childcare with your husband/
partner? How do you divide it? (e.g., getting up in the night,
bathing, feeding, changing diapers, childcare) How has this
division changed since you had your child?
Are you happy with the amount your husband/partner does? Is this
what you expected? Was this something that you had discussed
before having the baby? Would you like him to do more? What
sort of things, specifically? Have you asked him to do more? Do
you think he should do more?
How do you think your husband/partner compares with other
fathers you know?
Does anyone else help you with the housework or with looking
after the child? Are you satisfied with that help?

(iv) Leisure time together

Do you have as much time on your own with your husband/
partner as you would like?
What do you do during that time?

8. Social Networks and Support

(i) Mapping of social networks

I would like you to draw a map of the people who are important to
you in your life at the moment. Put yourself in the middle of the page
and then draw the people close or far away from you, depending on
how important they are to you.[3]

[Nature of contact (does it revolve around the children, around the
couple, is it a one-to-one contact)]
[Frequency of contact]
To whom would you turn for advice about childcare?
For someone to baby-sit while you go out?

For material or financial help?

If you had a personal problem?

What kind of support have you found most helpful since you had the baby?

Overall, who would you say has offered you the most support since you had the baby?

How have these networks changed since you had the baby?

Did you find that you mixed more with other mothers once you became a mother yourself? How did you meet them? How often do you see them? What is it you value about your friendships with other mothers?

(ii) Your own mother

Has your mother been an important source of support? In what ways?

Has your relationship with your mother changed since you had a child? In what ways?

9. Employment Situation

(i) Antenatal employment history

[Occupation just before and during pregnancy]

[Hours of work/study]

[Reasons for working/studying (e.g., financial, social contact, intellectual stimulation)]

What did you enjoy most about work/studying?

[Stage in pregnancy when stopped work/studying]

Did you intend to return to work/study? How did your husband/partner feel about this?

How did you feel after you stopped working/studying? Did you miss work/study? What aspects?

(ii) Postnatal, and current, employment status and preferences

If currently employed/studying

[Resumed at what stage postpartum; hours; preferred employment/study status]

How did you decide to return to work (i.e., in whose terms)? Was it a difficult decision to make?

How did your husband/partner feel about your working/studying?

How does your husband/partner feel generally about mothers
   working/studying when their children are young?
[Childcare arrangements and satisfaction with these]
Ideally, what arrangement of paid work and childcare would you
   want for yourself and your husband/partner?

If not employed/studying

[Preferred employment/study status]
How did you make the decision (i.e. in whose terms)? How did
   your husband/partner feel about your staying at home/not going
   back to work/study?
How did/do you feel about being economically dependent?
Did/do you miss work/study? What aspects?
Ideally, what arrangement of paid work and childcare would you
   want for yourself and your husband/partner?

(iii) Combining employment and motherhood

Do you think it is important for a child to have one of his/her
   parents, rather than someone else, taking care of him/her during
   the day? Do you think it makes any difference whether that
   parent is the mother or the father?
Do you think it can be harmful to a child if the mother goes out to
   work? In what ways?
Do you think it can be good for some mothers if they go out to
   work? In what ways?

(iv) Future employment plans

10. Looking to the Future—Debriefing

Would you like to have another child? Is this something that you
   and your husband/partner have discussed?
Are there any things that you would want to do differently next
   time?
Is there anything that concerns you about having another child
   (e.g., further changes in the marital relationship; feeling
   depressed again)?

There's just a few factual details I'd like to ask you:

[Life events during pregnancy and postpartum period (e.g., moving house; death of family members, friends, pets; illness in family, among friends)]

[Housing conditions during and since pregnancy: house/flat; rented or owner-occupied, whether happy there, central heating, telephone, size, noise, neighbors, length of residence there]

[Financial situation/difficulties during and since pregnancy]

[Transportation: car or public transportation; frequency and efficiency of service; difficulties of using public transportation with a baby]

11. Conclusion

Is there anything else that we haven't spoken about that you would like to mention?

How did you feel about taking part in the interview?

notes

INTRODUCTION

1. For popular literature on difficulties in motherhood and on postpartum depression, see Vivienne Welburn, *Postnatal Depression* (London: Fontana, 1980); Carol Dix, *The New Mother Syndrome: Coping with Post-Natal Stress and Depression* (London: Allen and Unwin, 1986; first published in 1985); Maggie Comport, *Towards Happy Motherhood: Understanding Postnatal Depression* (London: Corgi, 1987); Jane Price, *Motherhood: What It Does to Your Mind* (London: Pandora, 1988); Fiona Marshall, *Coping with Postnatal Depression* (London: Sheldon Press, 1993); Ann Dunnewald and Diane G. Sanford, *The Postpartum Survival Guide: It Wasn't Supposed to Be Like This* (Oakland, Calif.: New Harbinger Publications, 1994); Karen R. Kleinman and Valerie D. Raskin, *This Isn't What I Expected* (New York: Bantam, 1994); Sally Placksin, *Mothering the New Mother: Your Postpartum Resource Companion* (New York: Newmarket, 1994); Siobhan Curham, *Antenatal and Postnatal Depression: Practical Advice and Support for All Sufferers* (London: Vermillion, 2000); Jane Feinmann, *Surviving the Baby Blues: Recognising, Understanding and Overcoming Postnatal Depression* (London: Ward Lock, 1997).
2. G. Combes and A. Schonveld, *Life Will Never Be the Same Again: A Review of Antenatal and Postnatal Health Education* (London: Health Education Authority, 1992).
3. Janet Stoppard, *Understanding Depression: Feminist Social Constructionist Approaches* (London and New York: Routledge, 2000).
4. R. York, "Pattern of Postpartum Blues," *Journal of Reproductive and Infant Psychology,* 8 (1990): 67–73.

5. R. E. Kendell, "Emotional and Physical Factors in the Genesis of Puerperal Mental Disorders," *Journal of Psychosomatic Research,* 29 (1985): 3–11.

6. James A. Hamilton, "The Identity of Postpartum Psychosis," in Ian F. Brockington and Ramesh Kumar, eds., *Motherhood and Mental Illness* (London: Academic Press, 1982).

7. B. Pitt, "'Atypical' Depression following Childbirth," *British Journal of Psychiatry,* 114 (1968): 1325–1335.

8. J. L. Cox, D. Murray, and G. Chapman, "A Controlled Study of the Onset, Duration and Prevalence of Postnatal Depression," *British Journal of Psychiatry,* 163 (1993): 27–31.

9. J. M. Green, "Postnatal Depression or Perinatal Dysphoria?" *Journal of Reproductive and Infant Psychology,* 16 (1998): 143–155.

10. R. Kumar and K. M. Robson, "A Prospective Study of Emotional Disorders in Childbearing Women," *British Journal of Psychiatry,* 144 (1984): 35–47.

11. David A. Karp, *Speaking of Sadness: Depression, Disconnection, and the Meanings of Illness* (New York and Oxford: Oxford University Press, 1996), p. 174.

12. "New Motherhood; for the Partum Blues, a Question of Whether to Medicate," *New York Times,* June 25, 2000.

13. Karp, *Speaking of Sadness,* p. 175.

14. Martha McMahon, *Engendering Motherhood: Identity and Self-Transformation in Women's Lives* (New York: Guilford Press, 1996); Sharon Hays, *The Cultural Contradictions of Motherhood* (New Haven and London: Yale University Press, 1996).

15. Evelyn N. Glenn, "Social Constructions of Mothering: A Thematic Overview," in Evelyn N. Glenn, Grace Cheng, and Linda R. Forcey, eds., *Mothering: Ideology, Experience, and Agency* (New York and London: Routledge, 1994), p. 11.

16. Jessica Benjamin, *The Bonds of Love* (London: Virago, 1990), p. 208.

17. A. Doucet, "Gender Equality and Gender Differences in Household Work and Parenting," *Women's Studies International Forum,* 18 (1995): 271–284.

18. Harriet Marshall, "The Social Construction of Motherhood: An Analysis of Childcare and Parenting Manuals," in Ann Phoenix, Anne Woollett, and Eva Lloyd, eds., *Motherhood: Meanings, Practices and Ideologies* (London: Sage, 1991), p. 73.

19. Hays, *The Cultural Contradictions of Motherhood.*

20. Natasha S. Mauthner, "Postpartum Depression: A Relational Perspective" (Ph.D. diss., University of Cambridge, 1994).

21. In Britain, a home healthcare provider, known as a health visitor, is a nurse who has responsibility for the welfare of mothers and children until the children are five years old. She visits families on a regular basis during pregnancy and in the months following childbirth.

22. See also Verta Taylor, *Rock-a-by Baby: Feminism, Self-Help, and Postpartum Depression* (New York and London: Routledge, 1996).

23. M. W. O'Hara and A. M. Swain, "Rates and Risk of Postpartum Depression—A Meta-Analysis," *International Review of Psychiatry,* 8 (1996): 37–54.

24. I met the American women as a participant observer in a postpartum depression support group they were attending, which meant I could not systematically collect their sociodemographic details.

25. For example, see N. S. Mauthner, "Postpartum Depression: The Significance of Social Contacts between Mothers," *Women's Studies International Forum,* 18 (1995): 311–323; N. S. Mauthner, "Suffering in Silence," *Association for Postnatal Illness Newsletter* (1996): 45; N. S. Mauthner, "Postnatal Depression: How Can Midwives Help?" *Midwifery,* 13 (1997): 163–171; N. S. Mauthner, "'It's a Woman's Cry for Help': A Relational Perspective on Postpartum Depression," *Feminism and Psychology,* 8 (1998): 325–355; N. S. Mauthner, "'Feeling Low and Feeling Really Bad about Feeling Low': Women's Experiences of Motherhood and Postpartum Depression," *Canadian Psychology,* 40 (1999): 143–161.

1. LIFTING THE VEIL OF SILENCE

1. To ensure anonymity, I have changed the names of the women, their partners, their children, and all individuals mentioned by them. In certain cases I have also changed some of the identifying characteristics of the women, and occasionally I have edited their words for the sake of clarity.

2. For example, see Lynne Murray, "Effects of Postnatal Depression on Infant Development: Direct Studies of Early Mother-Infant Interactions," in Ian F. Brockington and Ramesh Kumar, eds., *Motherhood and Mental Illness* (London: Academic Press, 1982); Lynne Murray, "The Cambridge Study of Postnatal Depression and Infant Development," in John L. Cox, Eugene S. Paykel, and M. L. Page, eds., *Childbirth as a Life Event* (Southampton: Duphar Medical Relations, 1989); L. Murray, "The Impact of Postnatal Depression on Infant Development," *Journal of Child Psychology and Psychiatry,* 33 (1992): 543–561; L. Murray and A. Stein, "Postnatal Depression and Infant Development," *British Medical Journal,* 302 (1991): 978–979; Lynne Murray and Peter Cooper, eds., *Postpartum Depression and Child Development* (London: The Guilford Press, 1997).

3. L. Murray and C. Cooper, "Effects of Postnatal Depression on Infant Development," *Archives of Disease in Childhood,* 77 (1997): 99–101.

4. Anne Woollett and Ann Phoenix, "Psychological Views of Mothering," in Ann Phoenix, Anne Woollett, and Eva Lloyd, eds., *Motherhood: Meanings, Practices and Ideologies* (London: Sage, 1991); E. Ann Kaplan, *Motherhood and Representation: The Mother in Popular Culture and Melodrama* (London and New York: Routledge, 1992); Jane Ribbens, *Mothers and Their Children: Towards a Feminist Perspective on Childrearing* (London: Sage, 1994).

5. On mothers as "shadowy figures" see Woollett and Phoenix, "Psychological Views of Mothering"; on mothers as "absent presence" see Kaplan, *Motherhood and Representation*.

6. Michael Rutter, "Commentary: Some Focus and Process Considerations Regarding the Effects of Postnatal Depression on Children," *Developmental Psychology,* 26 (1990): 60–67.

7. Edward Z. Tronick and Andrew F. Gianino, "The Transmission of Maternal Disturbance to the Infant," in Edward Z. Tronick and T. Field, eds., *Maternal Depression and Infant Disturbance* (San Francisco and London: Jossey-Bass, 1986).

8. Rozsika Parker, *Torn in Two: The Experience of Maternal Ambivalence* (London: Virago, 1995), p. 196.

9. Adam Phillips, *On Kissing, Tickling, and Being Bored* (Cambridge, Mass.: Harvard University Press, 1993).

10. For the purposes of discussing existing research on postpartum depression, I am drawing a distinction between the medical model of postpartum depression and social science perspectives. The former includes medical, psychiatric, and experimental psychological studies, which tend to adopt a quantitative, positivist approach. Social science perspectives include social psychological, sociological, and feminist studies located predominantly within a phenomenological and qualitative tradition. The boundaries between these traditions are, in one sense, becoming increasingly blurred. For example, "medical" researchers are beginning to show interest in the social and cultural context of motherhood and its influences on postpartum depression (see, for example, R. Kumar, "Postnatal Depression," *Maternal and Child Health,* 19 [1994]: 354–358; J. L. Cox, "Perinatal Mental Disorder—A Cultural Approach," *International Review of Psychiatry,* 8 [1996]: 9–16). There is a growing appreciation of the value and necessity of qualitative, ethnographic methods for understanding postpartum depression. This move parallels a shift within the fields of medicine and psychiatry more generally, in which the value of lay or subjective perspectives is being highlighted and the use of qualitative research is being legitimized (see, for example, N. Britten, "Qualitative Interviews in Medical Research," *British Medical Journal,* 311 [1995]: 251–253; C. Pope and N. Mays, "Reaching the Parts Other Methods Cannot Reach: An Introduction to Qualitative Methods in Health and Health Services Research," *British Medical Journal,* 311 [1995]: 42–45; K. Buston, W. Parry-Jones, M. Livingston, A. Bogan, and S. Wood, "Qualitative Research," *British Journal of Psychiatry,* 172 [1998]: 197–199; V. A. Entwistle, M. J. Renfrew, S. Yearley, J. Forrester, and T. Lamont, "Lay Perspectives: Advantages for Health Research," *British Medical Journal,* 316 [1998]: 463–466). In other words, researchers within both medical and social science traditions use quantitative and qualitative methods, and attend to individual and sociocultural contexts. However, I would argue that these two traditions still remain distinct because, in practice, they differ in the value

and status they accord to women's perspectives, in their views about the fundamental nature of mental health problems, and in the extent to which they regard them as either individual or sociocultural in origin.

11. M. W. O'Hara and A. M. Swain, "Rates and Risk of Postpartum Depression—A Meta-Analysis," *International Review of Psychiatry,* 8 (1996): 37–54; A. R. Lane, R. Keville, M. Morris, A. Kinsella, M. Turner, and S. Barry, "Postnatal Depression and Elation among Mothers and Their Partners: Prevalence and Predictors," *British Journal of Psychiatry,* 171 (1997): 550–555.

12. John Cox and Jeni Holden, *Perinatal Psychiatry: Use and Misuse of the Edinburgh Postpartum Depression Scale* (London: Gaskell, 1994).

13. E. S. Paykel, E. M. Emms, J. Fletcher, and E. S. Rassaby, "Life Events and Social Support in Puerperal Depression," *British Journal of Psychiatry,* 136 (1980): 339–346, quote p. 340.

14. Ibid., p. 340.

15. R. D. Laing and Aaron Esterson, *Sanity, Madness and the Family* (Harmondsworth: Penguin Books, 1986; first published in 1964); Erving Goffman, *Asylums* (London: Penguin Books, 1987; first published in 1961).

16. B. Pitt, "'Atypical' Depression following Childbirth," *British Journal of Psychiatry,* 114 (1968): 1325–1335; J. Hopkins, S. B. Campbell, and M. Marcus, "Role of Infant-Related Stressors in Postpartum Depression," *Journal of Abnormal Psychology,* 96 (1987): 237–241.

17. J. M. Green, "'Who Is Unhappy after Childbirth?': Antenatal and Intrapartum Correlates from a Prospective Study," *Journal of Reproductive and Infant Psychology,* 8 (1990): 175–183; R. S. Small, S. Brown, J. Lumley, and J. Astbury, "Missing Voices: What Women Say and Do about Depression after Childbirth," *Journal of Reproductive and Infant Psychology,* 12 (1994): 89–103.

18. For reviews of some of these studies see M. W. O'Hara and E. M. Zekoski, "Postpartum Depression: A Comprehensive Review," in Ramesh Kumar and Ian F. Brockington, eds., *Motherhood and Mental Illness 2: Causes and Consequences* (London: Wright, 1988); O'Hara and Swain, "Rates and Risk of Postpartum Depression."

19. N. S. Mauthner, "Re-assessing the Importance and Role of the Marital Relationship in Postnatal Depression: Methodological and Theoretical Implications," *Journal of Reproductive and Infant Psychology,* 16 (1998): 157–175.

20. O'Hara and Swain, "Rates and Risk of Postpartum Depression."

21. Katharina Dalton, *Depression after Childbirth: How to Recognize and Treat Postnatal Depression* (Oxford: Oxford University Press, 1989; first published in 1980).

22. Research on the hormonal etiology and treatment of postpartum depression is extensive (for a review see J. Wang, F. R. de Boer, C. Zhang, E. Bruck, N. Tang, F. T. Yang, M. Abou-Saleh, R. Ghubash, L. Karim, M. Krymski, and I. Bai, "Hormonal Aspects of Postpartum Depression," *Psychoneuroendocrinology,* 23 [1998]: 465–475). It explores links between postpartum de-

pression and a history of premenstrual mood change (see Pitt, "'Atypical' Depression following Childbirth"; K. Dalton, "Prospective Study into Puerperal Depression," *British Journal of Psychiatry,* 118 [1971]: 689–692); other biochemicals such as monoamines (see Merton Sandler, ed., *Mental Illness in Pregnancy and the Puerperium* [Oxford: Oxford University Press, 1978]); plasma concentrations of the steroid cortisol (see S. L. Handley, T. L. Dunn, G. Waldron, and J. M. Baker, "Tryptophan, Cortisol and Puerperal Mood," *British Journal of Psychiatry,* 136 [1980]: 498–506); and thyroid depletion (see S. Clayton, "Postpartum Thyroiditis—An Undiagnosed Disease," *British Journal of Obstetrics and Gynaecology,* 93 [1986]: 1121–1123). Several cross-cultural studies have been carried out in an attempt to evaluate the relative contributions of biological and cultural factors (for example, Y-C. Huang and N. Mathers, "Postnatal Depression—Biological or Cultural? A Comparative Study of Postnatal Depression in the UK and Taiwan," *Journal of Advanced Nursing,* 33 [2001]: 279–297). Some studies have also investigated hormonal treatments for postpartum depression, with some suggesting that estrogen may be an effective treatment (see A. J. P. Gregoire, R. Kumar, B. Everitt, A. F. Henderson, and J. W. W. Studd, "Transdermal Oestrogen for Treatment of Severe Postnatal Depression," *International Journal of Gynecology and Obstetrics,* 55 [1996]: 88). Overall, however, these studies indicate mixed and inconclusive results, and there is little evidence for any direct or indirect links between postpartum depression and hormones (A. Gregoire, "Hormones and Postnatal Depression," *British Journal of Midwifery,* 3 [1994]: 99–104). Furthermore, the mechanisms by which biochemical or hormonal changes affect the mother's mood are rarely explained. For example, all mothers experience these hormonal changes but only some become depressed. Postpartum depression can develop any time within the first twelve months after the birth and can persist over time, long after the mother's body has physiologically recovered from childbirth. The hormonal theory is also difficult to square with evidence suggesting that postpartum depression is not an experience restricted to the biological mother. Fathers, grandmothers, and adoptive parents are said to experience depression following birth or adoption (see S. S. Asch and L. J. Rubin, "Postpartum Reactions: Some Unrecognized Variations," *American Journal of Psychiatry,* 131 [1974]: 870–874; A. Atkinson and A. Rickel, "Postpartum Depression in Primiparous Parents," *Journal of Abnormal Psychology,* 93 [1984]: 115–119; D. Quadagno, L. Dixon, N. Denney, and H. Buck, "Postpartum Moods in Men and Women," *American Journal of Obstetrics and Gynecology,* 154 [1986]: 1018–1023; J. A. Richman, V. D. Raskin, and C. Gaines, "Gender Roles, Social Support, and Postpartum Depressive Symptomatology: The Benefits of Caring," *Journal of Nervous and Mental Disease,* 179 [1991]: 139–147; C. G. Ballard, R. Davis, P. C. Cullen, R. N. Mohan, and C. Dean, "Prevalence of Postnatal Psychiatric Morbidity in Mothers and Fathers," *British Journal of Psychiatry,* 164 [1994]: 782–788; S. Gair, "Postnatal Depression and the Birthing Process: Contrary Evidence from the Experience of Adoptive Mothers," *Australian Social Work,* 47 [1994]: 37–42; S. Gair, "Distress and Depression in New Motherhood: Research with Adoptive Mothers Highlights Important Contributing Factors," *Child and Family Social Work,* 4 [1999]: 55–66).

23. Susan P. Penfold and Gillian A. Walker, *Women and the Psychiatric Paradox* (Montreal: Eden Press, 1983); Elaine Showalter, *The Female Malady: Women, Madness and English Culture, 1830–1980* (London: Virago, 1987; first published in 1985); Jane M. Ussher, *Women's Madness: Misogyny or Mental Illness?* (Hemel Hempstead: Harvester Wheatsheaf, 1991).

24. Dalton, *Depression after Childbirth,* p. 27.

25. Ibid., p. 20.

26. Ibid., p. 40.

27. C. T. Beck, "The Lived Experience of Postpartum Depression: A Phenomenological Study," *Nursing Research,* 41 (1992): 166–170; C. T. "Teetering on the Edge: A Substantive Theory of Postpartum Depression," *Nursing Research,* 42 (1993): 42–48; J. McIntosh, "Postpartum Depression: Women's Help-Seeking Behaviour and Perceptions of Cause," *Journal of Advanced Nursing,* 18 (1993): 178–184; Small, Brown, Lumley, and Astbury, "Missing Voices."

28. On feminist analyses of postpartum depression, see Ann Oakley, *Women Confined: Towards a Sociology of Childbirth* (Oxford: Martin Robertson, 1980); Patrizia Romito, *La Naissance du Premier Enfant: Étude Psychosociale de L'Expérience de la Maternité et de la Dépression Post-partum* (Lausanne: Delachaux and Niestle, 1990); Verta Taylor, *Rock-a-by Baby: Feminism, Self-Help, and Postpartum Depression* (New York and London: Routledge, 1996); Paula Nicolson, *Post-Natal Depression: Psychology, Science and the Transition to Motherhood* (London: Routledge, 1998); Janet Stoppard, *Understanding Depression: Feminist Social Constructionist Approaches* (London and New York: Routledge, 2000). On broader feminist critiques of psychiatry and medicine, see Ussher, *Women's Madness;* Janet Stoppard, "Women's Bodies, Women's Lives and Depression: Toward a Reconciliation of Materialist and Discursive Accounts," in Jane Ussher, ed., *Body Talk: The Material and Discursive Regulation of Sexuality, Madness and Reproduction* (London: Routledge, 1997); J. Stoppard, "Dis-ordering Depression in Women: Toward a Materialist-Discursive Account," *Theory and Psychology,* 8 (1998): 79–99.

29. Oakley, *Women Confined;* Romito, *La Naissance du Premier Enfant;* Nicolson, *Post-Natal Depression.*

30. Oakley, *Women Confined;* Nicolson, *Post-Natal Depression.*

31. Nicolson, *Post-Natal Depression,* p. 109.

32. Ibid., p. 695.

33. Stoppard, *Understanding Depression,* p. 140.

34. Paula Nicolson, "Developing a Feminist Approach to Depression following

Childbirth," in Sue Wilkinson, ed., *Feminist Social Psychology: Developing Theory and Practice* (Milton Keynes: Open University Press, 1986); Ann Oakley, *Telling the Truth about Jerusalem* (Oxford: Blackwell, 1986); Patrizia Romito, "Unhappiness after Childbirth," in Iain Chalmers, Murray Enkin, and Marc J. N. C. Keirse, eds., *Effective Care in Pregnancy and Childbirth*, vol. 2 (Oxford: Oxford University Press, 1989).

35. Taylor, *Rock-a-by Baby*; Stoppard, *Understanding Depression*.

36. Taylor, *Rock-a-by Baby*.

37. Oakley, *Women Confined*; Stoppard, *Understanding Depression*.

38. Taylor, *Rock-a-by Baby*.

39. Adrienne Rich, *Of Woman Born: Motherhood as Experience and Institution* (London: Virago, 1986; first published in 1977); Rozsika Parker, *Torn in Two: The Experience of Maternal Ambivalence* (London: Virago, 1995); Wendy Hollway and Brid Featherstone, *Mothering and Ambivalence* (London and New York: Routledge, 1997).

40. Sue Wilkinson, *Feminist Social Psychologies: International Perspectives* (Buckingham: Open University Press, 1996), p. 13.

41. For relational work on boys and men see S. J. Bergman, *Men's Psychological Development: A Relational Perspective*, Work in Progress, no. 48 (Wellesley, Mass.: Stone Center Working Paper Series, 1991); S. J. Bergman and J. Surrey, *The Woman-Man Relationship: Impasses and Possibilities*, Work in Progress, no. 55 (Wellesley, Mass.: Stone Center Working Paper Series, 1992); Niobe Way, *Everyday Courage: The Lives and Stories of Urban Teenagers* (New York: New York University Press, 1998).

42. Judith V. Jordan, *Women's Growth in Diversity* (New York: Guilford Press, 1997).

43. Jean Baker Miller, *Toward a New Psychology of Women* (London: Penguin Books, 1986; first published in 1976); C. Gilligan, "In a Different Voice: Women's Conceptions of Self and of Morality," *Harvard Educational Review*, 47 (1977): 481–517; Carol Gilligan, *In a Different Voice: Psychological Theory and Women's Development* (Cambridge, Mass.: Harvard University Press, 1982).

44. Ian Burkitt, *Social Selves: Theories of the Social Formation of Personality* (London: Sage, 1991), p. 1.

45. The notion of humans as intrinsically social and relational beings has been put forward by scholars within other theoretical traditions (see Burkitt, *Social Selves*), including: symbolic interactionism (see George Herbert Mead, "The Genesis of the Self and Social Control," in A. J. Reck, ed., *Selected Writings: George Herbert Mead* [Chicago: Chicago University Press, 1924]); developmental psychology (see Daniel Stern, *The First Relationship: Mother and Infant* [Cambridge, Mass.: Harvard University Press, 1977]; Colwyn Trevarthen, "Descriptive Analyses of Infant Communicative Behaviour," in H. Rudolph Schaffer, ed., *Studies in Mother-Infant Interaction* [New York: Academic Press, 1977]; John Bowlby, *Attachment and Loss. Volume II. Loss:*

Sadness and Depression [London: The Hogarth Press, 1980]; Robert Emde, "Levels of Meaning for Infant Emotions: A Biosocial View," in W. Andrew Collins, ed., *Development of Cognition, Affect, and Social Relations* [Hillsdale, N.J.: Lawrence Erlbaum Associates, 1980]); feminist political theory and philosophy, including work on the "ethic of care" (see Sara Ruddick, *Maternal Thinking: Toward a Politics of Peace* [Boston, Mass.: Beacon, 1989]; Seyla Benhabib, *Situating the Self* [Cambridge: Polity Press, 1992]; J. Tronto, "Care as a Basis for Radical Political Judgements," *Hypatia*, 10 [1995]: 141–149); and in legal theory as a discussion of relational rights and responsibilities (see M. Minow and M. L. Shanley, "Relational Rights and Responsibilities: Revisioning the Family in Liberal Political Theory and Law," *Hypatia*, 11 [1996]: 4–29).

46. Gilligan, *In a Different Voice.*
47. Miller, *Toward a New Psychology of Women*, p. 83.
48. J. B. Miller, J. V. Jordan, A. G. Kaplan, I. P. Stiver, and J. L. Surrey, *Some Misconceptions and Reconceptions of a Relational Approach*, Work in Progress, no. 49 (Wellesley, Mass.: Stone Center Working Paper Series, 1991), p. 5.
49. J. L. Surrey, *The 'Self-in-Relation': A Theory of Women's Development*, Work in Progress, no. 13 (Wellesley, Mass.: Stone Center Working Paper Series, 1985).
50. Dana Jack, *Silencing the Self: Depression and Women* (Cambridge, Mass.: Harvard University Press, 1991).
51. A. G. Kaplan, *The 'Self-in-Relation': Implications for Depression in Women*, Work in Progress, no. 14 (Wellesley, Mass.: Stone Center Working Paper Series, 1984); I. P. Stiver and J. B. Miller, *From Depression to Sadness in Women's Psychotherapy*, Work in Progress, no. 36 (Wellesley, Mass.: Stone Center Working Paper Series, 1988); Jack, *Silencing the Self;* Catherine Steiner-Adair, "The Body Politic," in Carol Gilligan, Nona P. Lyons, and Trudy J. Hanmer, eds., *Making Connections: The Relational Worlds of Adolescent Girls at Emma Willard School* (Cambridge, Mass.: Harvard University Press, 1990); Ann Willard, "Cultural Scripts of Mothering," in Carol Gilligan, Janie V. Ward, and Jill M. Taylor, eds., *Mapping the Moral Domain: A Contribution of Women's Thinking to Psychological Theory and Education* (Cambridge, Mass.: Harvard University Press, 1988).
52. Stiver and Miller, *From Depression to Sadness;* Jack, *Silencing the Self;* Lyn M. Brown and Carol Gilligan, *Meeting at the Crossroads: Women's Psychology and Girls' Development* (Cambridge, Mass.: Harvard University Press, 1992); Jill M. Taylor, Carol Gilligan, and Amy Sullivan, *Between Voice and Silence: Women and Girls, Race and Relationships* (Cambridge, Mass.: Harvard University Press, 1995).
53. Jean B. Miller, Irene P. Stiver, Judith V. Jordan, and Janet L. Surrey, "The Psychology of Women: A Relational Approach," in James Fadiman and Robert Frager, eds., *Personality and Personal Growth* (New York: Longman, 1994).
54. Ibid., pp. 167–168.

55. Ibid., p. 170.
56. David A. Karp, *Speaking of Sadness: Depression, Disconnection, and the Meanings of Illness* (New York and Oxford: Oxford University Press, 1996), p. 15.

2. THE LANDSCAPE OF MOTHERHOOD

1. The National Childbirth Trust (NCT) was first established in 1956 to promote Grantly Dick Read's teachings about childbirth. It is now the largest British lay organization concerned with childbirth. It runs prenatal classes, postnatal groups, and offers a wide range of support services to parents, including advice on breast-feeding, groups for parents of twins and other multiples, and support for women experiencing postpartum depression. For further details on the history and current organization of the NCT see Jenny Kitzinger, "Strategies of the Early Childbirth Movement: A Case-Study of the National Childbirth Trust," in Jo Garcia, Robert Kilpatrick, and Martin Richards, eds., *The Politics of Maternity Care: Services for Childbearing Women in Twentieth-Century Britain* (Oxford: Oxford University Press, 1990).
2. Rozsika Parker, *Torn in Two: The Experience of Maternal Ambivalence* (London: Virago, 1995); Wendy Hollway and Brid Featherstone, *Mothering and Ambivalence* (London and New York: Routledge, 1997).
3. Verta Taylor, *Rock-a-by Baby: Feminism, Self-Help, and Postpartum Depression* (New York and London: Routledge, 1996), p. 153.
4. J. L. Cox, "Postnatal Depression: A Serious and Neglected Postpartum Complication," *Baillere's Clinical Obstetrics and Gynaecology,* 3 (1989): 839–855; J. M. Green, "Postnatal Depression or Perinatal Dysphoria?" *Journal of Reproductive and Infant Psychology,* 16 (1998): 143–155; P. Nicolson and W. Woollett, "Postnatal Depression: Context and Experience," *Journal of Reproductive and Infant Psychology,* 16 (1998): 85–89.
5. American Psychiatric Association, *Diagnostic and Statistical Manual of Disorders, 4th ed.* (Washington, D.C.: American Psychiatric Association, 1994); World Health Organization, *ICD-10* (Geneva: WHO, 1992).
6. Martha McMahon, *Engendering Motherhood: Identity and Self-Transformation in Women's Lives* (New York: Guilford Press, 1996), p. 8.
7. Nancy Chodorow and Susan Contratto, "The Fantasy of the Perfect Mother," in Barrie Thorne and Marilyn Yalom, eds., *Rethinking the Family* (New York and London: Longman, 1982); Lynn Segal, *Is the Future Female: Troubled Thoughts on Contemporary Feminism* (London: Virago, 1987); A. Snitow, "Feminism and Motherhood: An American Reading," *Feminist Review,* 40 (1992): 32–51.
8. Evelyn N. Glenn, "Social Constructions of Mothering: A Thematic Overview," in Evelyn N. Glenn, Grace Cheng, and Linda R. Forcey, eds., *Mothering: Ideology, Experience, and Agency* (New York and London: Routledge, 1994), pp. 22–23.

9. Chodorow and Contratto, "The Fantasy of the Perfect Mother"; Glenn, "Social Constructions of Mothering"; Jane Ribbens, *Mothers and Their Children: Towards a Feminist Perspective on Childrearing* (London: Sage, 1994); Parker, *Torn in Two.*

10. Evelyn N. Glenn, Grace Cheng, and Linda R. Forcey, eds., *Mothering: Ideology, Experience, and Agency* (New York and London: Routledge, 1994).

11. Ann Oakley, *Essays on Women, Medicine and Health* (Edinburgh: Edinburgh University Press, 1993), p. 85.

12. Paula Nicolson, *Post-Natal Depression: Psychology, Science and the Transition to Motherhood* (London: Routledge, 1998), p. 8.

13. McMahon, *Engendering Motherhood,* p. 268.

14. Mary G. Boulton, *On Being a Mother: A Study of Women with Preschool Children* (London: Tavistock, 1983); Lydia O'Donnell, *The Unheralded Majority: Contemporary Women as Mothers* (Lexington, Mass.: Lexington Books, 1985); L. Bell and J. Ribbens, "Isolated Housewives and Complex Maternal Worlds—The Significance of Social Contacts between Women with Young Children in Industrial Societies," *Sociological Review,* 42 (1994): 227–262; Parker, *Torn in Two.*

15. This is why feminists have, for some time, been advocating and putting into practice "reflexivity"—critical thinking about the links between our private lives and our research (see A. Doucet, "Interpreting Mother-Work: Linking Methodology, Ontology, Theory and Personal Biography," *Canadian Women Studies,* 18 [1998]: 52–58; Natasha S. Mauthner and Andrea Doucet, "Reflections on a Voice-Centred Relational Method: Analysing Maternal and Domestic Voices," in Jane Ribbens and Rosalind Edwards, eds., *Feminist Dilemmas in Qualitative Research: Public Knowledge and Private Lives* [London: Sage, 1998]; N. S. Mauthner, O. Parry, and K. Backett-Milburn, "The Data Are out There, or Are They? Implications for Archiving and Revisiting Qualitative Data," *Sociology,* 32 [1998]: 733–745). For example, in *Engendering Motherhood,* Martha McMahon points out that representations of motherhood, including in academic work, are often implicit representations of personal and collective identities.

16. Ann Oakley, *Becoming a Mother* (Oxford: Martin Robertson, 1979), p. 6.

17. Jonathan Smith, "Pregnancy and the Transition to Motherhood," in Paula Nicolson and Jane Ussher, eds., *The Psychology of Women's Health and Health Care* (London: Macmillan, 1992).

18. K. Paradice, "Postnatal Depression: A Normal Response to Motherhood?" *British Journal of Midwifery,* 3 (1995): 632–635, quote p. 632.

19. T. G. Arizmendi and D. D. Affonso, "Research on Psychosocial Factors and Postpartum Depression: A Critique," *Birth,* 11 (1984): 237–240; J. McIntosh, "Postpartum Depression: Women's Help-Seeking Behaviour and Perceptions of Cause," *Journal of Advanced Nursing,* 18 (1993).

20. Whether postpartum depression is regarded as normal or not partly depends on how it is defined, and to what range of feelings and experiences the label is applied. In particular, the label can be used to describe any form of low

mood, or it can be used to describe only the more severe end of the spectrum, which is generally regarded as clinical depression (see George W. Brown and Tirril Harris, *Social Origins of Depression* [London: Tavistock, 1978]; James C. Coyne, "Ambiguity and Controversy: An Introduction," in James C. Coyne, ed., *Essential Papers on Depression* [New York: New York University Press, 1985]; I. P. Stiver and J. B. Miller, *From Depression to Sadness in Women's Psychotherapy*, Work in Progress, no. 36 [Wellesley, Mass.: Stone Center Working Paper Series, 1988]). A possible reason some feminist scholars argue that postpartum depression is a normal response to motherhood is that they have used the term *postpartum depression* in a broad and inclusive way. Indeed, these scholars recognize that the term *depression* is used by mothers to describe different experiences and feelings, but they do not refer to these distinctions within their models of postpartum depression (see Ann Oakley, *Women Confined: Towards a Sociology of Childbirth* [Oxford: Martin Robertson, 1980]; Patrizia Romito, *La Naissance du Premier Enfant: Étude Psycho-sociale de L'Expérience de la Maternité et de la Dépression Post-partum* [Lausanne: Delachaux and Niestle, 1990]; Paula Nicolson, "The Social Psychology of 'Postnatal Depression'" [Ph.D. diss., London School of Economics, 1988]). Yet it is not clear whether the women in these studies were experiencing postpartum depression or simply feelings of low mood. The fact that these studies were longitudinal suggests that only about one in ten of the women would be expected to develop postpartum depression. This represents a small number of women in these studies. It might be that these studies focused mainly on women experiencing low mood rather than more debilitating forms of depression. If this is the case, then their argument that women are not necessarily happy when they have a baby, and that the expression of a range of emotions should be regarded as normal, makes sense. It also follows that these studies may have failed to adequately address women's experiences of postpartum depression.

21. Brown and Harris, *Social Origins of Depression;* Dorothy Rowe, *Depression: The Way Out of Your Prison* (London: Routledge, 1983); Kathy Nairne and Gerrilyn Smith, *Dealing with Depression* (London: The Women's Press, 1984); Stiver and Miller, *From Depression to Sadness.*

22. Coyne, "Ambiguity and Controversy," p. 3.

23. Stiver and Miller, *From Depression to Sadness,* p. 2.

24. Ibid., p. 4.

25. A. G. Kaplan, *The "Self-in-Relation": Implications for Depression in Women*, Work in Progress, no. 14 (Wellesley, Mass.: Stone Center Working Paper Series, 1984); T. Bernardez, *Women and Anger—Cultural Prohibitions and the Feminine Ideal,* Work in Progress, no. 31 (Wellesley, Mass.: Stone Center Working Paper Series, 1988); N. M. Fedele and E. A. Harrington, *Women's Groups: How Connections Heal,* Work in Progress, no. 47 (Wellesley, Mass.: Stone Center Working Paper Series, 1990); Dana Jack, *Silencing the Self: Depression and Women* (Cambridge, Mass.: Harvard University Press, 1991).

26. Stiver and Miller, *From Depression to Sadness*, p. 4.
27. See Parker, *Torn in Two*.

3. THE PERFECT MOTHER

1. Ann Willard, "Cultural Scripts of Mothering," in Carol Gilligan, Janie V. Ward, and Jill M. Taylor, eds., *Mapping the Moral Domain: A Contribution of Women's Thinking to Psychological Theory and Education* (Cambridge, Mass.: Harvard University Press, 1988).
2. Elizabeth Badinter, *The Myth of Motherhood: An Historical View of the Maternal Instinct* (London: Souvenir Press, 1981); Denise Riley, *War in the Nursery: Theories of the Child and Mother* (London: Virago, 1983); Patricia H. Collins, *Black Feminist Thought: Knowledge, Consciousness, and the Politics of Empowerment* (London: Routledge, 1990).
3. Evelyn N. Glenn, Grace Cheng, and Linda R. Forcey, eds., *Mothering: Ideology, Experience, and Agency* (New York and London: Routledge, 1994).
4. Ibid.; Martha McMahon, *Engendering Motherhood: Identity and Self-Transformation in Women's Lives* (New York: Guilford Press, 1996); Sharon Hays, *The Cultural Contradictions of Motherhood* (New Haven and London: Yale University Press, 1996).
5. Hays, *The Cultural Contradictions of Motherhood*.
6. Harriet Marshall, "The Social Construction of Motherhood: An Analysis of Childcare and Parenting Manuals," in Ann Phoenix, Anne Woollett, and Eva Lloyd, eds., *Motherhood: Meanings, Practices nd Ideologies* (London: Sage, 1991).
7. On the fantasy of the perfect mother see Nancy Chodorow and Susan Contratto, "The Fantasy of the Perfect Mother," in Barrie Thorne and Marilyn Yalom, eds., *Rethinking the Family* (New York and London: Longman, 1982).
8. McMahon, *Engendering Motherhood*.
9. On the ideology of privatized caring see McMahon, *Engendering Motherhood*, p. 261. The construction of childcare as primarily women's personal responsibility also renders caregiving work invisible and valueless, and means that other types of childcare are seen as inferior to privatized nuclear families and consequently receive little structural support (ibid.).
10. Ibid., p. 270.
11. Sigmund Freud, "Mourning and Melancholia," in Edward Jones, ed., *Collected Papers, Volume IV: Papers on Metapsychology. Papers on Applied Psycho-Analysis* (London: Hogarth Press, 1995; first published in 1917), p. 157.
12. Dana Jack, *Silencing the Self: Depression and Women* (Cambridge, Mass.: Harvard University Press, 1991), p. 94.
13. McMahon, *Engendering Motherhood;* Hays, *The Cultural Contradictions of Motherhood*.
14. D. S. Gruen, "Postpartum Depression: A Debilitating yet Often Unassessed

Problem," *Health and Social Work,* 15 (1990): 261–270; G. Combes and A. Schonveld, *Life Will Never Be the Same Again: A Review of Antenatal and Postnatal Health Education* (London: Health Education Authority, 1992); Kathleen A. Kendall-Tackett with Glenda Kaufman Kantor, *Postpartum Depression: A Comprehensive Approach for Nurses* (Newbury Park: Sage, 1993).

15. See also Combes and Schonveld, *Life Will Never Be the Same Again.*

16. Ibid., p. 96; see also Gruen, "Postpartum Depression."

17. Combes and Schonveld, *Life Will Never Be the Same Again,* p. 96.

18. S. A. Elliott, M. Sanjack, and T. J. Leverton, "Parent Groups in Pregnancy: A Preventive Intervention for Postnatal Depression?" in Benjamin H. Gottlieb, ed., *Marshaling Social Support: Formats, Processes and Effects* (Calif.: Sage, 1988); J. L. Cox, "Postnatal Depression: A Serious and Neglected Postpartum Complication," *Baillere's Clinical Obstetrics and Gynaecology,* 3 (1989): 839–855; Gruen, "Postpartum Depression."

19. It is worth pointing out, however, that only a minority of women (15–28 percent) attend a full, or nearly full, program of prenatal classes (Combes and Schonveld, *Life Will Never Be the Same Again*). These women are most likely to be first-time, older parents with higher self-esteem and socioeconomic status than other mothers (ibid.; M. Langer, B. Czermak, and M. Ringler, "Couple Relationship, Birth Preparation and Pregnancy Outcome: A Prospective Controlled Outcome Study," *Journal of Perinatal Medicine,* 18 [1990]: 201–208).

20. Adrienne Rich, *Of Woman Born: Motherhood as Experience and Institution* (London: Virago, 1986; first published in 1977), p. 23.

21. S. Prendergast and A. Prout, "What Will I Do . . . ? Teenage Girls and the Construction of Motherhood," *Sociological Review,* 28 (1980): 517–535, quote p. 524.

22. Dana Breen, *The Birth of a First Child* (London: Tavistock, 1975), p. 192.

23. Hays, *The Cultural Contradictions of Motherhood.*

24. For example, Ann Oakley describes women as "helpless victim[s]" of medical control and the institution of motherhood (see Ann Oakley, *Women Confined: Towards a Sociology of Childbirth* [Oxford: Martin Robertson, 1980], p. 271). The possibility that women might engage with, and resist, the social context is also denied, as Oakley clearly states: "both medical control and [women's] subordinate group status militate against self-determination and encourage helplessness" (ibid., p. 272). Paula Nicolson also sees women as "passive objects," victims of patriarchal society who "on an unconscious level . . . accept the dominant ideology: that mothering and loss of personal autonomy is the 'natural' female experience" (see Paula Nicolson, "Towards a Psychology of Women's Health and Health Care," in Paula Nicolson and Jane Ussher, eds., *The Psychology of Women's Health and Health Care* [London: Macmillan, 1992], p. 27). Nicolson argues that the "internalization of passivity . . . is central to understanding the psychology of women's health" (ibid., p. 9). Women, she suggests, are regulated by and subjected to medical

discourses of postpartum depression (see Paula Nicolson, "Explanations of Postpartum Depression: Structuring Knowledge of Female Psychology," *Research on Language and Social Interaction,* 25 [1991/92]: 75–96).

25. Verta Taylor, *Rock-a-by Baby: Feminism, Self-Help, and Postpartum Depression* (New York and London: Routledge, 1996).

4. KEEPING UP APPEARANCES

1. Carol Gilligan, "Prologue: Adolescent Development Reconsidered," in Carol Gilligan, Janie V. Ward, and Jill M. Taylor, eds., *Mapping the Moral Domain: A Contribution of Women's Thinking to Psychological Theory and Education* (Cambridge, Mass.: Harvard University Press, 1988), p. xxiii.

2. Dana Jack, *Silencing the Self: Depression and Women* (Cambridge, Mass.: Harvard University Press, 1991), p. 187.

3. Vivienne Welburn, *Postnatal Depression* (London: Fontana, 1980), p. 154.

4. Rozsika Parker, *Torn in Two: The Experience of Maternal Ambivalence* (London: Virago, 1995).

5. Jessica Benjamin, *The Bonds of Love* (London: Virago, 1990), p. 214.

6. Hilary Graham, "Coping: Or How Mothers Are Seen and Not Heard," in Scarlet Friedman and Elizabeth Sarah, eds., *On the Problem of Men: Two Feminist Conferences* (London: The Women's Press, 1982).

7. Janet Finch and Jennifer Mason, *Negotiating Family Responsibilities* (London and New York: Tavistock/Routledge, 1993).

8. Frances and Celia knew each other, and it was Celia who introduced me to Frances.

9. Cry-sis is a U.K.-based registered charity that offers telephone support to parents dealing with a crying baby.

10. Graham, "Coping," p. 103.

11. Ibid., p. 105.

12. Ibid.

13. Carol Gilligan, *In a Different Voice: Psychological Theory and Women's Development* (Cambridge, Mass.: Harvard University Press, 1982); Gilligan, Ward, and Taylor, eds., *Mapping the Moral Domain;* Jack, *Silencing the Self;* J. V. Jordan, *Relational Resilience,* Work in Progress, no. 57 (Wellesley, Mass.: Stone Center Working Paper Series, 1992).

14. I. P. Stiver and J. B. Miller, *From Depression to Sadness in Women's Psychotherapy,* Work in Progress, no. 36 (Wellesley, Mass.: Stone Center Working Paper Series, 1988), p. 2.

15. Jordan, *Relational Resilience,* p. 5.

5. MOTHERS AND DAUGHTERS

1. The women spoke less about their fathers, possibly because I asked fewer questions about them, but also because they appeared less involved in their daughters' lives around the time of pregnancy and childbirth than were the

mothers. For example, it was often the mother alone who spent time with the daughter following the birth.

2. Rozsika Parker, *Torn in Two: The Experience of Maternal Ambivalence* (London: Virago, 1995).

6. MEN, WOMEN, AND RELATIONSHIPS

1. See N. S. Mauthner, "Re-Assessing the Importance and Role of the Marital Relationship in Postpartum Depression: Methodological and Theoretical Implications," *Journal of Reproductive and Infant Psychology,* 16 (1998): 157–175. Although researchers point out that evidence of an association between a poor relationship and postpartum depression does not imply a causal link, in practice they often assume that it does. Dwenda Gjerdingen and her colleagues, for example, write that correlational studies "do not shed light on which came first—depression or lack of social support" (D. K. Gjerdingen, D. G. Froberg, and P. Fontaine, "The Effects of Social Support on Women's Health during Pregnancy, Labor and Delivery, and the Postpartum Period," *Family Medicine,* 23 [1991]: 370–375, p. 373). However, they go on to say that "the hypothesis developed in our paper implies a cause-and-effect relationship between support and health" (ibid., p. 374).

2. I. H. Gotlib, V. E. Whiffen, P. M. Wallace, and J. H. Mount, "Prospective Investigations of Postpartum Depression: Factors Involved in Onset and Recovery," *Journal of Abnormal Psychology,* 100 (1991): 122–132, quote p. 123.

3. M. Sheppard, "Postnatal Depression, Child Care and Social Support: A Review of Findings and Their Implications for Practice," *Social Work and Social Sciences Review,* 5 (1994): 24–46, p. 38.

4. These women were Dawn, Fiona, Frances, Helen, Monica, Sandra, Sonya, and Tina.

5. These women were Caroline, Celia, Louise, Marcia, Pam, Penny, Petra, Rachel, and Vera.

6. A. Doucet, "Gender Equality and Gender Differences in Household Work and Parenting," *Women's Studies International Forum,* 18 (1995): 271–284.

7. Ibid.

8. Lorna McKee and Margaret O'Brien, eds., *The Father Figure* (London: Tavistock, 1982).

9. N. S. Mauthner, "Re-Assessing the Importance and Role of the Marital Relationship."

10. See also A. G. Kaplan, *The 'Self-in-Relation': Implications for Depression in Women,* Work in Progress, no. 14 (Wellesley, Mass.: Stone Center Working Paper Series, 1984); J. V. Jordan, *Relational Resilience,* Work in Progress, no. 57 (Wellesley, Mass.: Stone Center Working Paper Series, 1992).

11. L. Wandersman, A. Wandersman, and S. Kahn, "Social Support in the Transition to Parenthood," *Journal of Community Psychology,* 8 (1980): 332–342.

12. Lorna McKee, "Fathers' Participation in Infant Care: A Critique," in McKee and O'Brien, eds., *The Father Figure;* Charlie Lewis and Margaret O'Brien, *Reassessing Fatherhood: New Observations on Fathers and the Modern Family* (London: Sage, 1987); Julia Brannen and Peter Moss, *Managing Mothers: Dual Earner Households after Maternity Leave* (London: Unwin Hyman, 1991); Doucet, "Gender Equality and Gender Difference."
13. E. H. Boath, A. J. Pryce, and J. L. Cox, "Postnatal Depression: The Impact on the Family," *Journal of Reproductive and Infant Psychology,* 16 (1998): 199–203; Robert Hickman, "Husband Support: A Neglected Aspect of Postpartum Psychiatric Illness," in James A. Hamilton and Patricia N. Harberger, eds., *Postpartum Psychiatric Illness: A Picture Puzzle* (Philadelphia: University of Pennsylvania Press, 1992).

7. MOTHER TO MOTHER

1. C. E. Cutrona, "Social Support and Stress in the Transition to Parenthood," *Journal of Abnormal Psychology,* 93 (1994): 378–390.
2. Research on women (not mothers specifically) also highlights the importance of female friendships. Pat O'Connor's work shows that women who lack a confiding relationship with a female friend are just as likely as those who lack a confiding relationship with a spouse to experience psychological problems (see P. O'Connor, "Women's Confidants outside Marriage: Shared or Competing Sources of Intimacy?" *Sociology,* 25 [1991]: 241–254). Further studies suggest that friendships with other women are important in times of stress and psychological difficulties (see Y. Keeley-Robinson, "Women's Concepts of Depression," *Health Visitor,* 56 [1983]: 11–13; Agnes Miles, *Women and Mental Illness: The Social Context of Female Neurosis* [Brighton: Wheatsheaf Books, 1988]).
3. For example, M. Sheppard, "Postnatal Depression, Child Care and Social Support: A Review of Findings and Their Implications for Practice," *Social Work and Social Sciences Review,* 5 (1994): 24–46.
4. Verta Taylor, *Rock-a-by Baby: Feminism, Self-Help, and Postpartum Depression* (New York and London: Routledge, 1996).
5. Ann Oakley, *Women Confined: Towards a Sociology of Childbirth* (Oxford: Martin Robertson, 1980); Paula Nicolson, "The Social Psychology of 'Postnatal Depression'" (Ph.D. diss., London School of Economics, 1988); P. Nicolson, "Counselling Women with Postnatal Depression: Implications from Recent Qualitative Research," *Counselling Psychology Quarterly,* 2 (1989): 123–132; Patrizia Romito, *La Naissance du Premier Enfant: Étude Psycho-sociale de L'Expérience de la Maternité et de la Dépression Post-partum* (Lausanne: Delachaux and Niestle, 1990).
6. L. Bell and J. Ribbens, "Isolated Housewives and Complex Maternal Worlds—The Significance of Social Contacts between Women with Young Children in Industrial Societies," *Sociological Review,* 42 (1994): 227–262, p. 228.

7. Ibid.; Lydia O'Donnell, *The Unheralded Majority: Contemporary Women as Mothers* (Lexington, Mass.: Lexington Books, 1985).

8. Other studies show that individuals experiencing psychological problems feel that other people going through similar experiences come nearest to understanding their own feelings and, if available, are the best choices for confidences and support (see Miles, *Women and Mental Illness*).

9. Rozsika Parker, *Torn in Two: The Experience of Maternal Ambivalence* (London: Virago, 1995).

10. For example, Oakley, *Women Confined.*

11. Premenstrual tension, which is the same as premenstrual syndrome, or PMS.

12. Adrienne Rich, *Of Woman Born: Motherhood as Experience and Institution* (London: Virago, 1986; first published in 1977), p. 40.

13. Parker, *Torn in Two.*

14. Cathy Urwin, "Constructing Motherhood: The Persuasion of Normal Development," in Carolyn Steedman, Cathy Urwin, and Valerie Walkerdine, eds., *Language, Gender and Childhood* (London: Routledge and Kegan Paul, 1985).

15. For research studies see J. B. Morris, "Group Psychotherapy for Prolonged Postnatal Depression," *British Journal of Medical Psychology,* 60 (1987): 279–281; S. A. Elliott, M. Sanjack, and T. J. Leverton, "Parent Groups in Pregnancy: A Preventive Intervention for Postnatal Depression?" in Benjamin H. Gottlieb, ed., *Marshaling Social Support: Formats, Processes and Effects* (Calif.: Sage, 1988). For anecdotal accounts see J. McKears, "Group Support for Young Mothers," *Health Visitor,* 56 (1983): 16; C. Jones, "A Postpartum Support Group," *Birth,* 11 (1984): 244. J. B. Morris's research on group psychotherapy (above) similarly shows that the move out of postpartum depression is accompanied by shifts in mothers' constructs of the "actual" versus the "ideal" self as mother, and the "actual" versus the "ideal" child. Research on befriending schemes is also relevant here (see A. D. Cox, "Befriending Young Mothers," *British Journal of Psychiatry,* 163 [1993]: 6–18). Programs such as Home-Start and Newpin (The New Parent Infant Network) have developed in Britain to provide services to disadvantaged mothers (see W. van der Eycken, "Home-Start: A Four-Year Evaluation" [Leicester: Home-Start Consultancy, 1990]; R. Evans, "Newpin: The New Parent Infant Network. National Development Strategy, 1992–1995" [London: Newpin, 1991]; M. Mills and A. Pound, "Mechanisms of Change: The Newpin Project," *Marcé Bulletin,* 2 [1986]: 3–7; A. Pound and M. Mills, "A Pilot Evaluation of NEWPIN: Home Visiting and Befriending Scheme in South London," *Association of Child Psychiatry,* 114 [1985]: 1325–1335). These services, which cater to families with children under five years of age, were established with the stated aim of preventing child abuse and neglect. They are relevant to this discussion, however, because most of those who take advantage of these services are, in fact, depressed mothers with children under one year of age. Newpin, for example, is an independent voluntary organization working with parents or other main caregivers suffering from de-

pression or emotional distress. It is a professionally run program, but the service is provided by volunteers from the same background as the women they befriend. Through this service mothers in difficulty are provided with intensive one-to-one support by volunteers. This program has been particularly successful for depressed mothers. Pound and Mills in their "Pilot Evaluation of NEWPIN" found that one-third of mothers who had been clinically depressed at an initial interview had completely recovered, and the remainder had improved, by the follow-up interview six to twelve months after entry into the program.

16. The Association for Postnatal Illness, another British organization with charitable status, aims, through telephone support, to help mothers experiencing emotional and psychological difficulties following childbirth.

8. JOURNEYS TO RECOVERY

1. J. L. Cox, J. M. Holden, and R. Sagovsky, "Detection of Postnatal Depression: Development of the 10-Item Edinburgh Postnatal Depression Scale," *British Journal of Psychiatry,* 150 (1987): 782–786.

2. R. Kumar and K. M. Robson, "A Prospective Study of Emotional Disorders in Childbearing Women," *British Journal of Psychiatry,* 144 (1984): 35–47.

3. In Britain, a community psychiatric nurse is a nurse with psychiatric training who visits people in their homes.

4. Side effects include dry mouth, drowsiness, constipation, urinary hesitancy, blurred vision, and confusion (see J. Cookson, "Side-Effects of Antidepressants," *British Journal of Psychiatry,* 162 (suppl. 20) [1993]: 20–24). Since the early 1990s, several newer classes of antidepressants have appeared with far fewer side-effects.

5. In Britain, talking treatments tend to be perceived by individuals with mental health problems as desired alternatives or adjuncts to medical treatment (see Ann Rogers, David Pilgrim, and Ron Lacey, *Experiencing Psychiatry: Users' Views of Services* [Basingstoke: Macmillan, 1993]). In the case of postpartum depression, interpersonal psychotherapy has been shown to be an effective treatment (see S. Stuart and M. W. O'Hara, "Interpersonal Psychotherapy for Postpartum Depression: A Treatment Program," *Journal of Psychotherapy Practice and Research,* 4 [1995]: 18–29). The positive effects of antidepressants are also enhanced when combined with therapeutic listening and social support (see J. M. Holden, R. Sagovsky, and J. L. Cox, "Counselling in a General Practice Setting: Controlled Study of Health Visitor Intervention in Treatment of Postnatal Depression," *British Medical Journal,* 298 [1989]: 223–226). However, it is possible, at least in some cases, to avoid antidepressants altogether if mothers are encouraged and enabled to talk at the very early stages of their depression, and even before their difficult feelings turn into depression. Antidepressants may then only be necessary when the depression is quite advanced.

6. Failure of healthcare professionals to detect postpartum depression is a

widely recognized problem (see John L. Cox, *Postnatal Depression—A Guide for Health Professionals* [Edinburgh: Churchill Livingstone, 1986]; D. S. Gruen, "Postpartum Depression: A Debilitating yet Often Unassessed Problem," *Health and Social Work,* 15 [1990]: 261–270; R. Kumar, "Postnatal Depression," *Maternal and Child Health,* 19 [1994]: 354–358). The most important development in the early detection of postpartum depression has been the Edinburgh Postpartum Depression Scale (EPDS), developed in Britain but now used worldwide. This is a ten-item rating scale that primary care workers can use as a screening questionnaire to detect mothers who are depressed (see Cox, Holden, and Sagovsky, "Detection of Postnatal Depression"). The scale is administered at the six-week postnatal check-up, is generally accepted by mothers, and can be completed within five minutes. Use of the EPDS has been shown to improve healthcare professionals' awareness of postpartum depression, aid in the diagnosis, and increase the likelihood that these professionals will refer women for treatment (see A. M. Schaper, B. L. Rooney, N. R. Kay, and P. D. Silva, "Use of the Edinburgh Postnatal Depression Scale to Identify Postpartum Depression in a Clinical Setting," *Journal of Reproductive Medicine,* 39 [1994]: 620–624).

7. Levels of knowledge and awareness of postpartum depression vary across healthcare professionals of different ages and genders. A North American study, for example, found that obstetric nurses were more aware than obstetricians of the emotional impact of postpartum depression. Older male obstetricians were the least likely to recognize the psychological antecedents of postpartum depression (see H. S. Lepper, R. DiMatteo, and B. J. Tinsley, "Postpartum Depression: How Much Do Obstetric Nurses and Obstetricians Know?" *Birth,* 21 [1994]: 149–154). Provision of information about postpartum depression (and training in counseling skills) is critical as research suggests that it enables health professionals to detect, manage, and help women overcome postpartum depression (see Holden, Sagovsky, and Cox, "Counselling in a General Practice Setting"; S. Seeley, L. Murray, P. J. Cooper, "The Outcome for Mothers and Babies of Health Visitor Intervention," *Health Visitor,* 69 [1996]: 135–138).

8. Many of the mothers saw several doctors, and, in some cases, they might have had a difficult encounter with one doctor and a positive encounter with another.

9. Gerrard and colleagues found that visiting nurses trained in the detection, treatment, and prevention of postpartum depression could positively influence the emotional well-being of postnatal women. They were trained in use of the EPDS and given information about the value and practice of non-directive counseling and preventative strategies (see J. Gerrard, J. M. Holden, S. A. Elliott, J. McKenzie, and J. L. Cox, "A Trainer's Perspective on an Innovative Programme Teaching Health Visitors about the Detection, Treatment and Prevention of Postnatal Depression," *Journal of Advanced Nursing,* 18 [1993]: 1825–1832). Other intervention studies also show the value of visit-

ing nurses' allowing women to talk about their feelings and providing a "listening ear" in reducing levels of depression (see Holden, Sagovsky, and Cox, "Counselling in a General Practice Setting"; S. A. Elliott, M. Sanjack, and T. J. Leverton, "Parent Groups in Pregnancy: A Preventive Intervention for Postnatal Depression?" in Benjamin H. Gottlieb, ed., *Marshaling Social Support: Formats, Processes and Effects* [Calif.: Sage, 1988]; Seeley, Murray, and Cooper, "The Outcome for Mothers and Babies"). Through their close contact with pregnant women, their involvement in labor and delivery, and their early contact with mothers in the first few days after the birth, midwives can also play a potentially critical role in identifying women experiencing difficulties (see N. S. Mauthner, "Postnatal Depression: How Can Midwives Help?" *Midwifery,* 13 [1997]: 163–171).

10. Y. Keeley-Robinson, "Women's Concepts of Depression," *Health Visitor,* 56 (1983): 11–13, quote p. 12.

11. Interestingly, several researchers have put forward similar proposals. John Cox, for example, a British psychiatrist and leading researcher in the field, argues that "there should be identified within each health district at least two community psychiatric nurses who have a particular concern for the prevention and treatment of postpartum mood disorder and can provide essential back-up to other health professionals such as health visitors and midwives" (J. L. Cox, "Postnatal Depression: A Serious and Neglected Postpartum Complication," *Baillere's Clinical Obstetrics and Gynaecology,* 3 [1989]: 839–855, quote p. 852).

12. Dana Jack, *Silencing the Self: Depression and Women* (Cambridge, Mass.: Harvard University Press, 1991), p. 190.

13. Dana Breen, *The Birth of a First Child* (London: Tavistock, 1975), quotes p. 192, p. 11.

9. VOICES FROM A DIFFERENT CULTURE

1. "Innocents Lost," *Newsweek,* Nov. 14, 1994, pp. 26–30.
2. "Condemned to Life," *Newsweek,* Aug. 7, 1995, pp. 19–23.
3. "Innocents Lost."
4. Ibid.
5. "Condemned to Life."
6. Ibid.
7. As we can see in the case of Susan Smith, media representations of postpartum depression tend to sensationalize the condition or present extreme cases of women who kill their children. This sensationalization of PPD is unhelpful to women because it presents a terrifying image of what is assumed to be "postpartum depression" but may, in some instances, be cases of puerperal psychosis. These sensational stories misrepresent the vast majority of cases of postpartum depression in which women do not harm their children.
8. Rozsika Parker, *Torn in Two: The Experience of Maternal Ambivalence*

(London: Virago, 1995), believes that the feelings of guilt mothers experience have their origins in the experience and handling of this ambivalence, and the difficulty mothers have accepting ambivalence within a culture that neither acknowledges nor tolerates such feelings.

9. See Patricia N. Harberger, Nancy G. Berchtold, and Jane I. Honikman, "Cries for Help," in James A. Hamilton and Patricia N. Harberger, eds., *Postpartum Psychiatric Illness: A Picture Puzzle* (Philadelphia: University of Pennsylvania Press, 1992); Verta Taylor, *Rock-a-by Baby: Feminism, Self-Help, and Postpartum Depression* (New York and London: Routledge, 1996).

10. Taylor, *Rock-a-by Baby,* notes that the postpartum depression movement more generally is dominated by white, middle-class women.

11. Ibid., p. 140.

12. Ibid.

13. Ibid.

14. David A. Karp, *Speaking of Sadness: Depression, Disconnection, and the Meanings of Illness* (New York and Oxford: Oxford University Press, 1996).

15. Taylor, *Rock-a-by Baby.*

APPENDIX 2

1. Using this technique meant that several mothers in the study knew each other. Three women had been friends before becoming depressed, although, interestingly, they did not know about each other's depression at the time. Three women met through a postpartum depression support group. Two mothers lived in the same village and had been put in touch with each other by their visiting nurse, who knew they were both depressed. Another two women were in telephone contact; one was counseling the other as part of the support provided by the Association for Postnatal Illness.

2. For a more detailed account of how I analyzed the data see Natasha S. Mauthner and Andrea Doucet, "Reflections on a Voice-Centred Relational Method: Analysing Maternal and Domestic Voices," in Jane Ribbens and Rosalind Edwards, eds., *Feminist Dilemmas in Qualitative Research: Public Knowledge and Private Lives* (London: Sage, 1998).

3. L. M. Brown, D. Argyris, J. Attanucci, B. Bardige, C. Gilligan, K. Johnston, B. Miller, R. Osborne, M. Tappan, J. Ward, G. Wiggins, and D. Wilcox, *A Guide to Reading Narratives of Conflict and Choice for Self and Relational Voice* (Cambridge, Mass.: Harvard Graduate School of Education, 1988); Carol Gilligan, Lyn M. Brown, and Annie Rogers, "Psyche Embedded: A Place for Body, Relationships, and Culture in Personality Theory," in A. I. Rabin, R. Zucker, R. Emmons, and S. Frank, eds., *Studying Persons and Lives* (New York: Springer, 1990); Lyn M. Brown and Carol Gilligan, *Meeting at the Crossroads: Women's Psychology and Girls' Development* (Cambridge, Mass.: Harvard University Press, 1992); Jill M. Taylor, Carol

Gilligan, and Amy Sullivan, *Between Voice and Silence: Women and Girls, Race and Relationships* (Cambridge, Mass.: Harvard University Press, 1995).

4. Brown and Gilligan, *Meeting at the Crossroads,* pp. 27–28.

5. Ibid.

6. I consolidated the work in these four readings by writing up case studies of individual women. In addition to these case studies, I compiled summaries for each woman: summaries of the key issues raised by these four readings; summaries of the key points in each woman's experiences and circumstances; and summaries of each woman's sociodemographic, educational, and employment details.

7. On the notion of "interpretive community" see Taylor, Gilligan, and Sullivan, *Between Voice and Silence.*

8. See N. S. Mauthner and A. Doucet, "Reflexive Accounts and Accounts of Reflexivity in Qualitative Data Analysis," *Sociology* (forthcoming).

9. Elliot G. Mishler, *Research Interviewing: Context and Narrative* (Cambridge, Mass.: Harvard University Press, 1986); Karen Pidgeon and Nick Henwood, "Using Grounded Theory in Psychological Research," in Nicky Hayes, ed., *Doing Qualitative Analysis in Psychology* (Hove: Psychology Press, 1997); Mauthner and Doucet, "Reflections on a Voice-Centred Relational Method."

APPENDIX 3

1. This interview guide is not designed to be followed sequentially.

2. I used the same term used by the mother.

3. This mapping out of the mothers' social networks is based on Jane Ribbens's use of this technique (see Jane Ribbens, *Mothers and Their Children: Towards a Feminist Perspective on Childrearing* [London: Sage, 1994]).

acknowledgments

Many people have helped me over the course of the last ten years as I researched and wrote this book. My deepest thanks go to the many women and men who gave generously of their time to tell me about their experiences of parenthood. I am deeply indebted to them for their willingness to share painful memories and for allowing me to tell their stories.

In Britain, I am grateful to the National Childbirth Trust, Cry-sis, and the Association for Postnatal Illness for helping me find mothers to take part in my research. In the United States, my work would not have been possible without the help of Depression after Delivery, and the support, interest, and commitment of Karen Glennon, Gerri Piatelli, and members of the postpartum depression support group I attended. I am particularly grateful to Karen and Gerri for their friendship.

Financial assistance for the research in Britain was provided by a doctoral studentship from the Medical Research Council. In the United States, my work was supported by an International Fellowship from the American Association of University Women, and Wingate and Fulbright Scholarships.

My research in Britain could not have taken place without the support and commitment of Martin Richards. In the early stages of my work he provided a much-needed intellectual environment. I have drawn enormous strength from Carol Gilligan's support, encouragement, and belief in my work. She has been a loyal colleague and friend, a constant source of inspiration, and I continue to learn from her wisdom and vision. Andrea Doucet has been my dearest friend and colleague since I first embarked on this research. She has generously given me emotional and intellectual support, which have been invaluable in helping me see this book through to completion. My sister, Melanie, and my father, Martin, have provided excellent company along this journey as we have each confronted the challenges of writing a first book. Kathryn Geismar was a very good friend to me when I was in the United States, and has remained so. Over the years, I have benefited from fruitful discussions with her about my research. Lorna McKee helped me carve out the time and space to complete this book. I am also deeply indebted to her for her careful reading of the entire manuscript, and for her insightful comments. Odette Parry's pragmatism and sense of humor have helped me at many points along the way. I thank my cousin Julia MacKenzie for her encouragement and for her editorial advice. Her insider knowledge of the publishing world, and of the time it takes most books to see the light of day, has provided much needed reassurance.

At Harvard Press, I am grateful to Angela von der Lippe for showing interest and belief in my work and for providing valuable advice on turning a doctoral thesis into a book. I thank Elizabeth Knoll for her patience, editorial insights and suggestions, and her commitment to publishing this book; and I thank Christine Thorsteinsson for her meticulous editing and many improvements to the manuscript.

My husband, Dave, has been supportive and reassuring throughout. He helped create a space for me to write and complete the book and has provided emotional support in times of desperation. My final thanks go to Sam, for giving me the experience of motherhood and a more personal understanding of the lives of the women about whom I have written.

index